The Winds Call

BOOKS BY CARLETON MITCHELL

Islands to Windward

Yachtsman's Camera

Passage East

Beyond Horizons

Summer of the Twelves

Isles of the Caribbees
(A Special Publication of the National Geographic Society)

The Winds Call

The Winds Call

CRUISES NEAR AND FAR

CARLETON MITCHELL

Charles Scribner's Sons   New York

Contents

The Winds Call

Foreword

There are almost as many facets of life in small boats as there
are courses to steer. For some, it is a summons beyond far
horizons, a landfall less important than the lengthening track
astern, the visible world a tumbling waste of empty water; for
others, it is swinging at anchor in a pine or palm girt cove,
snug in the embrace of the land, the next harbor no more
distant than the next joggle in the coast. It can be escape for
a weekend, or an endless succession of new places and peo-
ples. There is the high tension of an afternoon 'round the
buoys, or the long continued challenge of an ocean race.
Whatever gives the sailor pleasure is part of life afloat, the
finest of lives for those in tune.

Looking back, I find my most precious memories are of
cruises, near and far. The size and type of boat have been less
important than the fact of being afloat. Distance has been
unimportant: as the sea has spoken with many voices, its call
has known no boundaries. Wherever the tide pulsed was the

sea, from a mid-ocean waste definable only by latitude and longitude, to the innermost gunk-hole at the end of a creek off a river leading from a bay. Being on the water and able to enjoy was what counted, and identifying with the neighboring shore: eating the food, drinking the wine of the country —be it *vin blanc, ouzo, saki,* or rum—trying to speak the language, reading of the past and living in the present.

The sixteen stories in this volume add up to a circumnavigation, without the passages between. Many were originally published in an abridged form. Some have been updated, although most have stood the test of time—except, perhaps, in references to shores no longer virgin and harbors now less remote, as humans flee the urban civilizations they have created. And how better to escape than aboard your own portable castle?

Somewhere around the age of twelve, when contemporaries were choosing careers ranging from western sheriffs to railway engineers, I declared my intention of becoming a ship captain and a writer. I had already begun sailing on Lake Pontchartrain—my first nickname was "Skeet," after an uncle was reminded of a mosquito as I hauled on a jib sheet— and had already begun receiving rejection slips as manuscripts made the rounds. Neither goal was achieved as I then envisioned the future, but after all these years I do still find myself basically living my boyhood dream.

In this book are no accounts of storms and other perils of the deep, no reports of races, across oceans or around the America's Cup buoy off Newport, no technical how-to or detailed piloting instructions. Instead, I have tried to share some wonderful moments afloat in a few of the favored cruising areas of the world. May they revive memories for those who have sailed the same waters, but equally bring pleasure to those who must make their voyages without leaving a chair by the fire.

I wish to thank the editors and publishers of the magazines

named on the copyright page for their permission to repub-
lish these articles, and also for their encouragement and guid-
ance when they were originally written. Above all, I desire
to thank my shipmates through the years, who made possible
the happy memories.

C.M.

Aboard *Sans Terre*,
Virgin Gorda, B.V.I.
10 June, 1971

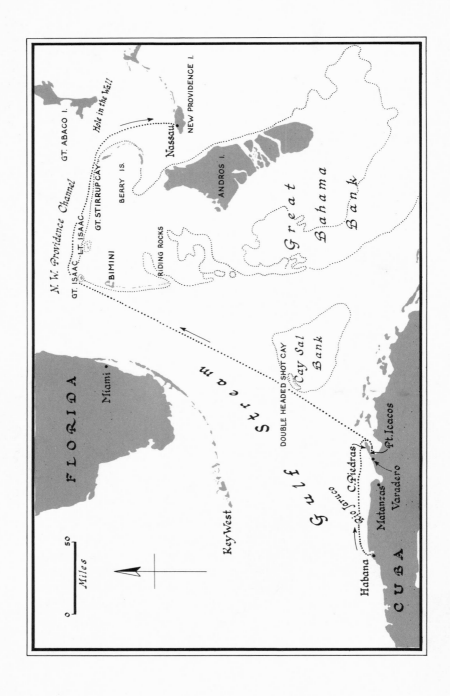

1
At Home Offshore
THE CARIBBEAN

It was blowing hard when we left Havana. It had been blowing hard for several days. The flags over Morro Castle stood out rigid, bright rectangles against a bright sky. We had moved *Carib* over under the lee of the northern shore of the harbor to ease a nasty chop. There was no sign the wind would drop.

"Hell," said Hod, "it's never going to let up."

"No," I answered, "I guess not."

So we took my wife Zib ashore to Zaragozana's for a last lunch of morro crabs, and stopped by to pick clearance papers for Nassau, and bought a baked ham and a case of Mexican Carta Blanca beer, and got out through the entrance just at sunset. The fortress looked massive and impregnable, typifying the solidity of the land.

Outside there was quite a slop of a sea, but it was worse close in than farther out. By the time we were a mile off the beach there were no tops on the seas. They looked big in the strange light of dusk but there was no weight in them. *Carib* rose easily to each, hardly wetting her deck. As the lights ashore winked on we saw that we were getting a set from the Gulf Stream.

At first we were steering about north, which would take us to Key West. That wasn't our destination. Our idea was to get east along the Cuban coast to the resort town of Varadero. We hadn't seen a good swimming beach since leaving Grand Cayman. Varadero sounded fine. But it looked as if the wind had other ideas. *Carib* was a ketch, 46 feet 8 inches overall, heavy and short rigged. She had begun life as John Alden's *Malabar XII*, and embodied the requisite nautical virtues save one: she was reluctant to go to windward. We came about and did no better than east-southeast.

About an hour later the wind gave one last gasp and died. There was a sudden squall and then no wind. Not a breath. We expected it to come back, but after awhile started the engine. It stayed calm all night. The sea dropped off entirely. Ashore towns and lights with musical names slid steadily astern: Rio Jaruco, Santa Cruz del Norte, Puerto Escondido, Matanzas.

At dawn Hod Fuller called me. Hod was still on terminal leave from the Marines; he had risen from private to brigader general on retirement, and had seen service from Guadalcanal to Normandy. His pre-war sailing career included a circumnavigation after graduating from Harvard. When Hod was on watch, the skipper could sleep soundly.

Just ahead a light dominated a cay. "Piedras," said Hod, by way of identification. He had turned off the engine. *Carib* had bare steerageway. Below perhaps six or seven fathoms, the bottom was plain: hard sand dotted with occasional humps of coral.

We turned in and picked up some buoys. Nothing checked with the Pilot Book. The water became murky. Finally we discovered that Bahi Cárdenas is a big place. We worked in behind a long low point called Icacos; it had begun to blow hard again, this time from almost due north, so we decided that Varadero could wait for another cruise and beat up into the lee of Icacos. Close under the land the water was flat but wind howled through the rigging. In the worst puffs the whole boat trembled.

It blew the whole day. Two men sculled by in a dinghy and we bought a pargo, which was still flapping. We were content. We swam over the side and ate fish for lunch, slept through the afternoon, ate fish for dinner, and went right back to sleep.

That dawn was like the last, all the colors any painter ever dreamed but no wind. A wonderful tropic smell came off the land. We sat on top of the deckhouse, waiting for enough light to see our way out. When things began to resume their shapes we got in the anchor.

After dropping the Cuban coast the horizon was empty. We were sailing waters that had known the whole incredible streaming of life from the Old World to the New. Before us had passed explorers, colonists, traders, soldiers, priests and buccaneers, a ghostly procession inspired by greed, by lust, by power, by religion, and by all the other motives and dreams that can send men forth into the unknown.

To the east stretched the Old Bahama Channel, a shimmering chasm of blue lying between the pale green water of the Great Bahama Bank and the dark green mountains of Cuba; to the west, beyond the Gulf Stream, extended the peninsula of Florida. Ahead, except for a tangle of reefs and uninhabited low cays forming the Cay Sal Banks, our way was clear.

Observations of the sun during the afternoon put us east of the estimated reckoning. Cay Sal is no place to approach after dark. Since the days of sailing ships ended the light on Double Head Shot Cay had not been lighted. Hod climbed the mast. He waved and pointed; as he signalled I swung the bow until it was in line with the abandoned tower, and read the bearing from the compass. It was somehow an unreal procedure. I never saw the cay from the deck. But I pictured it from an earlier visit: the sun baking down on the rocks and thousands of screaming sea birds rising ahead as we walked among the nests, the tracks of turtles across the beaches, the grave of a light keeper desecrated by seekers after treasure.

A strange thing was the calm. The rising sun had not brought wind. We ran the engine during periods when no air was stirring, turned it off as soon as there was enough breeze for steerageway. For hours at a time the Gulf Stream lay unruffled. No ripples, no underlying swell. Nothing. The sun went down and the stars came out. They reflected in the water. We kept on through the night and the next day, paralleling the unseen coast of Florida. Nothing came over the sharp bright ring of the horizon. Then before sunset we angled towards the east and small humps appeared, and when it became dark twin flashes glowed ahead. We had reached Great Isaac Cay, guardian of Northwest Providence Channel. Here we swung sharply to the east for Nassau.

A moderate breeze struck in from the west, letting us free sheets. It was a slant most unusual in trade wind latitudes, consequently doubly appreciated. Off to starboard in the darkness were the rock forms of the Brothers, East and West, and the Isaacs, Little, Middle and East; and farther along the hidden teeth of Gingerbread Ground Reef; and still farther the wondrous sand plateau of the Great Bahama Bank.

Early in the morning we rounded Great Stirrup, a final turn. The breeze was still in the west, lighter with the sun. We held in close along the fringe of cays, following the line of soundings. Between small islands the pale green of the Banks shone with unreal brilliance.

During the afternoon the breeze gradually faded. Before it trailed off entirely, a tiny hump broke the flat line of the sea: the top of the watertower above Fort Fincastle, the highest point on New Providence.

We could have been at anchor within three hours. There was gas in the tanks. Instead we drifted. Ahead was the land, the sheltered harbor and fine town of Nassau. Still we drifted. Being out on the water was best. There was no hurry. It was too good to end. . . .

That, like most accounts of passages, is a relation of conditions and progress. We left Havana, we covered four hundred miles—painlessly, in this case, because of a freak of weather —and we fetched Nassau. But that is only part of the story: the rest is what makes sailing a way of life.

Carib lying a few miles offshore was more than a boat becalmed. To the four of us aboard, she was home: man's portable castle. We happened to be in the Providence Channel. Under similar conditions, we would have been just as content off Montauk Point or the Golden Gate or Land's End. Life aboard would have been about the same, and we would have had the same feeling of completeness.

During our passage every moment of every day had been filled. There is always something to do for a small boat on the open sea. Giant steamers are likened to cities: so many kilowatts of electric power, so many loaves of bread baked, so many gallons of water consumed. But no one has attempted to find a comparison for cruising boats poking about the lonely places.

Aboard we had the goods and services taken for granted by civilized man. We pressed a button and had electric light; we turned a valve and had drinking water; we ate hot food and slept on spring mattresses and drank our fruit juice chilled. If we had a headache there was aspirin in the medicine chest. If we felt like reading there were shelves of books. Rotating a knob brought us the noises and doings of mankind. Torn pants could be mended, shoes shined, cocktails mixed. Into an object some forty-six feet long and twelve wide was compressed all the items of a well stocked house: food, beverages, linens, clothes; pots, dishes, glasses, silver, medicine, cosmetics; books, writing paper, pictures—everything. And in quantities to last several people for days or weeks—no running to the corner drug store for castor oil or to the grocery for mustard!

But few houses have to manufacture their own electricity, or carry fresh water in the basement. Even if they do, they are hardly called upon to furnish and accommodate their own means of propulsion. Or to take along the equipment to find where they are. So into that same space, a space of considerably less cubic footage than the most modest of cottages, was also placed an engine, a generator, batteries, tanks for fuel and water and an intricate maze of pipes and wires. Plus a few other items not generally found in houses: sheets and sails and halyards, squares of canvas and bags of blocks, awnings and covers and such things required by the Coast Guard and common sense as life jackets, fenders, fire extinguishers and code flags. . . .

So as we made our way along we were a complete unit. A part of our pleasure came from our knowledge of independence. Part came from having the skills that kept everything functioning. Part came from pride in our boat, and our relation to her. We tended her needs and she kept us safe and comfortable. Our time was filled. We lived four happy days, days of peace and content. We saw the dawn lighten the eastern sky, we saw the sun shafting deep into the blue water, we saw the day fade and the night begin. We did our daily tasks and lazed in the shadow of the sails, we finished our night tricks at the wheel and slept deeply. We trailed fishing lines astern and watched bos'n birds wheel overhead. There were bucket baths under the bowsprit and long involved discussions in the cockpit. We sat alone with our thoughts when we wanted to be alone, we gathered by the helmsman when we wanted companionship. The day and its events were sufficient in themselves.

To desire nothing beyond what you have is surely happiness. Aboard a boat it is frequently possible to achieve just that: that is why sailing is a way of life, one of the finest of lives.

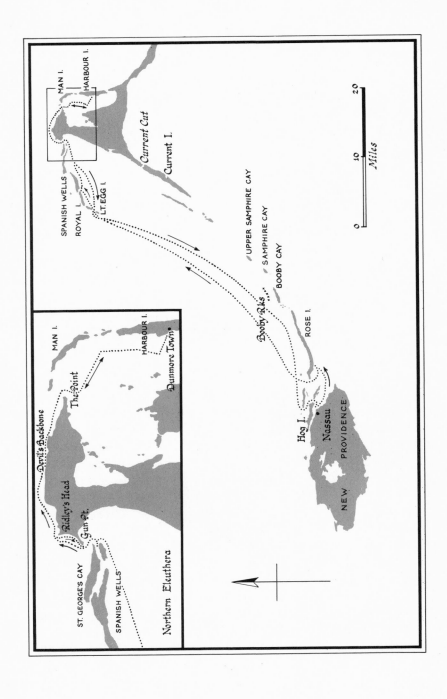

2
At the Wind's Call
THE BAHAMAS

A personal philosophy is nothing more than a point of view evolved by experience and conditioned by temperament, readily applicable to most situations without the burden of additional thought. It is a very handy thing to have on tap. Mine, covering the major divisions of sailing, may be simply stated: a race without a windward leg is no race at all, but cruising to windward is a pain in the neck.

Before dropping our mooring in Nassau harbor I said to Zib: "If we want to get to Georgetown for the Out Island Regatta we had better leave *Gigi*. We're late starting, we're alone, and I'm sure this wind will hold. We'll have to go into Exuma Sound at Ship Channel Cay Cut if we can make it by dark and then we'll have to keep going outside all night. But we shouldn't be towing a boat of more than half our waterline length."

Our winter schedule had been hectic. A friend had commented it was a race getting *Finisterre* ready for the next race.

After coping with the logistics of the Southern Circuit I had been in no mood to make long range plans. Hence our lack of crew.

"Don't you want to take *Gigi?*" asked Zib.

"Sure," I replied. *Gigi* was a 16 foot fiberglass Glamour Girl runabout, built by Bill Dyer's Anchorage. A good seaboat, yet with her propeller protected by a tunnel stern and heavy skeg, she could go almost anywhere. The previous year we had towed her through the Exumas, and she had added a new dimension to our Bahamian cruising. In her we explored tidal creeks not previously suspected, crossed flats teeming with bonefish, and anchored over coral reefs and heads where crawfish and grouper lurked, otherwise beyond reach. With *Gigi* astern, there was never an empty icebox.

"Sure," I repeated.

"Then why don't we start with her and see what happens?" asked Zib reasonably.

So we secured *Gigi* astern and dropped the mooring and powered east through Nassau's back door. Beyond The Narrows, the sea quickly built, the short steep sea of shallow water. *Gigi* plunged like a restive stallion subjected to the indignity of a halter, and we slowed to bare steerageway. It was nearly noon before the slim spire of Porgee Rock light was abeam. The buildings of Nassau were still plain astern.

A mild hangover deteriorated into a mood of black pessimism. We could never get across the Yellow Banks before dark, I told myself: we would find ourselves in a maze of rocky heads without visibility, and then have to beat out through the tidal rips of the cut in pitch darkness, relying on a single bearing from the light. There would be no sleep for either of us. The sea in the open ocean would be much worse than on the banks.

"Zib!" I suddenly heard myself calling down the companionway.

She came on deck. It was windy and wet. Spray was flying.

"Look." I pointed. "See those casurinas on Rose Island? Wouldn't it be nice? . . ." My voice trailed away. An especially juicy dollop drove aft, soaking us both.

"It would be better than this," agreed Zib.

She took the helm as I hoisted the mainsail. A reluctance to short tack had kept it in stops until that moment. But reaching downwind would be different. Quietly we slid off to leeward, *Gigi* now trotting happily astern.

That was Wednesday, a warm early April Wednesday in 1956, clouds white and soft against a deep blue sky, open water white and crinkled under the trade wind. Even in the anchorage at Lower Harbour we rolled to the sea which curled around the low cay protecting *Finisterre* from the full sweep to the south and east. We had a long swim, a nip of Añejo rum left over from Cuba, lunch, a nap, another swim, some music, and watched the sun set through misty cirrus, which blew away with the last purple afterglow to leave stars bright and close.

The evening broadcast from radio station ZNS promised diminishing winds. I did not believe it. Nor did I apply the yachtsman's usual cynical 180 degree correction to the prediction of southeast. The Exumas lay in that direction. When a forecaster comes up with what you don't want, he is infallible. Once I awakened as the change of tide introduced a new rhythm to our roll. The wind had not fallen off. Halyards slapped, sail covers rattled, wavelets broke against our hull. Exuma Sound would be utter hell. In a lazy luxury I pulled the covers tighter around my neck and went back to sleep.

In the morning the weather was the same. Cautiously I opened an eye to see the angle of the sun through the ports: wind southeast, still piping.

Southeast, I thought. Dead on the nose. A hard wet slug all the way to Georgetown. By the time we arrived, the regatta would be nearly over. So why go at all? Lying there, I conjured up in my mind a chart of the Bahamas. To the west,

Andros, but across the open water of Tongue of the Ocean; to the northwest and north, the Berrys and Abaco—but again only after an ocean passage. East? The Bight of Eleuthera; all on the banks, but the wind was hardly far enough south to let us fetch. Then suddenly I remembered: why not outside along the line of cays to Royal Island? Following the edge of soundings, *Finisterre* would be in the lee. There would be no sea, and no pilotage headaches, either. Course should be about northeast; a fine fast beam reach. . . . Not only Royal Island, but Spanish Wells and Harbour Island close beyond. Good swimming. New spearfishing territory. Interesting settlements.

Full of enthusiasm I pulled a chart from the drawer over my head without leaving the bunk. My recollection was correct. The course was approximately northeast, and we could hug the edge of the banks the whole way. Perfect! But how to broach it to Zib? I suspected she took for granted we would go on to Georgetown.

We swam, and had a cup of tea in the cockpit. "Nice morning," I ventured.

"It is," she agreed.

Finisterre trembled to a sudden gust. "Windy, though," I pursued.

"It is," she replied. "Do you want to get under way now, or after we have had breakfast?"

Desperately I squinted at the sky trying to find a threatening omen. Not a cloud as big as a baby's hand marred the serene brilliance overhead. Piled cumulus ringed the horizon, an almost certain indication of continuing fair weather and fresh easterlies.

"Remember Royal Island?" I asked suddenly.

"Yes."

"And Spanish Wells? And the fishing Aziel Pinder showed us?"

"Certainly."

"Wouldn't you like to try it with a spinning rod? And see Harbour Island? You've never been there: wonderful place. Pink sand beach . . . And there's a new dredged channel into Spanish Wells. Remember what a nice little town that was? . . ." I looked at her hopefully.

"But what about the Exumas? What about the regatta?" Her tone was doubtful.

"We were there last year," I said firmly. "We don't want to get into a rut. Here, let me show you the chart. . . ."

So a little later we were sliding along almost dead off before the wind, main boom against the shrouds, skirting the shore of Rose Island to avoid the clump of heads off the casurinas, coming back in close to clear the shallow bank near the western end. While Zib at the wheel responded to my hand signals from the bow I hummed a silly tune about the music going 'round and 'round and coming out here, as I clipped on the working jib.

Soon *Finisterre* passed Chub Rock, and we were off soundings. Even after all the years of Bahamian cruising I still had a feeling of wonder at the beauty of it, the transition from shoal to deep water: on the banks, plateaus of clean white sand, the water was shallow, perhaps from one to three fathoms. There the coloring was all pale greens and blues, with random patches of dark purple-green over the grassy areas, and purple-brown marking the reefs. A really shallow bar was silver white. But then, in a few yards as you sailed through a cut, the bottom fell away—visibly, on a clear calm day—and the water took on the deep greens and blues of ocean depths, sometimes shading in a few more yards to the magnificent indescribable blue of the true ocean abyss, for in places were canyons of more than a thousand fathoms just off the shore.

Clear of the land, *Finisterre* heeled to the wind. A centerboard yawl, 38 feet 7 inches overall, she was the physical embodiment of dreams spun during lonely night watches through the years, all the doodles on paper transmuted to wood and metal reality. *Finisterre* was the symphony I could not otherwise compose, the vision I could not capture on canvas, the Great American Novel forever unwritten. Before she had even taken form I had confessed I was trying to build a boat that had everything. And now I was not being disappointed.

Astern, the towing line to *Gigi* was a taut bar. A fan of spray rose at either side of her bow and jetted outwards along the curve of her flare. Deep blue water patterned by foam whiter than whipped cream rushed past the lee rail; tiny droplets glittered in our bow and stern waves. As penance for yesterday's sloth I pulled the mizzen staysail from its bag and hauled it aloft.

The distance from Chub Rock to Royal Island is thirty miles. A line of cays and reefs extended the whole distance. With the wind southeast, they formed a barrier behind which we could sail in smooth water. Looking to windward, I could see spray flying as waves broke over exposed rocks, but the open Atlantic was calm, so calm I revised my earlier plan of hugging the bank. As the cays formed an arc, a direct course would take us some eight miles offshore at the midway point, but no sea would build in deep water that could bother us, wind abeam.

So we slid along, the rail occasionally scooping up dark blue liquid from overside which miraculously became as transparent as air when flowing along the deck. The sun lay on bare shoulders like a warm friendly hand, and the miles spun astern. At noon, Zib put her head in the companionway to say lunch was ready. Gladly I turned the ship over to The Ape, our automatic pilot, for nothing could be hit that couldn't be seen, and nothing interrupted the clean sharp circle of the horizon.

When I came back on deck, little humps were in sight over the bow. Walking forward to the main shrouds I felt my usual sadness at the end of a passage, no matter how long or short: something is over which never will be exactly repeated, and can never be wholly recaptured: a little piece of life is finished. Not long afterwards the bottom began to appear. Where there had been only a nothingness of changing dark hues, there appeared a shadowy pattern of rock and sand. It was still deep, though. Ten fathoms. Perhaps more.

A sudden gust funneled through the cut between Little and Great Egg Islands, where we would come on the bank north of Eleuthera. *Finisterre* heeled and gathered way, rushing towards pastel shoals ahead. The bottom seemed to leap up. It looked so shallow I almost called a warning to the wheel, but instead exhaled and quit making like a pilot, as reason told me there was a good six feet to spare.

A house became visible on Royal Island. Zib steered for it. Wind aft, jib and mizzen staysail collapsed, so I lowered everything but the mainsail. *Finisterre* barely crept through the narrow harbor entrance. The wind was dropping. It is pleasant to have it die at the end of a sail, for then you feel you are missing nothing. Inside, we jibed and drifted west, only the upper part of the main finding breeze. The entrance closed astern. We were wholly within the shelter of the land.

Next morning, the sky was overcast. Although our anchorage remained glassy, the masthead fly snapped audibly over the growl in the upper rigging. Wind south-southeast, maybe south-by-east. A solid Force 6, maybe more outside. Plenty fresh. Seas were breaking white on the small cay in the entrance to the harbor. Exuma Sound would be worse than yesterday. It was no day to go anywhere unless you had to, and I was content. I puttered on deck through the morning, reading a little at times, but Zib interrupted the siesta I planned after lunch by announcing there was nothing for dinner. I sighed, reflecting it was ever thus for the poor male, even when sabre-toothed tigers snarled around the entrance to the cave.

Tossing mask and spear into *Gigi*, we put-putted along the shore of Royal Island. The spray coming over the bow was cold. Scanning the bottom for nearby heads, they were embarrassingly absent. Yesterday I had signalled Zib around several dark patches, but now we saw only growths of weed.

Finding nothing on the bank, we continued through the cut between Royal and Great Egg Island, over a bottom scoured bone bare by currents. It was smoother on the ocean side, under the lee of the cays, and warmer, sheltered from the wind. I shed my oilskin jacket.

Here, too, the bottom was mostly clear sand. We drifted, looking down through the glass-bottom bucket, until finally we arrived over a curious rock formation, almost like a pile of flat boulders, where a few minnows hovered. I was about to give up when the feelers of a crawfish showed under a ledge. A big fellow. Over the side I went. While below, I saw a small grouper peeping at me from behind a sea fan, so went down again to add him to the pot. Back aboard and dry, I readied the spinning outfit for Zib. After a few casts, we trolled slowly along the shore. Soon the identical twin of my grouper was reeled in, and we decided there was food enough.

After returning to *Finisterre*, Zib rewarded me with a drink. Tilting my head, I noticed the masthead fly showed the wind had hauled west of south, and thought: "Now it is sure to go on around; all the way around. The wind and the music go 'round and 'round, and if you go with them, you never have to go to windward," and began to sing the silly tune until Zib came on deck and asked, "Do you hear a strange noise?" I said no, slicing a filet from a grouper, and she listened awhile and said she couldn't hear it any more, either; perhaps she had imagined it.

In the morning the wind was southwest.

A milky veil of cirrus had been drawn across the sun. We swam and breakfasted in the cockpit, and lazily I hoisted the main to reach onto the bank. Outside, it was smooth, and colors were vivid. As a landscape takes its character from nature's building blocks of rock and soil, fields and forests, mountains and plains, so does crystal clear water reveal the type and depth of bottom. Nowhere does the term seascape have greater validity than in the Bahamas.

Feeling the breeze, *Finisterre* began to walk and talk. There was a gentle plash from the bow wave, and tiny little slaps along the hull, and a low murmur under the stern. Quiet but sibilantly insistent sounds came from the mainsheet and blocks. Above, the flags moved languidly, ends not whipping, but lifting and snapping in idle flicks. Astern, the roiled water of our wake was cut by *Gigi*'s sharp bow, while behind her the combined wakes lay as a trail of tiny bubbles.

Perhaps the greatest distinction between cruising and racing yachtsmen lies in a sense of pace. Your true cruiser sails by the calendar, not the clock. The moment is what counts: the fact he is afloat, a good little ship carrying him to another place; there is no need to be impatient, nor to fret—only to enjoy. But your racing sailor never escapes the ticking second hand. It is probably his most necessary competitive attribute. In any given set of conditions, he feels how his boat should be going. When she is not doing her best, he suffers. He is goaded into action by an overwhelming compulsion: he fiddles with the trim or changes headsails. If nothing helps he glares at sea and sky, feeling some malign force is at work. He must be efficient to be happy.

As these thoughts came to me I looked at the Kenyon speed indicator in the cockpit. It stood a hair over 3 knots. Generous. In the St. Petersburg–Havana Race it had read 10 percent high. Change from cruising jib to light genoa, and we might go up to 5 knots. Shift to ballooner, maybe 5½. Break out the Hood red-head spinnaker, probably touch 6 knots. Maybe with the 'chute trimmed just right, plus the mizzen staysail, maybe reach 7. Maybe. Close, anyway. Suddenly I found myself grinning. I realized I didn't give one fractional infinitesimal damn. It would be time enough to start caring in June when Brenton Reef Lightship came abeam, with the finish line in Bermuda over the bow. Now we were cruising.

When *Finisterre* neared Spanish Wells a dinghy came through the old channel. Two small boys sat in the bow, a man on the after thwart. I had an impression of glasses and flashing teeth under a large and floppy straw hat. "Need help?" asked the man.

A pilot, the mortal enemy of the cruising yachtsman, I thought: bearers of false witness from the North Channel to the Boca del Sierpe; a confident "Plenty water, cap, *plenty-y* water!" usually the prelude to a grounding. . . . "No," I replied with reasonable politeness.

The man began to wind a starter cord around the flywheel of an ancient outboard. "Just a minute," I called. "Can you tell me where to find Aziel Pinder?"

He straightened up. "I'm Aziel," he said, looking at me more closely. "Bless the Lord, ain't that . . . ?"

So forthwith Aziel—which means "Whom the Lord Strengthens"—was signed to "carry" *Finisterre* to Harbour Island, that same afternoon. My general opinion of pilots did not include Aziel Pinder. He would make no mistakes on the reef passage to Harbour Island with a norther on the way.

Ahead the dredged channel into Spanish Wells stretched as clearly defined across shallow sand flats as a blue silk ribbon across an ambassador's dress shirt. Aziel called to tell us there was a basin to port, "two fathoms of water and the bottom like glue." Slowly we powered between a line of fingerboards to anchor off the settlement.

Legend has it Spanish Wells was a watering port for early navigators. It required little imagination to visualize fat merchantman or sleek privateer swinging in the multihued water, a rowing boat filled with casks approaching the beach. For Spanish Wells is by and of the sea; her men live on the sea, and her women look out across it, waiting. But gone were

the sails. As I stood on the foredeck of *Finisterre* paying out
the anchor rode I realized not one sloop or schooner was
moored in the harbor off the town. Even the dinghys no
longer had masts. Progress: outboards, inboards, automobile
conversions, diesels; smell of hot oil, scum in the bilge; stac-
cato exhausts at dawn and sunset; talk of miles per gallon and
waterpump packing. . . . But gone too the anxious hours of
midnight squalls and currents sweeping towards reefs; days
motionless under a shimmering sun, the sea mirrorlike reflecting; long sweeps and sculling oars, endless tacks, catch of
fish turning belly up in the well. . . . Progress, and the good
life. Gas in every tank, grouper in every pot.

The anchor snubbed, jerking *Finisterre*'s head like a curb
bit. *Gigi* ranged alongside, invitingly. We accepted. Ashore,
there was a new hotel and fuel pumps along the dock. Unchanged were the neat narrow streets, the neat small houses,
the neat courteous people, shy and quiet, but friendly. Spanish Wells is as clean as a town on the Zuider Zee.

As we walked I remembered we were greeting a true "four
hundred." The inhabitants are direct descendants of Royal-
ists from New York who chose to be resettled after our War
of Independence—or Rebellion, as their ancestors called it.
There has been much intermarriage, but virtually no dilution
of the pure Anglo-Saxon stock. Through the generations a
definite type has emerged: very fair, with skin that never
seems to tan even through a lifetime of exposure, blue eyes,
blond hair, slim and corded bodies. The children are beautiful.

As we powered back to *Finisterre* I looked astern at the little
town drowsing under the palms; looked at the boats careened
along the shore, at the blue sky and bluer water, at the shingle
roofs and dogs sleeping in the streets, nothing happening
through the turn of the seasons except the quiet fall of scarlet
hibiscus petals, and suddenly I could see and hear and smell
New York: the New York of Times Square, or Thirty-fourth

and Seventh, or Park Avenue and Sixty-eighth Street: brass and steel, piled masonry and aluminum facade, the very earth shaking from hurry on the surface and below the surface and in the air above, cacophony of sound and dollars to buy mink jackets, tranquilizers and phenobarbital wholesale and/or re-tail—same planet, another world.

The breeze had gone northwest before Aziel Pinder came aboard. Northwest, and very light. In the Bahamas, lying on the northern fringe of the trade winds, when the wind moves out of the east, it usually goes on around, clockwise. Sailors call the cycle a norther. It is predictable, but non-predictable: you generally know when one is coming, but never how hard or long it will blow; whether it will come in as a hard squall ahead of a gale which will rage for days, or whether the first burst will be followed by clearing skies and a shift to east and pleasant sailing; whether it will begin mildly as a gentle northwester, and only begin to howl when it gets to northeast, or never blow at all. . . .

Now, as we powered through the channel, I was aware of a vague distrust. The cirrus veil had vanished. The sky was very blue except for scattered cumulus; huge clouds, which towered to the stratosphere. The sun was bright. Everything sparkled. It was a day of perfection, an ideal Bahama day. But it wasn't right. Not with the wind northwest.

Ahead lay Gun Point, a low spit of sand topped by waving palms. I was curious. For many years I had heard of the reef passage from Spanish Wells to Harbour Island, but had never attempted it. Wide open to the whole Atlantic Ocean, a maze of coral heads and reefs, the beach under the turn of your bilge: a mistake and you've 'ad it, agreed all reports. Many had.

As *Finisterre* approached Gun Point I noted a sand shelf extended off, but also that the current had scoured a channel close to the shore. Beyond, the next point was marked on the chart as Ridley's Head: "See him?" asked Aziel. "There's the chin, there's the nose, the forehead." Running to it from Gun Point was a bank of white sand covered by perhaps three fathoms. Attempting to memorize the pilotage, I told myself: clear water on a line between the two points.

Nor was it too difficult to the next point. But somewhere beyond I gave up trying to remember. There was a tangle of reefs, some marked by iron pipes which had been twisted by the pounding of gales, some unmarked; some you left to port, others to starboard, others you ignored. There was a rock ledge called the Devil's Backbone extending almost to the shore, where a sand bank built out to meet it: you held close to the reef or the scend of the sea carried you among the palms; you swung out again at the proper moment, or you fetched up on the sand bank; but if you held too close to the reef, you would find sea fans waving in your bilge.

There is something barbaric and magnificent about venturing through a jungle of coral: here a black spot indicating a single head thrusting up abruptly through several fathoms, perhaps wider at the top than the bottom, as deadly as an erect cobra; there a purple-brown smudge, a jagged range of living rock not quite reaching the surface, ready to tear and rend at the first touch of a keel: shades of blue, hues of green, colors paling to crystal; curl of white in a lifting swell, ripples around a point, slow rise and heave in a motionless sea. Always the overtone of possible disaster, always the might of the ocean, waiting. And always implicit the courage and dignity of men, even the simplest men, who had risked and probed through the generations, learning.

No sooner had we threaded the reef and rounded The Point of Eleuthera than I wished *Finisterre* back in Spanish Wells. Me, I'm a snug harbor sailor. A five mile sweep of water opened northwest of Dunmore Town, and jagged limestone rimmed what would be a lee shore if the wind blew hard from the dangerous quadrant. We slowed for Aziel to bring his dinghy alongside for the trip home and agreed he would return the following afternoon. Morning was impossible, because he taught Sunday School. We proceeded towards town but I wasn't liking it one bit. Nor was I soothed when we came to anchor beyond the dock.

Ashore, I temporarily forgot my worries. Dunmore Town was not in the least like Spanish Wells, but in its way was a settlement of similar charm. Hidden among palms were the houses of winter visitors, as Harbour Island has its colony seeking the sun. It had not been spoiled by overbuilding, or bad building. There was the feeling of the not-so-many years ago Nassau I knew and loved, the Nassau of the thirties, before its postwar influx of English flight capital and American tourists in swarming packaged droves.

We bought supplies and walked across the island. Below us was the beach. "It *is* pink," exclaimed Zib in surprise. The reality of local phenomena rarely matches the promise of the resort advertisement.

The sand was like talcum powder: I scooped up a handful, and let it trickle through my fingers. Mixed with the white grains were tiny flecks of red, bits of shell and coral ground in the tireless mill of the sea. The effect was a delicate but definite pink, a lovely soft color which became more pronounced at a distance. To the south Eleuthera was a hazy blue shadow. Nearer, held in the curved arm of the beach, the shallows were an incredible green, a green sometimes seen in glass strongly backlighted. We sat to look, and became aware of a most amazing sight. The wavelets were pink. Each tiny transparent crest took on the color of the sand beneath. By contrast, the blues and greens became more vivid. We stared in a mood of childlike wonder and contemplation which did not end until the sun dropped below the dune behind us.

But as we crossed the high spine of the island and looked down on *Finisterre*, any lingering appreciation of beauty was lost in apprehension. A heavy milky veil had been drawn over the sky. Pale cirrus feathers radiated from a dark mass in the northwest. The wind had backed almost to south. Our stern had swung towards the dock.

Aboard, we put down a second anchor.

I was awake at dawn. The wind was west, very light. Rapidly it freshened, coming up with the sun. *Finisterre* began to move restlessly.

The old seaman's quandary: stay in a bad anchorage, or risk going to a better one? Take a chance getting caught among reefs, or remain in an uncomfortable but relatively safe position? If the front came in as a heavy squall as we were off the Devil's Backbone, with the body of the gale behind the first blast, what then? Within minutes the whole area would be a seething cauldron. But if the wind didn't go into the north until we made Spanish Wells we could sail through Current Cut and across the banks to Nassau, again sheltered by the line of cays, this time on the other side.

Activity on the mailboat at the dock made up my mind. She had come in shortly after dawn. Now she was ready to leave. On impulse I jumped in *Gigi* and raced alongside. The dock was crowded. Lines were beginning to snake aboard. Curious faces stared down. "Where is the captain?" I called.

A young man appeared at the wheelhouse window.

"Can I follow you out?" I asked. "Past Devil's Backbone?"

He looked down. "What boat you on?"

I pointed. He stared at *Finisterre*. "I guess so. But you better get goin'. We're leavin'. It's gonna blow."

When the mailboat backed clear of the quay our anchors were on deck. We fell in astern, engine wide open. From the first it was obvious we could not keep up. The gap of water between us steadily widened.

By now the whole sky was overcast, a steely gray. The wind had dropped to a whisper. Around us the water lay flat, taking on the same color as the sky. A few random drops of rain spattered on the deck.

The square stern of the mailboat continued to recede. We could hear and feel the pulse of her diesel diminish.

"We're losing her," said Zib. She had gone below for oilskins and had taken the wheel while I put on mine.

"Afraid so. *Gigi*'s a pretty heavy drag. We're making barely six knots."

I looked at the sky and the water. Despite the overcast, it was possible to judge depths fairly well. There was little surface reflection.

"Do you mind going on?" I asked, aware it might be a foolish decision. If it began to rain heavily when we were in the reefs, if a fifty knot squall should catch us at the Backbone, if there should be a big groundswell . . .

"No."

I slowed the engine to avoid overheating. Full power might be vital later.

Then I noticed we were closing the gap to the mailboat. It had been at least a half mile ahead. As we neared I saw a group of men at her rail, aft.

The captain waved us closer. "We can't wait for you," he shouted. "We got freight and mail for Nassau!"

"All right," I yelled back. "Thanks anyway."

He gestured for us to come alongside. "Harold Pinder from Spanish Wells'll go with you. He knows the water as good as anyone."

A pilot. I hesitated. But another hand in case of trouble, a seaman from Spanish Wells . . . My hesitation was only momentary.

Beyond The Point the ocean was calm. From deck level, looking seaward, there was no sign of movement. But as the bottom thrust upwards to sounding depth, undulations appeared on the surface, long lazy swells moving in from northwest. They shouldered us gently aloft as they passed under

Finisterre, then sped on towards shore to rear high and thunder on limestone promontories, or run hissing across sand beaches to the palms beyond. The sea, so innocent, so deadly. On both sides shallow coral patches showed white teeth.

From the first it was obvious Harold Pinder knew every rock and bar like the back of his hand. Flurries of rain which obscured landmarks and pelted the surface of the water into froth worried him not at all. He sat at the wheel, a chunky square figure in glistening oilskins, as unconcerned as a chauffeur driving along a familiar street. The wind held off. Jet black clouds looking like plums in a pudding came down on us in procession, but none had weight. I had the feeling of being part of a play whose climax had not arrived. On the fringe of the trades solid overcast, rain squalls, and calm contain the necessary elements of suspense. But nothing happened. The flags hung limp at the mastheads, or lifted only because of our speed through the water.

Then unaccountably behind a wet windless squall we found sunshine and a light northwest breeze. Anticlimax. The overcast peeled away like the opening of a trick nightclub roof. We blinked at each other, hot under our oilskins. "Beats me," said Harold. "This weather gone crazy. Now take when I was a boy. . . ."

After dropping the hook in the pool off Spanish Wells we put Harold ashore and raced back towards Harbour Island in *Gigi*, feeling cheated at missing our morning swim. I was anxious to atone to Zib for my mistaken judgment of the weather. Beyond Ridley's Head lay a cove, a small circle of beach protected by curving horns of rock, leaving only a narrow shallow entrance. Picking our way inside we found clear water, waving palms—and pink sand.

When we started back for lunch the day had again changed. The wind had clocked into the north and a peculiar smoky haze had crept across the sky. Whitecaps rolled through the entrance to the cove. They grew larger as we neared Gun

Point. "Zib," I called over the noise of the engine, "we're still going to get it. This is a weather breeder. It's going to blow like hell."

"When?"

I shrugged. "Damned if I know. Maybe tonight. Maybe tomorrow. But soon."

After lunch I put out a second anchor, listened to a recording of Bach's entire Art of the Fugue, and called Nassau on the radio-telephone, arranging for Bill and Nancy McWilliams, houseguests arriving from Annapolis, to fly to join us in the morning.

All afternoon and evening the wind moved around the compass: north-northeast; northeast; east-northeast, east. As it hauled it freshened. When I went on deck for a last look before turning in the rigging had begun to complain. Not a star showed. Overhead clouds were fused into a solid canopy; in the dark I could visualize the rolling gray bases, streaked with wisps of scud and blacker squalls.

And so it was at dawn, a diluted pale dawn of gray light filtering through a gray sky. The wind had gone almost southeast, not much stronger than during the night, but solid enough to lean slightly against, standing forward. When at 9:30 the McWilliams dropped out of the sky they received scant welcome. Within minutes we had cleared the dredged channel and hoisted main, mizzen and our reliable friend, the working jib. There are times when it pays to get a move on, even cruising.

Finisterre heeled although the wind was well aft. Immediately I felt better. Our arrival in Nassau had now become a race: our speed through the water against the falling barometer, the hauling wind, the advancing cold front. Standing on the bow I watched the bottom rush under our keel. There is no sensation of speed to equal the feeling of a boat driving through clear shoal water. I began to hum the silly tune, content. The wind had gone 'round and 'round, and we were still going with it; under us was a good ship, we were an adequate crew, and with any luck we would be on our mooring behind Hog Island before the wind went ahead and unleashed its full fury.

But as we neared the cut between Little and Great Egg Islands I was less certain we would win our race. The wind continued to work on around, little by little, as the sky became darker and more threatening. Beyond soundings, the deep water wore a black sullen look, as different from the normal blue as the leaden sky.

This time I wanted to be close to the lines of cays. We might need all the cushion to windward we could get. With *Gigi* astern it would be impossible to beat into the wind and sea we could expect when the shift came. There was no passage short of Chub Rock I would dare try. It was a case of having to win our race or sail back to Royal Island. And if we lost just short of our goal, we would not have time to sail back before dark. Which would mean a night at sea with a heavy boat in tow, the open Atlantic to weather, a pocket of low rock cays and sunken coral reefs to leeward.

As though sensing the challenge *Finisterre* put her shoulder down and went to work. This was what she was built for, my dream ship: to carry sail and go anywhere, fast and in comfort. My apprehensions about weather were only those of human frailty, not so much based on fear of actual danger as on a reluctance to undergo discomfort. It was impossible not to revel in the feeling of power under us. A short steep sea was coming off the bank. Close reaching, *Finisterre* drove through without lifting to the successive crests, knifing and smashing in one smooth continuous flow. Fanning sheets of spray rhythmically rose from the bow and blew off to leeward like horizontal rain.

As we closed the line of cays near Upper Samphire the wind abruptly shifted two points. Thankful for our windward position we rolled with it, more nearly paralleling the shore. Familiar shapes began to come into sight ahead: Booby Rocks, Booby Island, the eastern tip of Rose Island. We were nearing home waters, and I was grateful. For the sky was darker than ever, and the wind increasing. In the puffs we were forced to spill wind from the main by luffing, and even in the lulls were slightly overpowered. But the race was still not won. We were at the crucial point of no return.

Sandy Cay was in sight and we were under the beach of Rose Island when I saw a squall coming. White froth overlay the whitecaps to windward, blasting spindrift from the crests. Under the lash of the wind, the sea had a curious frosty look.

Bill McWilliams had been steering while I stood at the weather rail watching sea and sky. I shouted at Zib to take the wheel and scrambled forward to the main halyard.

I was not quick enough. A solid weight of wind pushed us down, down. I lost my footing while reaching for the winch handle and washed along the deck, up to my waist in rushing water. "Slack the main!" I yelled to Bill. "Zib! Bring her up! Luff!"

Overhead canvas slatted as the deck lifted and water flowed off. I struggled back to the mast and brought the mainsail down on the run.

With the squall the wind went into the south. Even under reduced sail *Finisterre* buried deeply. Astern *Gigi* seemed to leap from crest to crest.

Now the whole western sky was black, and the casurinas and palms ashore writhed in the rising gale. I felt only exhilaration. This time it was not for us to worry; this time it would howl for someone else.

We carried sail to the mooring, still with sheets eased. The wind had been behind us all the way, both ways. As Bill helped furl the mizzen I began to croon to myself, "Oh, you push the first valve down. . . ."

"What?" asked Bill, looking over the boom. "Did you say something?"

"No," I answered. "Nothing at all."

By midnight the wind was southwest. Some time before dawn it shifted to northwest in a blast that shook the house. In the morning even the sheltered waters of Nassau harbor were covered with whitecaps. *Finisterre* and the other boats plunged at their moorings. It was the hardest blow of the winter.

It blew three days before hauling east. Then it blew some more.

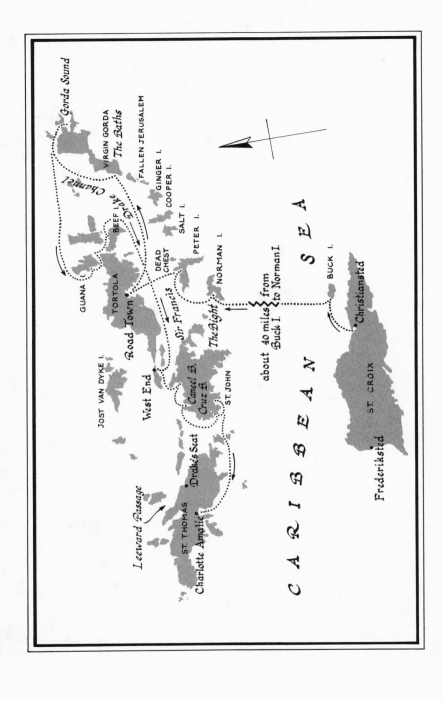

3
New Magic in an Ancient Sea
THE VIRGIN ISLANDS

Down in the Virgin Islands they have a saying that there are two kinds of time, "clock time and Cruzan time." The former is the variety which we all know too well, the scurrying second hand adding up to minutes and the minutes to hours, each a reminder of appointments to be kept and each carrying a sense of destiny.

But Cruzan time is something else again. It sounds like "cruising" spoken in the softly slurred West Indian dialect; and it stems from Santa Cruz, the name Columbus bestowed on his first landfall in the archipelago, now St. Croix. Cruzan time means slow down, take it easy, old boy, enjoy the sun and the view and the tall glass in your hand. It's later than you think only by clock time.

It seems the most natural thing in the world for time to have a special quality in the Virgin Islands. They lie against the dark blue velvet of the sea like a handful of emeralds scattered by a careless pirate. Some are low and framed by beaches of dazzling white sand, while others are rocky and steep enough to defy a browsing goat. Some await their Robinson Crusoe with an air of never having known the tread of man, others are dotted by houses riding the saddles of the hills, or snuggled under palms in sheltered coves. There are nightclubs in the towns with calypso music and on the outer islands ruins of ancient plantations being recaptured by creeping growth; and modern bungalows close to weathered stone houses almost hidden by hibiscus and bougainvillaea. Around the next headland from the settlement is almost always the deserted anchorage. Everywhere is contrast in color and form and character: palms waving against a background of blue, slow-moving people, and an overwhelming sense of *mañana*.

Here also, for those who want them, can be curved sails overhead and a wake creaming astern, for no area anywhere in the world offers better cruising conditions during most of the year. The entire archipelago of some 100 islands and cays is within the magic band of the tropics, yet is not far enough south to experience searing equatorial heat. Nor do the tail end of blizzards occasionally reaching Florida and the Bahamas as "northers" extend so far. Thus there is little difference in temperature between January and June, because the surrounding ocean acts as a vast air conditioner.

Almost constantly there is a breeze from the east, the trade wind of the era of commercial sail. Rare is the day when it does not come up with the sun, ready to drive a cruising yacht to the next harbor. True, there are times when it falls to a whisper, and other occasions when it pipes a mite too pert for comfort, but generally the trade wind is close to just right for a husky little vessel, especially in sheltered water. And a beneficient Providence has provided even that.

I had come down to the Virgin Islands remembering all this from previous visits. I was beaten by snow and the book I was writing and the telephone, and found myself suffering mirages of sparkling water and waving palms. *Finisterre* was laid up for the winter, but suddenly I remembered the Caribbean had known the finest flowering of that post-war phenomenon, the charter boat. The Virgin Islands had become home base for a fleet of infinite size and type, so all I had to do was make a choice to become an instant yachtsman.

"Look," I said to myself, "you can fly down, have a day to prowl around a major American island, sail a chartered boat through the British Virgins for a week, have another day at another American island on the other end, and be back in ten days. Or compress it into a week of solid sailing."

So one gray morning I left New York ankle deep in slush, and got off my airplane blinking at the sunshine like a hibernating bear whose tree has been pulled apart. Partially due to the schedule of the boat I chartered on short notice, I was to begin my cruise from St. Croix. I was content, as I planned ten days in the islands, and on Cruzan time that is a long holiday.

St. Croix is a narrow island, shaped somewhat like a weathervane pointed towards the prevailing breeze. The eastern end receives scant moisture; it tends to be arid, but its compensations are good beaches and virtually unfailing sunshine. The central and western section is a garden of fertile soil, tended through the centuries. Cane fields run in a green and brown checkboard from the shore to the central ridge of mountains, whose heights are cool and shadowy in liana-festooned rain forests. Conical stone towers of ancient windmills dot the slopes, reminders of a glamorous past, when West Indian planters lived as rich and pleasant a life as any in history.

Few islands have had a more varied background. Successively it has flown seven flags—Spanish, British, Dutch, French, Knights of Malta, Danish and United States. Traces of each culture are visible. It is the least Americanized American possession of my experience. Here are no four lane highways, no garish signs, no inharmonious civic structures. Traffic moves on the left, British fashion; the streets of the towns are called *gades*, from the days of Danish occupancy; houses front the sidewalk with gardens behind, as customary in French colonies; and the policeman on the corner may address pedestrians in Spanish.

"St. Croix is a place which grows on you," mused my friend Lee Platt as we later sat looking out over the harbor at Christiansted. It had grown on him, certainly, as it has on many others. He had sailed in one day for a look around, and swallowed the anchor. "It is as different from St. Thomas as town and country. We don't have tourists in the usual sense, but we do have the gracious life." St. Croix, home of Cruzan time, is determined to remain that way.

Christiansted is the principal town. A squat red fortress with white trim, built by the Danes in 1734, still commands the harbor, looking like an oversized Christmas package. Schooners and inter-island freight boats unload at the quay, and carts piled high go rumbling off to dim shops. Sidewalks are shaded by overhanging upper floors, supported by coral block and brick arches along the street line. Houses are painted in pastels, pink and yellow and green, colors which fade quickly in the sun to harmonize with weathered ancient walls. Open doors afford glimpses into patios brilliant with flowers. All is quiet and cool and unhurried, probably changed little in appearance or feeling from the days when Alexander Hamilton clerked for a local merchant.

Barnabus, a 48-foot steel ketch chartered by mail, arrived on schedule. Built in Holland, *Barnabus* looked capable, comfortable, sea-kindly, and—slow. She was. "We never has to reef," boasted Captain Ronnie as I came aboard, a sure indication of a vessel undercanvassed for normal conditions. But this wasn't racing, and I had left the mental stopwatch firmly behind, buried in the snow with *Finisterre*.

Anchor up, *Barnabus* heeled to a glorious fresh easterly. It

was a brilliant day, with small white clouds scurrying overhead, and each wavelet reflecting myriad points of sunshine.
We had the choice of a 35-mile sail across open ocean to the
main group, or lazing for a night behind nearby Buck Island,
5 miles along the coast. Offshore the trade wind white horses
were kicking up their heels. *Mañana*, I decided, and chose the
low road in smooth water to a wide beach and snug anchorage
in the lee of an uninhabited tropic isle, complete with waving
palms. For the energetic, behind the reef at the other end of
Buck Island is an underwater trail, complete with signposts
and tame fish. Such choices are among the joys of cruising,
Cruzan style.

But next morning the high road beckoned. After an early
swim—and what is a greater luxury while others shiver than
to swim in warm clear water, so clear you can see the anchor
on the bottom below, so warm you stand on deck drying in
the breeze?—the main was hoisted, and sedately *Barnabus* ambled around the fringing reef.

Away from the lee the seas were long, but without malice,
gentle rollers topped by crests which slapped lazily at our
ample flanks. The water was the deep purple blue of the
abyss, for not far offshore were depths exceeding 2000 fathoms, over 2 miles. Trade wind clouds ringed the horizon but
never seemed to come overhead. Flying fish skittered away.
Patches of brown Sargossa weed drifted past, and around
them dolphin darted.

St. Croix is entirely separate from the other Virgins. In
fact, old books of sailing directions did not even list it as part
of the group. Where St. Thomas and St. John and the British
islands of the northern archipelago lie on a single bank of
soundings running westward to Puerto Rico, so they form
and share a common shelter, St. Croix rides by itself as an
isolated peak. It is one of the few islands in the outer perimeter of the West Indies wholly within the Caribbean, unlike

the Windwards and Leewards, which are washed on one side
by the Atlantic Ocean.

We were sailing in the wake of history. Through these same
waters had streamed the whole forgotten procession of men
from the Old World to the New, ghostly men in ghostly ships,
from carvels to galleons to clippers. And almost paralleling
our course passed the first and the greatest; as Christopher
Columbus had voyaged north in 1494 from St. Croix on the
Second Voyage he had seen over the bow an astonishing
number of islands, beyond count as peaks merged and broke
apart through changing perspective, and he was reminded of
the legend of St. Ursula and the Eleven Thousand Virgins.
Ursula, a princess, had persuaded her father to allow her a
cruise before becoming the bride of a neighboring monarch.
She asked a few young ladies to accompany her, but multi-
tudes desired to sign on. It took eleven ships to accommodate
them all, but their final landfall was unfortunately timed. The
fleet dropped anchor in Cologne as the city was being sacked
by the Huns. A famous painting leaves no doubt as to the fate
of the virgins. Ursula was canonized, while the whole crew
was immortalized by Columbus. And that, despite lewd
speculation to the contrary, was how the archipelago received
its name.

Our course was slightly east of north for Norman Island,
at first indistinguishable from others of the group. The wind
was east-southeast, about 15 knots, making it an easy fetch.
Occasionally *Barnabus* rolled her rail down almost to the water, while a smother of white foam boiled off to leeward. It
was lovely, lazy sailing, and gradually the islands ahead lifted
and separated, meanwhile changing from the hazy blue of
distance to bright patterns of green vegetation and brown
rocks.

Behind the point at the southwest corner of Norman lay a
cove shown on the chart as Privateer Bay. This made out into
a long peninsula called Treasure Point, perhaps in recogni-

tion of the legend that in caves near the tip a Spanish chest crammed with gold and jewels was found a half-century ago. Beyond this point extended a snug anchorage, The Bight. A long half-moon of white sand curved around water which paled as it shoaled, while above palms moved in the soft warm breeze. Two small yachts lay anchored close to the shore; another swung near the point, her crew spearfishing over coral clumps.

To understand cruising the Virgins, it is necessary to visualize the pattern of the archipelago between St. Thomas and Virgin Gorda. Two parallel lines of islands extend almost east and west, forming the Sir Francis Drake Channel, named for that intrepid Elizabethan sea predator when he proceeded through in 1585 to attack Hispaniola. In the words of the *New Sailing Directions for 1818,* "Nature has so arranged the islands as to form a grand basin . . . wherein ships may lie at anchor, land-locked, and sheltered from every wind." Thus when the trade is blowing northeast, the water is smooth under the lee of Tortola; when it blows southeast, better conditions exist along the shores of the southern islands. This is not to say that during the heaviest weight of the trade wind Drake Channel cannot get rough, but it is the sea of, say, Long Island Sound or Chesapeake Bay, rather than the open ocean. And distances between islands are short, and harbors plentiful. As Reed Chambers of *Merposal III* put it, "You could anchor in a different harbor every night for 30 nights and each would be perfect." Further, in only a very few places—well charted—is pilotage made hazardous by hidden dangers, such as coral heads or reefs. In the Virgins, if you can't see it, you aren't likely to hit it, a welcome change from many areas.

It seemed a shame to anchor in The Bight only long enough for a swim, but I remembered a cove on Peter Island I wanted to visit before sunset. Typical of distances in the Drake Channel, the passage between was two miles. Skirting the shore of Peter Island, we were tempted by another pair of anchorages,

Great and Little Harbors, before coming to Deadman Bay. This was it, a long-remembered dream of tropic perfection: multihued water, white sand beach, overhanging coconut palms, the works. And just offshore lay Dead Chest, a steep bleak island, an easy setting to imagine a band of drunken pirates singing "Fifteen men on a dead man's chest, yo-ho-ho and a bottle of rum!" Local legend has it that Blackbeard marooned part of a mutinous crew here, forming the inspiration for Robert Louis Stevenson's famous *Treasure Island* chant.

With the light fading, *Barnabus* crept into the harbor of Road Town, on Tortola, passing in the Channel a pair of spouting whales that were a match in both overall length and beam. Road Town is a port of entry for the British part of the group, which includes the islands and cays eastward of a line curving around the windward side of St. John. Formalities consisted merely of surrendering a crew list, despite our fracture of regulations by stopping at Norman before officially entering British territory.

Road Town was no longer familiar. In the '30's, and even immediately after the war, it had been a tiny settlement, oriented to the fields on the slopes above, and a fleet of fishing and cargo sloops swinging in the shallows. Boats were built under palms rimming the waterfront, alongside drying nets and lobster traps. Now by comparison Road Town was a bustling metropolis. At the head of the dock drivers of air conditioned taxis competed for attention—where not long before an automobile was a curiosity. What had been a sleepy main street fronted by frame houses had become a thoroughfare lined by stores, with the residential area moved to outskirts which were burgeoning into suburbs. Yet as a compensation for the loss of the picturesque, fresh supplies were available, and even hotels for those who might wish to linger.

But boats were made for escape by those who want it, and no sooner had the harbor of Road Town dropped astern than

we were back on an uncluttered highway, little changed since
Columbus had ordered the same waters explored by a task
force from his fleet. Slowly we tacked in long hitches. It was
a day when the trade wind was light, and *Barnabus* refused to
be hurried. I dozed atop the deckhouse, considering the
names on the chart, and wondered why they had been bestowed.

Virgin Gorda, our day's goal, was easy: *gorda* means fat
in Spanish, and the peak to the north made it a very obese
island indeed. On Virgin Gorda lay The Baths, supposedly
the scene of ablutions by generations of men-o'-war sailors,
and it is difficult to explain any other reason for it being
so labeled in British Admiralty publications. The rock
called Carvel would have taken its name from an ancient
type of ship—perhaps one of the very group Columbus
sent through while the main body of his fleet remained in
safe depths. Salt Island was the site of a pond where
seawater was allowed to evaporate. Round Island was
round, and Fallen Jerusalem equally appropriate: a freak of
nature had created huge squarish boulders and rock pinnacles, and then tossed them around to look like a ruined
city.

The Baths of Virgin Gorda are a similar formation.
Enormous rocks were left heaped on one corner of a curving beach by past geologic activity. Visitors must crawl
through a triangular gap to a pool in an inner cave. There,
like the Blue Grotto at Capri, the source of illumination is
sunlight reflected from a white sand bottom. As the rays
penetrate the seawater, they take on some of its color, so
The Baths are suffused by a pale green glow, heightening
the weird effect.

At the opposite end of Virgin Gorda lay Gorda Sound,
almost land-encircled, 10 fathoms and more deep in the
center, with clear water and scattered ledges in the shallows near shore. Claude, our cook from the French island

of St. Barts, promised good spearfishing. He also promised with the proceeds to concoct "a courtbouillon, a kind of bouillabaise we eats here."

In the water, with face mask and snorkel, it was clear that the pot would be filled. But despite the appeal to the gourmet side of my nature, the hunter was stilled as I looked around me. Nothing in nature quite compares to a tropic reef. The variety of form and color never can lose its magic through familiarity. For a long while I hung with a curious weightlessness, occasionally kicking down, seeing bright blue fish lazing under branches of coral, like birds in trees; noting how the sand was ridged into hills and valleys by the action of the sea; watching the strange semaphore of sea-urchins tucked in rock crevices. Then a margot fish just right for the galley moved slowly over a patch of open bottom, and my thoughts changed. I dived and missed. As I floated on the surface reloading a grouper swam from one coral head to another, going into a tiny cavern. I went down. Nothing. A fish can put on a better disappearing act than any Houdini, vanishing into what appears to be a solid mass of rock, or hiding completely in an open latticework where no shelter seems to exist. But on the third dive a handspan of mottled brown skin showed for an instant. One for the pot. And a crawfish whose feelers had poked from under the bottom ledge as I had stalked the grouper. Enough, especially as I saw Claude towing a string of smaller fry.

Back on *Barnabus*, sitting in the cockpit admiring the sunset through the amber filter of another of the products of St. Croix, I watched Claude fashion his West Indian bouillabaise. It was a dish worth recording: Brown 2 sliced onions and 3 diced garlic cloves in 1 tablespoon butter and 1 tablespoon cooking oil; add ½ small can tomato sauce, a "touch" of curry powder, salt and pepper, and about 3 pounds of fish—including the heads—scaled and cleaned, but unboned, cut in chunks. Pour over hot water to cover, and squeeze in the juice of 2 limes. Cook covered until the flesh of the fish begins to flake from the bones. Lift out the fish onto warm plates, and pour the liquid from the pot into separate bowls. The broth is served as a first course, although I recommend saving some to moisten the rice which accompanies the fish; it is rich, dark reddish-brown in color, and very savory. The fish will be moist and perfect. A superb combination with a salad on the side, especially eaten in the cockpit under the stars after a day of sailing and swimming.

Gorda Sound was my planned turning point, as it is for most cruising the Virgins. Beyond lay only Anegada, a lonely flat island surrounded by a maze of coral reefs which look like barbed wire entanglements on a chart. Now *Barnabus* would be scudding off before the trade wind, the happiest moments of tropic sailing.

Leaving to port a group of rocks with the lovely names of Seal Dog, George Dog, Great Dog, and West Dog, (but who named them, leaving out Fido?) *Barnabus* rolled gently along outside Great Camanoe to round the west end of Guana Island. Still guarding the approach to the harbor was the rock formation looking exactly like the outthrust head of a giant lizard, from which the island takes its name. High above on the saddle of the hill was the manor house, built on the foundations of a Quaker plantation of two centuries ago: to the north, it commanded a view of open blue ocean; to the south, the pale blue and green water of the harbor, with Tortola beyond. Flanked by the flame of an immortal tree in blossom, and the slightly less hot red of massed bougainvillaea, it seemed more like an aerie in the Mediterranean than any other of my Caribbean experience.

Guana Island is a club operated by Louis and Beth Bigelow, which may be entered on introduction by a member, but is only one of a number of places where visitors may get away from it all for days or weeks on an outer island, beyond even the relative bustle of St. Thomas or St. Croix. Most of these guest houses are happy to have visiting yachtsmen come ashore for drinks or a meal, to vary shipboard routine. While the Virgin Islands is a place where privacy still exists, and deserted beaches and uninhabited coves remain, during the past few years escapees from colder climes have found here their own ideal place to live, and many have provided guest facilities to supplement income.

Only a short run to the east is one of the most popular, Marina Cay, subject of the book, *Our Virgin Island*, by Robb White, later made into a movie starring Sidney Poitier. The present phase of its career began when Commander Allan Batham, Royal Navy, Retired, and his wife Jean sailed in during 1958 and dropped the hook as a break in a voyage round the world. The 34-foot ketch *Airey Mouse* was destined to remain over 10 years before continuing. Meanwhile Marina Cay had become a magnet drawing other small cruisers. Rare is the sunset when a fleet does not swing in the perfect shelter of a fringing reef, while the crews go ashore to have a drink on the terrace, and later dine.

From Marina Cay, we had the choice of sailing eastward along the Atlantic Ocean side of Tortola, passing inside Jost Van Dyke and cutting into Pillsbury Sound through the Windward Passage; or beating the short distance around the windward tip of Beef Island to run the Sir Francis Drake Channel. Unhesitatingly I choose the latter: there is much ocean in the world, looking pretty much alike, but nothing to compare with Drake's Channel.

Rounding The Bluff, we came off until *Barnabus* was wing-and-wing, rolling along as windships had before us for centuries. Islands extended in a semi-circle from bow to stern on either hand, fair little islands in a shimmering sea, so closely spaced ahead there seemed no place for *Barnabus* to go. Soon Road Town was on the starboard beam, and the gap between Tortola and St. John became visible. Piled high over The Narrows were cumulus clouds, fantastic shapes towering into an incredibly blue sky, reflecting in the water as long pale tongues. The miles spun slowly astern while vistas of beach and palms slid past as though on an unwinding screen, occasional red roofs breaking long stretches of untouched hillside. Sun warm, trade wind cool, a fishing line trailing astern; harbors ahead, harbors astern, water over the side for swimming—what price now glory or gain, or the distant metropolis?

St. John, as we approached, revealed itself as a mountainous island with strongly etched valleys running down to the sea. On all sides, many of these terminated in coves exactly right for the Cruzan cruiser, a new delight around each headland. We poked into them sampling beaches and spearfishing like connoisseurs tasting rare vintages, anchoring when and as we pleased. And perhaps one of the best things about St. John is that it is likely to remain in the future much as it is today. In 1956 Laurence Rockefeller turned over to the Secretary of the Interior the deed to approximately 5,000 of the island's 12,000 acres, and it has been set aside as a National Park. More area will probably be added, and meanwhile visitors can be accommodated in a lovely hotel at Caneel Bay, once maintained as a rest center by the Danish West India Company.

Cruz Bay is a port of entry, complete with Government House, docks, and a few shops. There is regular launch service to Redhook Bay in St. Thomas, and automobiles may be hired for the trip to Caneel Bay, and other points in the National Park.

Our final passage when even Cruzan time began to run out was across Pillsbury Sound, a spectacular body of water by any standards. Steeply beyond white beaches to the east and west thrust the towering green slopes of St. Thomas and St. John, while to the north and south were lesser islands with cuts between leading to the open sea—Atlantic and Caribbean, each equally blue and inviting, glinting in the sunshine as highways to distant horizons.

Barnabus slid through a gap between Water Point and a small scrubby cay bearing the imposing name of Great St. James Island. The trade wind had continued moderate, and under us the water lay almost flat. Below the keel we caught glimpses of bottom, and ahead and off to starboard St. Thomas was reflected, complete to cloud cover.

St. Thomas through the centuries has been a goal of seafarers, perhaps in part because of the delights of the shore. The town of Charlotte Amalie faces the sea, but runs up the mountainsides, perhaps symbolizing the sailor's duality—love of the water but need for the land, with alternating desire to escape from each. Houses cover the slopes of three low hills —Government, Berg, and French—which in the old windjammer days were called Foretop, Maintop, and Mizzentop. Some streets were too steep for ordinary paving, so became long flights of steps.

As early as 1765 Charlotte Amalie was declared a free port by the King of Denmark, and it soon became not only a center of legitimate trade for the West Indies, but a rendezvous of privateers and "such traffic as the French, English, Dutch, and Spaniards, dare not carry on publicly in their own islands," in the words of an old volume of sailing directions. It was also a favorite haunt of the Brethren of the Coast, the buccaneers. Dominating the town from a bluff is Bluebeard's Castle Hotel, where a pirate of that name is reputed to have maintained a lookout tower, and on another eminence was the stronghold of Edward Teach, better known as Blackbeard, one of the thoroughgoing rascals of history. He wore flowing whiskers done up in pigtails, through which slow-burning matches for setting off cannon were thrust; he traveled festooned with pistols, which sometimes during drinking bouts were suddenly fired in the direction of his companions; and a favorite pastime was to create a version of Hell by battening down the hatches of his vessel, igniting sulphur, and seeing who could take it longest. The winner was always

Blackbeard, giving rise to the theory he was the Devil incarnate, until his head decorated the bowsprit of a Royal Navy sloop in Carolina waters.

The pirates are gone, but Charlotte Amalie remains an open and broadminded city. It is still a free port; no customs duties are levied on incoming merchandise, and shops are stocked with the pick of the world at prices far below stateside levels. St. Thomas is much more of a tourist island than St. Croix, a crossroads of air and steamer traffic, with large modern hotels frankly oriented to the tripper and short-term visitor. Still, part of the city remains a pleasant place to wander and dream, a blend of Old World and West Indian architecture and atmosphere.

Barnabus swung to starboard when we were well into the embrace of the land, and I blinked with astonishment at the number and variety of the yachts moored in the marina at the head of Long Bay. Yacht Haven has become the center not only of the Virgin Islands charter fleet, but serves as a base in the West Indies for many cruising vessels wintering far from their ice-bound home ports. Not only are all the other Virgin Islands easily accessible from St. Thomas—as differentiated from St. Croix, which during periods of heavy winds can be virtually isolated from the rest of the group—but St. Thomas forms an ideal jumping off place for the whole of the curving bow of the Windward and Leeward Islands.

Ashore, I found much new, much remembered from visits extending back nearly twenty years, but little essentially changed. The facilities of Yacht Haven included a swimming pool flanked by restaurant and bar, with efficiency apartments behind, all recent; but at venerable Hotel 1829 the Planter's Punch tasted the same, and the view from Drake's Seat was just as magnificent as on my first climb, before the Virgin Islands boom—for such the present influx of visitors and residents must be considered, in part occasioned by the miracles of air transport, in part reflecting a changing economic and social philosophy, where having fun today is more important than building for the morrow.

From Drake's Seat, where the old sea-dog is supposed to have watched his fleet pass in review, Magen's Bay and a magnificent vista of the Atlantic patterned by islands opened to the north; on the opposite side lay Charlotte Amalie harbor with the blue Caribbean beyond. At the altitude, the trade wind blew strong, carrying a touch of chill, but in contrast the sun seemed even hotter. All timeless qualities, which will never change. Perhaps cement and chrome hotels will appear on more hillsides, and the streets of the towns will become more crowded, and more boats will swing at anchor in more harbors, but for the countable future there will remain the secluded beaches and deserted coves. Thus my final impression of the Virgin Islands remained much as my first: everywhere contrast, in color and form and character. A place to visit, to sail, to live—all on Cruzan time, of course.

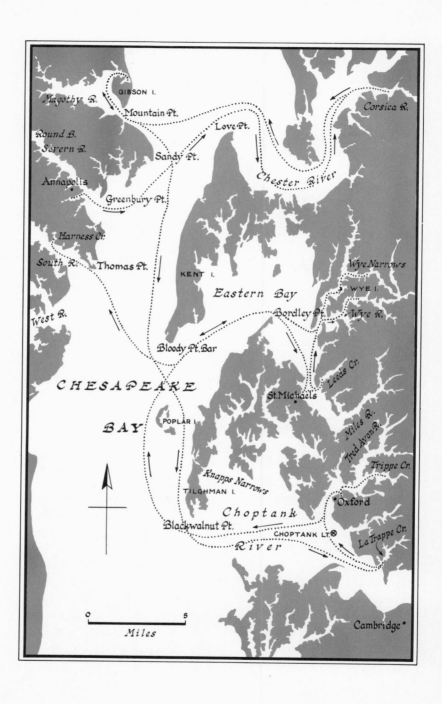

GIBSON I.

Magothy R.

Mountain Pt.

Love Pt.

Corsica R.

Round B.

Severn R.

Sandy Pt.

Chester River

Annapolis

Greenbury Pt.

Harness Cr.

South R.

Thomas Pt.

KENT I.

Eastern Bay

Wye Narrows

WYE I.

Bordley Pt.

Wye R.

West R.

Bloody Pt. Bar

Leeds Cr.

CHESAPEAKE

St. Michaels

BAY

POPLAR I.

Miles R.

Tred Avon R.

Knapps Narrows

Trippe Cr.

TILGHMAN I.

Oxford

Choptank

Blackwalnut Pt.

CHOPTANK LT.

La Trappe Cr.

River

0   5

Miles

Cambridge

4

Voyage into a Romantic Past
THE CHESAPEAKE

A gentle little southerly had begun to stir as *Finisterre* ambled across Annapolis harbor, the first breath of summer. Overhead, the sky was very blue, dappled with small clouds, the sky of a lazy June afternoon, yet in the shadow of the mainsail a chill was still in the air. Along the banks of the Severn newly unfurled leaves were pale green, accented by pink and white bursts of dogwood.

I stood in the cockpit, leaning against the mizzenmast. Occasionally touching the spokes of the steering wheel with a toe, half dozing in the spring sunshine, I reflected on the pleasures of getting back to familiar waters, surrounded by nice solid land, where if the breeze piped loud there would be no fetch for the seas to build, and harbors wherever you pointed the bow. I also ruminated on the joys of cruising: falling asleep hugging the thought there would be no rude summons on deck, getting up without knowing where I would be going, maybe letting the wind decide, sailing not caring if the proper jib was set and trimmed just so. . . .

"Hey, skipper," called Bill McWilliams, breaking into my reverie. "The jib's soft. Wind's come ahead. Shall I trim?"

I looked at the masthead fly, then at the wavelets, splintering the sun shafts into glittering points. As so often happens in fair weather, the breeze was advancing with the clock; it had been mirror calm at sunrise and through the early hours, with first catspaws appearing around ten, when we had gotten under way. Now it had freshened to good steerageway. Later, if it followed the usual cycle, it would strengthen through the afternoon, perhaps working up to a rousing rail-down slam around four, to taper off at sunset to a night of sibilant whispers in the tree tops.

Having gotten no answer about the jib, Bill strolled aft. "Where are we going, by the way?"

"I dunno," I replied lazily. "I haven't given it much thought."

What I really meant was that here on the Chesapeake there were so many delightful prospects I hadn't been able to choose. The whole area is such a lacy pattern of creeks and bays and rivers it is hard to decide whether it is water bounded by land or land bounded by water.

"Any suggestions?" I asked Bill.

Bill McWilliams squinted at the sky as though still on the bench. A lawyer, a judge, a raconteur, and an old Chesapeake hand, his opinion was not to be taken lightly. "If we go anywhere down the bay it will be a beat," he mused. "If we go up, we'll be reaching." So saying, he sat on the cabin and sprawled his legs across the lifelines, casting his ballot for sloth. The downwind vote was thereby unanimous. I flipped on the automatic pilot and went forward to join him, picking up a couple of cushions on the way.

Harbors literally lay in all directions. Even if we chose to turn around and sail west, up the Severn River instead of continuing into the open bay, we could pick from a multitude of anchorages. Typical of Chesapeake tidal rivers, although a lesser one by local standards, it winds on for miles, with a ladder of creeks and coves opening off, to finally blossom into a bay large enough to boast its own sailing club. Thus almost every Chesapeake tributary must be thought of as a microcosm of an infinitely varied cruising world.

When the radio towers on Greenbury Point dropped astern there came a moment of decision. So I let the wind suggest, gradually turning the bow to leeward until finally *Finisterre* slanted diagonally across the Bay, almost towards the northern tip of Kent Island.

"Heading for the Chester River?" inquired Bill, still sprawled on deck.

"Guess so," I answered. "If we come off for Gibson Island the wind will be dead aft. We'll have to set a spinnaker or start the engine to stem the tide."

Perish either thought. Discussion complete. Master and mate in accord. Bubbles slid along the hull and traced our wake, water furrowed by generations of ghostly ships. Where *Finisterre* now moved, Indians had passed in crude hollowed logs. Captain John Smith sailed by in 1608 to "perform his Discovery." Half a century later, Edward Lloyd of Wye House appeared in the first yacht, "a pleasure boat of 60 tons burthen," complete to "Ensign and pennant with 15 stripes, arms painted thereon, the field azure, the Lion gold . . . and 6 brass guns fixed on swivels to act in such a manner as to give the greatest report." And here also had passed each development of the age of commercial sail: the Chesapeake log canoe, the pungey, the ram, the bugeye, even the Baltimore tea clipper, white-winged marvel of the world's oceans.

As we drifted, I reflected on another of the charms of cruising: every area takes its character from the life along its shores, both present and past. The Caribbean, the South Pacific, the Aegean, the Baltic, the Mediterranean—each is different because of its own combination of geography and history.

The Chesapeake, too, is unique, as I was rediscovering. Here is a land of graciousness, of easy living, of uncluttered vistas, a legacy of cotton and tobacco and a plantation life when visits were measured in weeks, and it was necessary to pass legislation requiring that slaves not be fed terrapin too often. Here a small cruising yacht drifts across stretches of water bordered by trees or open fields, with perhaps an occasional glimpse of a lovely old house on a point. Here are anchorages disturbed only by the singing of birds and spreading rings following the splash of jumping fish. In the quaint, small villages people are hospitable and friendly. On the shores of the Chesapeake Bay still exists one of the nearest approaches to life on the other side of the Atlantic—a reasonable facsimile of rural England, modified by terrain and time.

As I mused, the breeze freshened. *Finisterre* leaned to it and spurted ahead. Gone was introspective indolence, to be replaced by the exhilaration of motion. Cruising is like that: a matter of mood stemming from weather and circumstance. Now we wanted to feel the boat go. The main was slacked a hair, the jib trimmed a few clicks, and *Finisterre* boiled along with the wind on the quarter, all hands fully awake to the perfection of the moment.

Love Point lifted rapidly. Swinging around the squat lighthouse marking the end of the shoals beyond Kent Island, we came hard on the wind. A beat could have been avoided by reaching a few miles to the fishing village of Rock Hall, or Swan Creek beyond. But we agreed a little windward work might not be amiss. "It will make us feel we've earned a drink," opined Bill bravely, not forgetting the distance was short, the water smooth, and that the jib could be roller-furled without wetting the feet.

Rail down, *Finisterre* drove across the river. This might be a good time to clear up a fairly general misconception of

Chesapeake cruising. Following normal pilotage procedures, a boat drawing six feet should have no real problems. True, there are areas where the water is spread thin, but in general the major tributaries of the Upper Bay—local name for the part north of the Potomac River—offer ample depths for care-free poking around. Pilotage aids are plentiful, fog infrequent, tidal range and current velocity slight, and in case of error the bottom is mud, not rock—lovely soft mud, so grounding is an inconvenience, not a catastrophe, just as a centerboard is a convenience, not a necessity.

The Chester River, across which we sailed, is fairly typical. Nearly three miles wide where it empties into the bay, depths average some 30 feet except close to the shores. Beyond, where it narrows, depths actually increase in places to 50 feet and more. Even after the Chester becomes a stream meandering through farmland, two fathoms still may be carried to the village of Chestertown, 25 miles above Love Point light.

Thus on *Finisterre* we had no navigational cares, and ahead the Eastern Shore stretched away as flat as the proverbial pancake, a peninsula 136 miles long, dangling like a bunch of grapes between the Atlantic Ocean and the Chesapeake Bay. It is shaped like a bunch of grapes, too, the northern stem part of Delaware, the center comprising nine counties of Maryland, the tapering tip in Virginia. It has borne its name for three centuries, ever since the first settlers established themselves on the western side of the bay and began referring to the land opposite as the Eastern Shore.

As we tacked and tacked again I remembered a day in autumn, when I had last sailed the Chester. It had been an afternoon of silver haze, smoky from burning leaves, and there had been a slight film of cloud over the sky, so it too was silvery. Yet somehow colors were intensified: the massed trees, turning russet and copper, the brown of cornstalks drying in the fields, the contrast of white barns and silos against evergreens, the steel gray of the water over which we crept.

Birds were everywhere, reminiscent of an earlier America. There were Canada geese in countless hundreds. They flew overhead in long trailing echelons, receding in perspective until the most distant were faint plumes on the horizon; they lifted from fields in waves; they floated in rafts on the water, watched over by wise old ganders, heads high and swiveling. Among the black and gray of the geese had been the pure white of wild swans, rare elsewhere, plentiful on the Chester. And shuttling through and over these noble birds were flights of lesser ones—ducks, coots, even gulls and fish hawks, eyeing patches of roiled water.

On that autumn cruise we had drifted by Grays Inn Creek, and on into the Corsica River. In the faint chill breeze *Finis-terre* had ghosted past gently rolling countryside in which sleek cattle browsed behind rail fences, to anchor finally where the river narrowed to a creek, the creek to a pond. After the sails came down with a rattle of slides, there had been only the sound of birds, wing beats and voices by the thousand, like the hum of a bumble bee's nest.

Now the hush of spring was upon the land. This time the Corsica was touched by the magic of bursting buds. The sun was low, and already the breeze had stilled; trees reflected, inverted, under the shore, and the creek took on the colors of the sky. Bill and I walked the deck, wordlessly, hands in pockets, and leaned against the rigging to watch.

Spring and fall, these are the magic times to cruise Chesapeake Bay. I have been under sail from the first warm days of late March to Christmas. When the New England coast, the Great Lakes, the Pacific Northwest, and even Long Island Sound are too frigid for pleasant cruising, the Chesapeake enjoys an additional month to six weeks on each side of summer. A boat brought down for winter lay-up, or en route to

58

Florida, can cash in on both. During these interim periods, days are likely to be warm and the nights cool, breezes are fresher and reasonably constant. There are few squalls. The water is clearer and more bracing for swimming. Air and waterborne pests—insects and jellyfish—are rare.

Summer has a different quality. Then, in the heat, there is a sense of almost voluptuous indolence, tempered always by an eye to squalls gathering over the western land. Crews laze under awnings, and screens are fitted at sundown. The water lies opaque and tepid. Boats anchor by the stern in creeks open to each vagrant puff of breeze. Fishermen sit patiently in rowboats, long cane poles extending like the antenna of insects. Cork bobbers float as immobile as racing fleets becalmed off the yacht clubs. The entire tempo of life slows. Some like it better.

Next morning it was still sunny, although a high haze softened shadows. Treetops waved, and a faint growl came from the upper rigging. The pen of the barograph traced a steady decline. Unmistakably a late season frontal system was on the way. We took our time over breakfast, for it was not the day for an open water passage. Hoisting sails, we drifted from our anchorage, feeling the breeze increase as the river widened, to find a wet beam reach across the bay to the shelter of the Magothy River. Anchoring in the lee behind Mountain Point, we had lunch, then reset sails for an afternoon of exploration of the headwaters. Gradually during the afternoon the clouds thickened and lowered, but well before sunset we swung on a mooring off the clubhouse of the Gibson Island Yacht Squadron.

Now I had my "harbors can be so nice" feeling. There was a chill edge to the wind on deck, but when I went below I was met by the snug coziness that exists only in the cabins of small boats. A coal fire burned in the bulkhead stove, a kettle simmered, oil lamp and candles shed a soft glow over books and polished mahogany. We settled on the cushions to listen to the hi-fi system, beginning with Heifetz playing Bach's Concerto in E-major for the violin, "the one with the bounce," as Bill put it. Sometime before dawn I was awakened by the patter of rain on deck. *Finisterre* shook to savage gusts as the front went through. Pulling the blanket tighter around my neck, I reflected briefly on the joys of cruising, especially the Chesapeake. Tonight others could struggle with flogging sails, somewhere offshore: for us the squall was a lullaby.

In the morning, we came on deck to find sky and earth scrubbed clean by the broom of a fresh nor'wester, clear cold air flooding down from Canada. *Finisterre* responded to the call of the wind, and soon we were past Mountain Point and into the open bay. It was a spring and fall day, both together: spring in the coloring of the shore and warmth of the sun, fall in the heft of the breeze. Wing and wing we skirted the beach to Sandy Point, speed diminishing as the Magothy dropped astern. As often happens, the wind had funneled down the western shore—a local phenomenon sought in light weather, especially by racing skippers, but to be remembered with caution when the wind is already heavy or when squall clouds gather.

A mid-summer Bay squall is not to be underrated. Three centuries ago John Smith wrote of the first encountered by a European sailor: "The winde and waters so much increased with thunder, lightning and raine, that our mast and sayle blew overbord and such mighty waves overwracked us in that small barge it was with great labour we kept her from sinking by freeing out the water."

Beyond Sandy Point, the course was almost south. Wind on the quarter, *Finisterre* romped along. The Severn opened to starboard, Kent Island slid by to port, Bloody Point Lighthouse ahead acting as a navigation aid and reminder of the past. On Kent was the first settlement of the Upper Bay, a trading post established by William Claiborne in 1631. In those virgin days the waters of the bay and its tributaries were as clear as the open ocean; fish swarmed the rivers, and every shoal was carpeted by oysters. Birds passed in flights to darken the sun. Trees stretched away in all directions, the forest primeval, individual trunks large enough to be hollowed into canoes capable of carrying forty Indians. Under the lofty canopy was little underbrush. Deer roamed in a cathedral peace of dim light and quiet.

Among the present generation of local sailors, there is an endless argument about the "best" of the rivers. Flowing into the bay are some 40 major estuaries, each fed by its own complex of branches, all feeling the pulse of the ocean to the remotest headwaters, for the entire Chesapeake is tidal. Devotees of the Upper and Lower Bay areas sing the delights of their own wide and lazy streams. Hidden harbors are played like cards, and always a secret gunk-hole is the final trump, perhaps only to be described, exact location and pilotage details too precious to be divulged, even to make a point.

Before us were my own twin favorites of the Chesapeake. Behind Kent Island stretched Eastern Bay, open mouth of the Wye, the Miles, and lesser streams; while a little farther along, past Tilghman Island, lay the Choptank River and its myriad feeders, wandering far across a peaceful countryside. Only from the air could the pattern be wholly comprehended, bringing visual reality to statistics of the United States Coast and Geodetic Survey, which show that the "tidal shoreline, detailed, of Chesapeake Bay and all its tributaries totals about 5,600 statute miles," against "4,840 statute miles of general coastline from Maine to Washington." In other words, measurement of each squiggle of each Chesapeake creek to the head of tidewater, or point where the water narrows to a width of 100 feet, exceeds the coastal outline of the continental United States. Nowhere can there be a straight line; everywhere there is one more creek and cove. And in the whole bay country the configuration was never more pronounced and thereby delightful for cruising than the waters over the bow of *Finisterre* that spring morning.

Again, it was the wind which decided our destination. It was too good a day not to sail as far as possible. Wordlessly, when Bloody Point lighthouse came abeam, course was altered for Poplar Island Narrows. Past Jefferson Island we sailed, looking somewhat wistfully at its lovely harbor, and ignored the shortcut of Knapps Narrows, a canal used by oystermen and crabbers to save distance. Avoiding the ever-present fish traps, we jibed off Blackwalnut Point, to enter the Choptank River by a well-charted channel. Not very far inside, the river is more than five miles wide, making it a rather respectable bay in itself.

Laying a course for Choptank light, I switched on the automatic pilot and sprawled back against the mizzenmast, nothing to hit that couldn't be seen, nothing in sight, nothing to do but consider the next choice. For at the lighthouse, now becoming visible ahead, we could swing to starboard and follow the Choptank past the small city of Cambridge as far as we cared to go—the river is navigated by commercial traffic for fifty miles into the heart of the Eastern Shore. Or at the light we could sharpen up to port and run the Tred Avon River beyond the village of Oxford, selecting an anchorage from an array of the loveliest creeks—on this, agreement is almost universal—of the entire Chesapeake.

We compromised, following the Choptank for a look into La Trappe Creek, then retracing our course into the harbor of Oxford. Here, in a snug inner cove, were tangible reminders of the golden age of sail. Maryland many years ago passed a law that oysters could not be dredged by powered vessels, so bugeyes and skipjacks, with their picturesque clipper bows and raked masts, still ply their ancient trade each winter, drowsing during the spring and summer tucked way in byways, refitting each fall.

Nor were these the only links with history. The village, with its spreading trees and smooth lawns, white picket fences and green shutters, bears a close resemblance to a New England town. Surrounding it is a countryside retaining much of the graciousness of an earlier era, fields running down to the water, colonial houses set back in flowering groves. And the flourishing boatyards rimming the harbor prove that it is continuingly oriented to the water.

Oxford was proclaimed a port of entry by Charles Calvert in 1669, when it was called Thread Haven, presumably because of ship chandleries. This modified into Third Haven, and later Tred Avon, which latter name applied to the river, while the village on its banks became known as Williamstadt, in honor of William of Orange. After Queen Anne ascended the throne of England in 1702, the name was changed to Oxford.

As is our wont when cruising. *Finisterre* poked in for supplies and a look, and poked out again in quest of a deserted anchorage. Passing Plaindealing Creek, which took its name from Quakers who traded fairly with the Indians, we continued up the Tred Avon to Trippe Creek, while the sun dropped towards the horizon and the sky changed from rose to palest violet, duly reflected in the water astern. Beyond Deepwater Point lay a sheltered bowl of a harbor, but it was almost regretfully that we dropped the anchor, hating to end so perfect a day.

If you live right, sometimes—sometimes—the gentle gods who watch over the affairs of Chesapeake creeks are kind. We awakened to a moderate easterly breeze, carrying with it the freshness of the ocean lying just beyond our rampart of land. The air was beginning to feel like summer. Gingerly I put a foot in the water, to be·rebuffed by the stored chill of winter. But never mind. Always cruising there are the compensations. The electric anchor winch whirred, and one heave on the sheet unfurled the jib. *Finisterre* heeled ever so slightly, and we began retracing our course to Eastern Bay, heading now for the Miles River and the town of St. Michaels.

Within the span of my acquaintance St. Michaels has changed, but principally to accommodate the expanding fleet of pleasure craft. At the end of World War II it was a drowsing harbor frequented principally by fishermen, crabbers, and oystermen, who fortunately have not been squeezed out by the burgeoning marinas. St. Michaels still plays a part in one of the principal joys of Chesapeake cruising: living off the land, or perhaps I should say water. Depending on the season, there are soft-shell crabs or steamers to buy, big bay busters transmuted from blue to bright red by steam and spices, or ready-picked back-fin meat, succulent lumps as big as your thumb. There are fresh shad and roe in the spring, and native rockfish in the fall. After the leaves begin to drop, oysters may be purchased ready-shucked, or by the barrel if your ship is big enough, the barrel to be lashed on the after deck and the oysters to be opened as you sit along the rail, tossing shells into the water alongside. Although local seafood can usually be bought, for fishing is still a major source of income to the area, there is also the do-it-yourself system. Few are the creeks which will not yield panfish and crabs aplenty. In fact, a long-handled crabnet chocked on deck is a standard Chesapeake cruising appendage.

It was nearly dark when we returned to *Finisterre* after a shopping expedition. Almost anywhere else it would be necessary to spend the night alongside a dock, whether we wanted it or not. But not on the Chesapeake. Starting the engine, we powered confidently forth as I scanned the chart. Quickly I found a creek named Leeds, less than a mile away. I had never heard of it before that moment, but as the red ball of the sun vanished without glare over the church spire of St. Michaels, *Finisterre* crept within the embrace of the first cove to appear to port, depth finder never showing less than the charted eight feet.

It was a harbor that might be famous elsewhere. After the anchor splashed down we lingered on deck, savoring perfection. Around us fish broke. Gulls almost too full to fly fluttered away. Crickets and frogs began their evening chorus and, with the fading of the last light, Venus shone like a suspended jewel, no more distant than the nearest treetop. Stars soon followed, tiny points of brilliance faithfully reflected under us. By my side, Bill said softly: "Think how few people today can know such moments. Most places there is noise and hurry. Here there are only stars—us and them."

With the morning, it was summer. Overnight through some miracle of nature the whole transformation had taken place. Even the tones of green ashore had darkened. Blinking at the brassy sun I rigged the cockpit table. It was the commencement of awning weather, meals on deck, tall glasses clinking, swimming over the side. Not a ripple broke the mirror of the harbor; the masthead burgee hung limp, and not a leaf stirred.

As we breakfasted on deck, we thought out the day: back to the Miles, then into the Wye as far as the Narrows, where the non-opening bridge would stop us; retrace course to Bordley Point, then up Wye East branch for the whole length of Wye Island—poking into creeks, glimpsing the magnificent colonial splendor of Wye Plantation, and on to the tip of one of the most beautiful islands in the world. So now it comes out, my favorite part of the Chesapeake, in its own way worthy of comparison with the Aegean, the Baltic, the Caribbean, the Pacific—a rambling few miles of solitude which seep into the soul, quiet green lanes of peace after the boisterous blue wastes of ocean *Finisterre* and I had known together.

It was a day when time was suspended, the morning passing quietly into noon, when the water didn't seem too cold for swimming after all, the afternoon sliding towards dusk and soft night. Faint airs carrying the essence of freshly tilled countryside moved us gently. When the breeze faded with the light, we dropped anchor where we were, for here the entire estuary was a harbor, snug and safe.

There was no anticlimax when the morrow brought back the fairweather cycle of southerlies. We slid to Tilghman Neck, enjoyed a brisk beat down Eastern Bay, and reached across the Chesapeake to South River. Once again, many choices opened, but we had already made up our minds. *Finisterre* crept into Harness Creek through an entrance barely two beams wide. Inside opened a haven no gale could ruffle, a sanctuary to visualize some screaming night offshore. Yet even better was to come. Beyond lay still another harbor, a hidden cove a stranger would not even suspect.

Slowly *Finisterre* rounded the final point to drop anchor in a veritable tea cup, a true gunk-hole, surrounded by land practically within stepping distance from the deck. We seemed a thousand miles west of nowhere, yet not far beyond the trees was Annapolis, a lovely colonial city which had gracefully made the transition to the modern age, a seat of government, learning, and culture, yet part of the stream of life, withal: automobiles bumper to bumper, neon signs, the electronic voices of the hucksters. But here in Harness Creek nothing stirred or sounded, not even the trees holding us in close embrace.

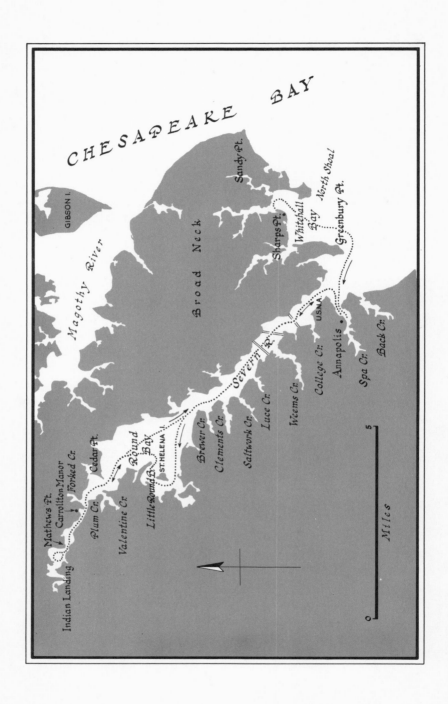

CHESAPEAKE BAY

GIBSON I.

Magothy River

Sandy Pt.

Broad Neck

Sharps Pt.

Whitehall Bay

North Shoal

Greenbury Pt.

Severn R.

U.S.N.A.

College Cr.

Back Cr.

Luce Cr.

Weems Cr.

Saltwork Cr.

Clements Cr.

Brewer Cr.

Annapolis

Spa Cr.

ST. HELENA I.

Little Round B.

Round Bay

Cedar Pt.

Valentine Cr.

Plum Cr.

Forked Cr.

Carrollton Manor

Mathews Pt.

Indian Landing

Miles

5

0

5

Winter Cruise to Nowhere
THE SEVERN RIVER

Me, I'm a hot weather boy. When the snow begins to fly I only want to know about it via Uncle Sam's post, or perhaps a copy of the *Times* three weeks old. But, as the Irishman said about whiskey, "All whiskey is good; some's just better'n others." All cruising is good, even when the frost is on the pumpkin.

I got away from the dock at Sharps Point about 11 o'clock one bright December morning, only three hours behind the planned departure hour. So far normal. This time the delay was the result of getting progressively colder and remembering more gear: sweaters, gloves, Nova Scotia hunting pants thicker than the butt end of a shingle, quilted jacket, wool socks, Navy watch cap, leather windbreak, and a suit of long-handled flannels relatively unperforated by moths. The cabin resembled the hold of a vessel about to winter in pack ice. Great mounds of clothes plus two weights of sleeping bags, plus a Primus stove with reflecting bell. Everything but huskies and a sled.

The wind was northwest and fresh. As soon as *Surprise* cleared the dock it became apparent there was going to be some difficulty between master and crew, both of which were me. It was all very well for captain to sit in the cockpit swaddled like a mummy but crew had to have a certain degree of mobility. Harsh words passed. Then the captain took off a few outer layers and became crew. Crew set mainsail. Boat heeled and forged ahead. Crew waddled aft; took tiller, reassumed raiment and dignity commensurable with rank of captain. Boat progressed out of Whitehall Creek. Breach healed. Class friction forgotten. Peace and good fellowship.

But cold. The wind whetted its blade on the whitecaps and plunged into my midsection. It whittled at my fingers and toes and lanced every chink in the woolies. Strictly from the tundras, I thought: and what am I doing here?

Surprise answered that one for me. She liked the breeze. With the main well started she got down to business; she put her shoulder into the bow wave and left a wide white trail astern. Soon the nun that supplants the summer flasher on North Shoal was abeam, and we were in the open Chesapeake. But not for long: the wind flawed ahead and dollops of spray wafted aft like well chilled shot; then Greenbury Point was abeam and we began a beat up Annapolis harbor, the shot becoming smaller and less frequent as we progressed. Without a jib the tiller kept me warm, and without a jib *Surprise* had all the wind she wanted.

Off the yacht club crew scrambled forward to drop the main, and captain made a satisfactory landing at the gas dock. No friction. All serene. Rapport established. But any contact with the shore is fatal to harmony. The few chores necessary to further progress dragged interminably; it was after three in the afternoon when the odds and ends were stowed, the phone calls made, the gas tank filled. As I chugged away the crew of a large powerboat at the dock was complaining loudly because the water lines were drained. They wanted to fill their tanks before heading south.

Beyond the gas dock, the Naval Academy anchorage was empty, the Midshipman fleet laid up until spring. Only the Florida-bound power cruiser and *Surprise* were astir. Perhaps that is what made me suddenly realize it was winter. Before it had been cold but now it was winter. The sun had vanished behind a thick bank of cloud; there had been little heat in the sun, but while it shone the day was at least cheerful. Now it was bleak. The breeze had dropped off entirely. So had the wavelets. On rounding the stern of the *Reina Mercedes* the Severn River stretched away without a ripple, gray under the sullen sky.

This is probably the proper time to establish locale and cast of characters, so this saga assumes a true perspective. *Surprise* was not a clipper, nor were we rounding Cape Horn; *Surprise III* was an Oxford 400, Oxford referring to the yard on the Eastern Sho' of Maryland where she was built, 400 designating the sail area in square feet. She was 28'10" overall, 22'6" on the waterline, had a beam of 8'4" and a draft of 4'6". Her layout provided a small aft cockpit opening into a raised deckhouse, which allowed full headroom in the galley, and a view of the outdoors through large/port windows. Forward were two settee/bunks, with a narrow walkway between. The whole could be encompassed in a telephone booth laid on its side, but somehow was spacious withal. I had chartered *Surprise* for a month to remain afloat while *Caribbee* awaited the Southern Circuit in Florida.

Distances involved were in keeping with the dimensions of the ship and the tastes of its company: so far we had covered about five miles. Now five miles isn't ordinarily very far to go. Hardly something to write about. But five miles on the Chesapeake can be a lot if you measure cruising in terms of variety: stretches wide and deep enough for good sailing, lovely countryside, and innumerable snug anchorages. Take the Severn River, for example. On its southern shore, even before you get to Annapolis, there is Back Creek; then Annapolis lying between Spa and College Creeks; then a whole row of creeks, just as nice. And then the Severn widens into Round Bay, a respectable body of water yet wholly sheltered, with Little Round Bay off on its western side, and Little Round Bay Creek beyond that. And off north of Round Bay the river continues another two miles, past other creeks, to finally end in another bay large enough for small boat racing. So the Severn could be thought of as more than a river: it is a veritable cruiser's Eden, scaled to the ship and crew engaged in this venturesome voyage.

Thinking such thoughts, I passed through the twin bridges beyond Annapolis, oblivious of conditions. Suddenly, on nearing the can buoy off Brewer Point, I came to with a start and glanced at my watch. Daylight was failing. Brewer Creek under its high banks was shrouded by dusk. It was almost impossible to make out the far shore of Round Bay: better anchor in Brewer rather than try to make the cove behind St. Helena Island, muttered captain to crew, damning timepieces which could not keep time.

But before the buoy came abeam the watch was exonerated: the sun had only been under a dense blanket of cloud spread flat across the sky. A corner of the blanket pulled back and the sun appeared as a blazing copper disk. The transformation was astonishing. A steel gray and haze blue landscape was suffused by warm amber light. High bluffs on the eastern side of the bay seemed almost of gold, and the weird light intensified and reflected by the bottom of the cloud heightened the colors of autumn. It became a landscape of bright yellow, warm orange and rich brown, a cheerful, happy landscape. Astern the wake lay as a long diagonal, the tiny undulations extending as far as I could see, picking up the color of the sky while the smooth surrounding water lay black. Ducks jumped ahead.

Yet it was really dusk when *Surprise* rounded St. Helena Island. Crew forward to drop anchor; skipper backing down to get a good bite. Motor off. Silence. Complete silence. Gone the sounds of summer: no outboards, no runabouts towing water skiers, no children squealing from the shallows. The houses dotting the shores of Little Round Bay were shuttered and empty. Only one light shone across the water. The night was silent and somehow lonely, and much colder.

From the cockpit I could almost see and smell the comfort soon to be mine: the Primus stove glowing cherry red, a venison stew bubbling, the first cocktail sipped from a reclining position on the bunk, feet up, back against the pile of gear, not a care in the world. Ah! Nothing so snug, so pleasant, as the cabin of a small boat! Nothing so relaxing. . . .

But on going below the smell I encountered was that of gasoline. Strong. I stuck my head up through the open hatch, cauterized my nostrils with oxygen practically cold enough to liquify, and took another sniff. Gasoline. No doubt about it. My dream of bliss underwent a swift retake: now I pictured myself spending the night in the cockpit huddled in a sleeping bag, eating cold beans straight from the can. . . .

Captain and crew into action, checking. Gas shut off at the tank. No sign of gasoline in the bilge. No special smell at the engine, no drip from the fuel line. But the cabin nevertheless heavy with fumes. Then I remembered the gasoline brought along for the pressure lantern, chocked away in the center of a coil of line under the cockpit seat. I had put it in a soda bottle having an impressive rubber gasket stopper, and then had stowed it safe from all contact. Fool proof. Now the stopper was intact, justifying my faith, but the bottle was not; it remained standing in the coil of line, and on first glance seemed perfect. But the glass had shattered into tiny bits.

By flashlight crew lifted out the wreckage, grunting an opinion of skippers who put gasoline in glass bottles. Skipper without rebuttal. Flooring battens up. And below, trapped behind a frame, a puddle of clear liquid. Pure gasoline! And pure luck: the limberhole was closed in that particular frame, so the gas had not drained forward. In almost friendly fashion

crew to work with a sponge, sopping, mopping, and squeezing over the side.

Thus not much later the first vision came to pass: the
Primus glowing, the stew bubbling, the cocktail warming;
candlelight soft, bunk softer. . . . Around *Surprise* the silence,
and the water stretching dark and still. The aloneness of a
little boat, the peace of a snug anchorage. Even when after
midnight wind began to shrill through the rigging there was
no motion below. Then, although I did not know it or I would
not have returned to sleep so easily, the big powerboat that
had earlier demanded water was getting water aplenty by
sinking with all hands off the mouth of the Potomac.

On awakening the next morning I lay quietly in my sleeping bag and looked up through the companionway. The sky
was a deep blue, an underexposed Kodachrome blue, like the
sky of far northern latitudes. My breath plumed. Lazily I
thought that electricity wasn't such a clever invention, after
all: what any small boat really needed on a frosty morning
was an old-fashioned lamp, complete with genie; one rub and
there he'd be, ready to light the stove and get the coffee going.
But the little man wasn't there and I had to shift for myself.
Craftily I planned each maneuver from the warmth of my
bunk. Then as though a whole swarm of bees had flown into
my sleeping bag, I popped out and leapt about the cabin, all
thumbs from urgency—to make a dive back into the bunk and
lie drowsing until the Primus had taken hold and my breath
no longer showed in the cabin air.

It was 10:45 before mainsail and jib went up. The breeze had
dropped off to a whisper, but what there was still came from
northwest. An hour—and less than three miles—later *Surprise*
had crossed Round Bay, passed Cedar Point and Forked
Creek, and approached the narrows below Carrollton Manor.
The wind was funneling down the river. Crew flattened sails
and settled back to watch captain beat through without
finding bottom. Wind here. Wind there. Tack. Tack again.

Back to the same place. Another tack. Four point wind shift. Always a header. Tack. The same bush on the shore ahead. Crew scornful. . . . *You and your four point shifts!* Captain apologetic. . . . *Honest! Very fluky! Honest!*

Back and forth. Some progress. Slow. Short boards. No time to go aground; no dinghy, no passing powerboats, water coolish for getting out to push. Then a long hitch into Rock Cove, and the breeze more off the shore. Chance to look around.

The banks of the Severn were covered by small summer cottages, tightly shuttered. On a point stood a bright yellow and pale green house with a cupola, exactly like a Bemelmanns drawing. Without the foliage and life of summer the little community looked dismal and forlorn.

Finally Matthews Point was abeam. Across a miniature bay lay Indian Landing, but captain and crew decided to enjoy the pleasure of downwind sailing. Turned around, it was immediately warm. Successive layers of clothes piled on the bridge deck. The wind was still tricky. Occasionally the main boom would swing from the shrouds to amidships as a catspaw flicked from dead ahead. Captain hoped crew noted. Fluky. Sixteen point shifts. Helmsman might be responsible for four point wind shifts, but not sixteen!

Back in Round Bay the breeze was slightly fresher. It was getting late. Thoughts shifted toward lunch. Why not poke into Brewer Creek, drop the jib, anchor, and heat some soup? Lazy and pleasant. Leave mainsail set. Maybe nap in the sun. . . .

Ahead a long black streak extended out from Brewer Point, looking like a mud flat uncovered by tide. Binoculars turned the streak into a raft of ducks, huddled around a rather scraggly blind I had noticed the afternoon before. Perhaps a picture, I thought, and began loading a camera. But the raft started to rise long before I came near, lifting with a beat of wings that echoed from the far shore.

Maybe it was thinking of the ducks, maybe it was being lulled by the peace of the scene, maybe it was just plain being cold, but I failed to notice the pattern of the puff on the water of Brewer Creek. When it hit *Surprise* heeled and jumped ahead. It was the first real wind of the day. The puff passed and *Surprise* straightened. Then another puff, slightly harder, and another lull. Still I thought nothing of it and kept going. The next gust had even more weight; it made a dark path on the water before striking. *Surprise* lay over, and I realized that there was far too much breeze in the creek to lie comfortably with mainsail set, so upped helm to bear off for the next point.

Half way 'round the wind gave up jabbing with its left and threw a hard right. *Surprise* took a knockdown for the count of nine. We both lived up to her name, but she climbed back on her feet bravely. It was with real respect that I looked to windward. This wasn't just a pushover of a preliminary; it gave signs of developing into a main event. Immediately there appeared a cleavage between captain and crew. On the knockdown captain had snarled: *Dummy, slack that mainsheet!* and the crew had answered: *Whydidntyuhtellmeto, nitwit!*

Single handed cruising should be a good cure for bellowing skippers. Or, to put it another way, single handed cruising teaches regard for a crew.

By now the wind was really smoking, a true winter nor'-wester whistling down the Severn. It came a-barreling and a-puffing, lacing whitecaps from shore to shore. *Surprise* was carrying too much sail. Studying the next move, there seemed to be something of a lee under the western bank, so we worked across to it.

Came the moment, an imagined lull: captain downed helm and crew hopped forward. Fingers too cold to uncleat main halyard smartly. . . . Captain: *Drop it, stupid!* . . . Crew: *Shut up and watch your helm!* . . . Canvas flailing, then jib full again, spinning *Surprise* back onto the tack. Crew running forward. Halyard clear. Boom sagging. . . . Captain: *Why didn't yuh set up on that topping lift, stupid?* . . . Crew: *Yeah? What about the main sheet?* Corner of sail in water. Chorus: *Now look what you've done!* Canvas inboard but ballooning. Chorus: *Whatcha do with the stops, cretin?* . . . Main stowed. *Surprise* flying off before it under jib. Real seas showing teeth astern. Sky innocent blue.

Ahead loomed a bridge tended by a gent on performance misanthropically inclined towards small boat sailors. I had never seen it open promptly. *Surprise* was coming down on its fast. Without much conviction I blew three blasts on the horn, long blasts, lungs full, eyes popping. My best effort sounded feeble even to me. Nothing happened. Jib down. Prayerfully I touched the starter button and the engine came into life. Such a handy thing to have around, sometimes!

Repeated blasts finally brought a languid figure to the window of the shack, but nothing more. Even with the engine it was difficult to keep *Surprise* under control. She heeled sharply when across the wind, and the engine had to be gunned hard to bring her bows into it. For long minutes nothing happened, then a Toonerville trolley creaked on the span, crawled across, and disappeared. Nine minutes later— by watch—the draw opened. *Surprise* boiled through. Captain and crew joined in sweet thanks to the operator. Common cause. Solidarity. Mainsail incident forgotten.

As *Surprise* rolled down the river the oyster fleet was coming up, seeking shelter from the seas of the open Chesapeake. Even the Severn was white in the harder squalls. Not a fit day for man nor beast—only ducks—and everything afloat seemed to have one thought: a snug harbor.

There are few places I can think of anywhere more sheltered than Spa Creek. Beyond the yacht club the water lay smooth, only slight riffles of white driving ahead of the blast. Crew forward to pick up a mooring off Arnie Gay's Yard, captain below to bend frozen fingers around bottle and glass. . . . Cold. No argument. Cold. . . . But not for long: Primus glowing, rum working, steak sizzling; early dusk, quiet night, wind lulling. . . .

And that is about the whole of it. Next morning when I opened my eyes it was snowing hard; I took a good look at the big white flakes drifting down past the ports and closed my eyes again right quick. Next time I opened them the snow clouds had gone. It was almost clear. My breath plumed. But I had learned at least one lesson: the Primus was within reach of my bunk and I lighted it without leaving the sleeping bag. Then had another nap.

This time when I awakened it was really clear. Fluffy cumulus clouds hung against a sky newly washed and polished. The wind had lightened. Outside the creek there was just a pleasant breeze, just enough to make the Small Craft Warning flag flying at the Naval Academy stand out and waggle as lazily as the tail of a Georgia houn' dawg. *Surprise* approved. After a circuit of the harbor sheets were eased. We ran off past Horn Point shoal, past Greenbury Point, reached into and across Whitehall Bay, and beat the last hundred yards up Whitehall Creek to home base.

Me, I'm a hot weather boy, as I said before. But I have to admit that cold weather cruising has its points. Even snow on the decks possesses a certain charm. Provided the next snug harbor isn't too distant.

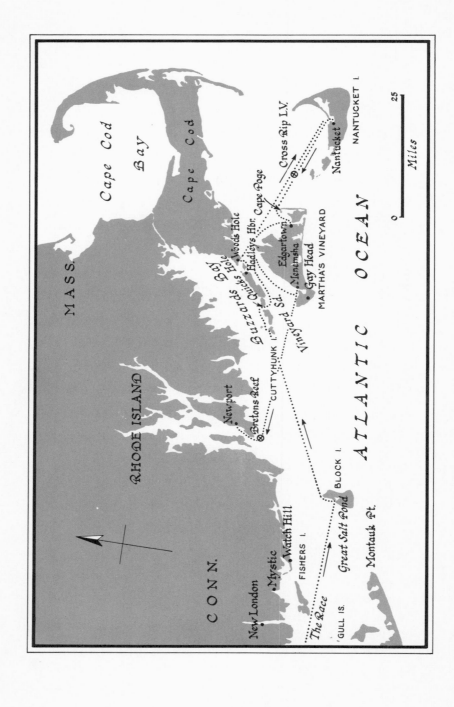

6

East of the Race and West of the Cape
THE AMERICAN ATLANTIC COAST

As *Finisterre* boiled past New London a long forgotten song began to run through my mind. "East of the sun and west of the moon," it went, and as I looked over the bow towards the squat stone lighthouse at the corner of Fisher's Island, the words changed to "east of The Race and west of the Cape."

Until that moment I had no handy way to describe my planless itinerary, embracing one of the most unique and delightful collections of little islands and coves and villages to be found in the world of sailing. The Elizabeth Islands, say some, taking the charted name of the string under the uplifted arm of Cape Cod. Vineyard Sound, say others, ignoring the equal claims of rival bodies of water from Montauk to Monomoy—Block Island Sound, Nantucket Sound, and Buzzards Bay, home of the afternoon sou'wester.

As though pleased that the problem was solved, *Finisterre* put her shoulder down to a puff and sped towards The Race. Under us the water began to churn and spin into giant whorls, silent reminder of the power of the sea. Twice each twenty-four hours millions upon millions of tons of water surge from the open Atlantic Ocean into Long Island Sound, running westward toward Manhattan, flowing through the arteries into the smallest capillaries, refreshing and revivifying every foot of shoreline. Then with almost clocklike regularity the cycle reverses, and the buoys begin to lean the other way as the tide rushes back out into the ocean.

We had caught the ebb just right, and *Finisterre* shot through The Race like an arrow from a bow. A crisp northwest breeze leaned against the sails above while the current gripped the keel below, both hurrying us in the same direction. As the elements were in accord, there were none of the steep, breaking waves that sometimes make the passage unhappy for small boat voyagers; instead, the water ran with a deceptively glazed smoothness, only patches of roiled white showing the forces at work. Fishing boats circled, now barely stemming the tide, now spurting downstream, until suddenly the water changed color and character, and we were through, east of The Race.

Almost as suddenly, there was a perceptible difference in the very air. For The Race is more than a tidal portcullis to trap racing fleets: it is a geographic and climatic boundary, as clearly defined as though Plum and Gull Islands were walls reaching to the sky. Behind, there is a feeling of the hinterlands of Connecticut and New York, crowded, dusty, and sometimes insufferably hot: people, noise, neons, and clogged highways. Beyond, there is the feeling of the open sea, a chill tang in the shadow of the mainsail even though the sun may lie warmly on bare shoulders at the wheel. Somehow this is part of the world of drifting ice, of long winter nights, of fog and rock and raging gales, just as the other side of The Race is the last stand of sand and rolling lowlands stretching all the way back to Florida.

On the port hand was Fishers Island, summer haunt of

names symbolizing wealth and position, a narrow irregular bastion behind which lay another exit from Long Island Sound, a passage to be preferred to The Race in strong winds and a foul tide. And Fishers Island Sound is something of a cruising microcosm in itself, with two good harbors on the parent island, and the picturesque towns of Stoningtown and Mystic across, the former a fishing port maintaining its character, the latter through the Marine Museum probably the closest link with the Golden Age of Sail to be found outside English Harbour, on the far-away isle of Antigua.

To starboard, distant but visible, was the eastern tip of Long Island, culminating in Montauk Point. Under it I visualized Gardiners Island and the bay of the same name, flowing toward and around Shelter Island to join the Peconic Bays, Great and Little, with such lovely nooks as Sag and Dering Harbors—another little cruising world in itself, so remote yet so close to great population centers, and not even requiring an open sea passage to attain. It is hard to think of any other area blessed with such variety for the boatman as the environs of New York City.

Yet despite these remembered blandishments *Finisterre* remained on course toward a smudge on the horizon that could only be Block Island. We 20th century voyagers were following in the wake of an almost forgotten little sloop called *Onrust*, Dutch for *Restless*, built under the waterfront trees in the village of Nieuw Amsterdam. Under the command of Adriaen Block, in 1614 *Onrust* made the first known passage through Long Island Sound. Groping his way eastward of The Race without benefit of charts or aids to navigation, the doughty Dutchman must have been relieved to find himself on open water, and he too sailed toward a smudge on the horizon, which ever after was known by his name.

Block Island is shaped like a sting-ray swimming south, the head a steep bluff topped by the green, blinking eye of a lighthouse, the tail a long trailing reef, cause of many maritime tragedies. It smells of seaweed tempered by small shrubs clinging to damp earth. Gulls wheel and cry above creeping tendrils of fog and the wash of surf on outlying rocks. Even the weathered shingle houses seem to huddle against the coming of savage winter gales. It is only when flying over in a small plane that another aspect appears, mute record of attempts to wrest the land from the sea. Patterning the surface are stone fences, monuments to vanished pioneers who cleared fields in hope of establishing farms.

Modern sailors have an advantage not enjoyed by Adriaen Block. In the old days there was no shelter. Now there are two harbors, man made, at opposite sides of the island and at opposite poles in character. To the west is Great Salt Pond, created by cutting a channel from a lake to open water. Extending over a mile into the land, bordered principally by rolling meadows, it has an air of spaciousness, of detachment from the hurrying throng. No matter how many boats may crowd in over a summer weekend, there is always a place to escape to anchor in solitude. Not so on the other side. Old Harbor, held fast in the embrace of stone breakwaters, is pure Baltic or Mediterranean, boats moored to the quay; it is in turn the focal point of the community, rimmed by restaurants and shops oriented to fish and fishing. Rarely uncrowded, Old Harbor can become so jammed when the swordfish fleet is in that the water may be crossed dry-shod by stepping from one deck to another.

Anyone doubting that boating has become a participating sport has only to arrive off Great Salt Pond in good weather on Saturday afternoon during the vacation season. Other sailing auxiliaries and assorted power vessels making for the entrance filed along with us, some with crow's nests, or outriggers, proclaiming them fishermen; others with TV antennas and an extra beer cooler on the afterdeck, identifying them simply as fellow escapees from the mainland. There were small sloops equipped with awnings and sleeping bags, and outboard cruisers carrying entire families. Big boats, little boats, sail and power, we all converged to slip past the sandspit at the Coast Guard station and debouch into the spacious anchorage, fanning out as our fancies dictated.

Always, coming into a harbor, be it familiar or strange, I like to sit a few minutes in the cockpit and let it seep into my soul, softening the transition from the sea to the land, as it were. It is a ritual best observed glass in hand, in this case preparing me for the *Alice in Wonderland* mixture I knew I would find ashore.

For while Block Island has a quality of aloof loneliness—houses widely scattered except for the two settlements around the harbors—it also manages an air of complete improbability. Perhaps this stems from the rambling wooden hotels dominating the urban landscape. In all stages of repair and disrepair, these faintly Victorian relics linger as reminders that people used to settle on a place for a holiday and then stay put. Ghostly battalions of guests in rocking chairs look out over cast-iron deer browsing on lawns running to weed.

Change, alas! is almost inevitable, I thought as I later made my annual pilgrimage by automobile to Old Harbor and Block Island Southeast lighthouse, passing the freshwater ponds—85 shown in color on the detail chart, but natives swear there is one for every day of the year if you count them all; passing the tiny old cottages, covered by beach roses and honeysuckle; smelling, too, the pungent fields of bayberry and clover. Block Island has a genuine quality of its own, culminating in the magnificent view from the base of the lighthouse, of restless ocean stretching unbroken across to Land's End.

After gorging on jumbo lobsters at Deadeye Dick's came the comfort of a snug berth in a sheltered harbor. There is something touching about small boats clustered like sleeping birds for the night, each a separate entity, a conveyance of gentle escape from workaday problems. Rowing out in the dinghy, long shimmering spears from riding lights mirrored in the dark water, while a thin veil of cirrus cloud high overhead blurred the stars without hiding them. From afar came the faint moan of a whistle, too soft to disturb the fleet, for it seemed everyone slept.

In the golden morning light there were new color values in the harbor: blue hulls, red hulls, white hulls, yellow hulls, topped by flags drooping lazily, while beyond, gently rolling hills formed a pattern of brown and green, accented by dark stands of trees. Slowly life began to blossom on decks, here a straggler sipping coffee in the cockpit, there an energetic skipper wielding a swab, even a few tousled heads bobbing alongside for a morning swim.

But at ten o'clock as though by signal the marine parade began in reverse, boat after boat dropping lines at the marina or hoisting anchor to make for the exit channel, much like twigs being swept along in a summer shower suddenly to disappear. *Finisterre* powered out as part of the procession, as for once the harbor breeze had failed to function. Great Salt Pond is one of those odd places in the world which funnels and concentrates whatever wind might be blowing, so often prudent crews reef before leaving, to find only a moderate breeze beyond the breakwater.

This time, though, nothing stirred outside, either. The bell buoy was mute as we passed, the automatic pilot set on course for the next buoy, beyond North Reef. Peacefully we putted past the scene of a tragedy famous in maritime lore, the wreck of the ship *Palatine* during a winter gale early in the 18th century. Bound for Philadelphia with German immigrants, she had been driven far off course by successive storms; the crew had mutinied, and forced the passengers to pay outrageous prices for food and water—over $50 for a biscuit, runs the tale. Some starved to death, others became walking skeletons. Then when land was sighted the crew deserted in the boats. The passengers tried to sail the *Palatine* to shelter, but fetched up on North Reef—lured, some say, by misleading lights shown by the natives of Block Island.

The first stirrings of a southerly breeze blew away thoughts of dark deeds. Hoisting sails is a good antidote to almost anything. With a faint murmur from bow and stern wave, *Finisterre* came 'round the corner at the buoy and again swung east, a whole selection of harbors over the bow, with Cuttyhunk getting the nod when I plotted a course on the chart.

As the sun lifted, the breeze freshened, part of a local phenomenon called the Buzzards Bay sou'wester, a wind so regular in settled summer weather it is claimed you can set your watch by it. During the night the land cools, to warm again as the sun climbs; the heated air rises, and in sweeps cold air from the water. The clearer the upper sky of clouds and the less diluted the sunshine, the stronger the wind, until some days it becomes very fresh indeed.

These are waters with special significance for a racing yachtsman. The biannual blue water trek to Bermuda starts from Brenton Reef Lightship, off Newport, and the rhumb line course of 149 degrees true carries the fleet not far to the eastward of Block Island.

Soon *Finisterre* cut through the vanished wakes she had left en route to triumphs which would ensure her place in yachting history: three successive firsts to The Onion Patch. Then we surfed across the course where during America's Cup years tall yachts meet to joust like knights in tournaments of old, starting and finishing off a special buoy set forth by the New York Yacht Club nine miles south-southeast of Brenton Reef.

Gradually the wind blew stronger, and as it did, a haze gathered, the phase of the local phenomenon called the smoky sou'wester. Rarely in these waters is there a golden day after the seabreeze appears. Instead, the sun takes on a frosty look. Land and buoys and other boats are seen as through a gauzy curtain. Colors are subdued. The sea turns a cold gray, and the sun path is silver. Visibility is restricted: there is none of the heart-clutching, blind groping of fog, but distant objects are swallowed, to appear unexpectedly with a bigger-than-life quality.

And so it was as *Finisterre* neared the Texas Tower replacing the lightship which for many years had marked the entrance to Buzzards Bay. We saw a shed atop spindle legs, looking, from our angle of approach, exactly like a fawn standing in shallows, an illusion heightened by the structure at one corner carrying weather instruments, representing the raised head and spike antlers. But closer the tower resolved into an ugly sumbol of functional modernity, helicopter landing field included.

Here the open water voyage ended. Soon *Finisterre* came under the shelter of Cuttyhunk, first of the Elizabeth Islands, and magically the sea smoothed. Running in close to the shore, we followed buoys to the entrance channel, narrow and deep as a stocking. And at the toe, like a child's delighted discovery on Christmas morning, there was a sailor's present of an almost perfect harbor, completely landlocked, restful in its perfection, with a little fishing village sprawling over a hillside at the far end, faintly reminiscent of the Mediterranean yet with touches that could only be New England: clapboard and shingle houses, weatherbeaten to a silvery grey, green shutters, rambler roses, and a church steeple prim as a Pilgrim maid.

These are waters dear to the fisherman as well as the sailing sailor, and at Cuttyhunk the striped bass reigns supreme. There is even a special breed of boat operating out of the harbor, rugged clinker-built craft which can be tiller steered from the bow, allowing the skipper to weave between rocks in boiling surf. For one who has spent a lifetime keeping clear of such dangers, it is something of a revelation to watch the boats at work—to say nothing of the surf casters, whose primary aim seems to be heaving a bit of lead as far as possible.

But both methods bring home stripers, as a stroll along the fishing dock will prove. Cuttyhunk, too, is the last refuge of some of the most dilapidated station wagons extant, wondrous specimens proving the survival characteristics of Detroit when exterior finish is ignored.

Beyond Cuttyhunk the Elizabeth Islands extend like steppingstones to Cape Cod. A variety of courses is possible. If time is ample, a side cruise may be made along the mainland shore of Buzzards Bay, touching New Bedford, Mattapoisett, and Sippican Harbors, before turning eastward to enter Vineyard Sound through Woods Hole. The opposite approach is to go back around Sow and Pigs Reef, off Cuttyhunk, and sail the entire length of Vineyard Sound, perhaps stopping at Menemsha Bight. Or it is possible to effect a combination of the two, starting in Buzzards Bay but swinging east to enter Vineyard Sound by one of the lesser channels.

It was the latter route we chose, partially to have a swim at a delightful beach on the south side of Quicks Hole. The "Holes" joining Buzzards Bay and Vineyard Sound are not like anything similarly named I have seen elsewhere: they are actually tidal channels, more millraces than the placid backwaters the term would imply. Except for a few places far Down East in Maine and Nova Scotia, Ushant off the coast of France, and Pentland Firth between Scotland and the Orkneys, there are few channels which give a more jet-propelled ride if the tide is fair, or can be more frustrating if it is foul.

It was against us as *Finisterre* rounded the corner of Nashawena Island. Back and forth we tacked, gaining precious little at the end of each hitch across, yet somehow it was the quintessence of sailing: swift blue water, warm sun, cool breeze, the genoa barely in flat on one side before it had to go to the other; squinting at landmarks and peering at the chart, gaining when close under the shore and losing in the full current sweep of mid-channel, until finally a long hitch among the rocks of Pasque Island let us fetch across to the other shore, dropping anchor off a crescent of white sand. Alone except for a distant red farmhouse on a hill beyond the dunes, we took our reward in a swim out of the tide, with mainsail and mizzen still set.

After resetting the genoa, a slant carried us beyond Quicks Hole and into Vineyard Sound, destination Tarpaulin Cove on Naushon Island, sanctuary for generations of sailors. The late John Alden once told me as we sailed past in *Malabar XIII* that as a boy he had counted more than one hundred coasting schooners sheltering within its protecting arms. Safe not only against the dread nor'westers and nor'easters of winter, the old windjammers bound for Long Island Sound also lay there during periods of strong summer sou'westers, as they could not make headway to windward when loaded. In our modern age of small pleasure boats, it is a magnet for picnics and overnight stops, as well as small craft awaiting milder weather.

It was a day for luncheon on deck, and the cockpit table was clamped to the binnacle. Living off the nearby land—and sea —makes a good cruising rule, so we sat down to clam chowder, cold lobster, and a salad of tomatoes and thin-sliced red onions grown by the Portuguese settled on the Narrangansett shore. The only interloper was a bottle from Alsace. Lunch extended lazily into the afternoon, while the sou'wester freshened and its frosty smoke thickened.

It was midafternoon before we set sail to reach along the shore of Naushon Island to Woods Hole. Something of a legend surrounds this particular channel joining Buzzards Bay and Vineyard Sound, a dogleg studded by rocks and swept by a tide transcending ordinary experience. I have been asked about Woods Hole by sailors as far away as the Baltic, and it seems to form a mental hurdle for many cruising the area.

Let it be said that although Woods Hole involves some

element of risk—woe betide the power vessel running out of gas or the sailboat of breeze at a critical point—on no account should it be missed. The fainthearted may prefer to make the passage at slack tide, easily determined from published tables, but then it is like almost any other body of water. Choose, rather, to arrive nearly at maximum flood or ebb; study the detail chart carefully, memorizing the placement of key marks and ranges, as later there may be scant time to divert attention from the helm. Prepare for surging crosscurrents, as ready to sweep the boat sideways out of the fairway as the main flow is to check progress entirely, and a radical change of orientation at the spindle marking sunken Grassy Island. Prepare, also, to make the critical mile in seemingly one minute flat if the tide is fair, an hour if not. And keep discreetly away in thick fog.

As *Finisterre* entered with a fresh breeze at her back, we were showing up to 7 knots on the Kenyon. Soon our progress over the bottom began to slow, as the current was running foul—slower, slower as we got farther in, then we came almost to a halt at the Grassy Island turn. With the puffs, *Finisterre* would forge ahead; in the lulls she would drop back, while around us the water ran with the curious serpentine undulations of a swift flowing river. Each exposed rock showed the white fangs of a sailor's nightmare, but more startling were the buoys: nuns and cans alike, huge steel cylinders no offshore sea could bury, behaving like errant porpoises, now sucking under, now breaching above the surface, a now-you-see-'em-now-you-don't fillip to the usual uncertainties of navigation.

It has undoubtedly already become apparent that cruising the waters east of The Race and west of the Cape bears little resemblance to indolent drifts on the Chesapeake. One is like a casual stroll through a garden, the other has aspects of an Alpine climb—easy enough in parts, but always requiring the necessity of paying attention, a succession of minor challenges represented by tide, fog, and swiftly altering weather patterns, making the harbors and the lazy moments even more pleasant by contrast.

And so it was for us after we had finally broken through. Off to port lay Hadley Harbor, teacup snug, where once in *Carib* I had ridden out a howling three day nor'easter with barely a strain on the anchor rode. *Finisterre* crept through the winding entrance almost at sunset, only the tops of the sails filling, to come to rest near another small yawl. Donning sweaters—for hereabouts the chill falls fast when the sun lowers—we sat in the cockpit watching the sky, its colors faithfully reproduced in the water. Golden rims outlined the clouds above the western horizon; slowly they turned a delicate mauve, almost exactly the color inside a Bahamian conch shell. Gradually the purple tints deepened, until Venus appeared framed in the pattern of rigging, soon to be joined by myriad stars, brighter than the riding lights of our fellow voyagers.

In the morning, a heavy haze was in the air, rendering indistinct the nearby shoreline. Moisture dripped from the boom. "Fog," predicted the radio during breakfast, "light rain and fog, visibility one-half mile, less in patches, clearing about noon. Light southerly winds."

I must confess distaste for one phase of boating: groping through fog. After doing my first sailing as a boy in the sunny South, it has always seemed compounding the cruelties of nature for fog to frequent the regions already made difficult by tide and rock. Still, half-mile visibility did seem to offer a sporting chance, to say nothing of the noon clearing. So finally we crept forth, agreeing that if the first buoy was hard to find we would return.

A black and red can soon showed over the bow, then the spindle off Penzance Point, and *Finisterre* was again in the current, at this hour flowing less strongly. The town of Woods Hole appeared briefly, and we had entered Vineyard

Sound. At the same instant we entered a dense thicket of fog. The limits of our world were reduced to a circle scribed as though by a sweep of dividers. It was a gray world, with unusual interests in a floating bit of driftwood, or a gull resting immobile on the mirror surface.

But before uncertainty could turn to worry, one of the buoys off West Chop appeared, and nearby loomed the shoulder of Martha's Vineyard. Now around the corner lay a snug harbor, Vineyard Haven, ours for the making, while beyond the next headland awaited Edgartown. Yet such is the perversity of the cruising yachtsman that the passage on to Nantucket seemed more alluring, despite being another 30 miles of swirling currents setting across rocks made no less soft by picturesque names from early Americana: Hedge Fence, Squash Meadow, Horseshoe Shoal, Cross Rip, and Tuckernuck.

We kept on and the reward came even before *Finisterre* had cleared Cape Poge. As though a celestial button had been pushed the overcast peeled back, the sun broke through in warming torrents, and the water changed from gray to blue. Tentatively a puff of breeze came from the west, then another, and soon all around us were dancing whitecaps. Mainsail, genoa, mizzen, mizzen staysail—one by one the sails went aloft, and Cross Rip lightship became a rapidly growing scarlet toy on the horizon, to recede almost as speedily after *Finisterre* rounded.

Whaling commenced for Nantucketers in 1672, it is recorded, because a boat launched from the shore brought in a small humpback. Offshore fishing began after 1712, when a sloop blown seaward during a gale took a sperm whale on the way home. In 1791 a vessel first rounded Cape Horn to open the vast fisheries of the Pacific, beginning a Golden Age. During the 1820–1830 decade, 237 ships showed the house flags of local merchants everywhere men and whales might venture. Altogether, between 1815 and 1860, an incredible 1,313,946

barrels of oil, plus other valuable whale products, were unloaded.

Ashore, evidence of past glory and the wealth harvested
from distant seas linger. Near the center of town, the Pacific
National Bank—its very name symbolizing the far-flung interests of bygone merchants—stand the homes of the merchants themselves. For a few blocks Main Street is one of the
most charming and gracious residential streets in the world.
White painted mansions are framed by towering elms, blue
hydrangeas, and clipped hedges. Perhaps the three most imposing were built in 1836 for the Starbuck brothers by the
patriarch of the clan, Joseph Starbuck. Door knockers and
knobs of solid silver still gleam in summer sunshine. Doubtless these doors swung open with great excitement on the
morning of April 20, 1859, when the news came that the ship
Three Brothers was off the bar, heavily laden. Even the rival
Coffins and Macys had to congratulate the Starbucks, as the
6000 barrels in her hold was the largest single catch ever
brought home.

It blew hard while *Finisterre* lay at one of the guest moorings of the Nantucket Yacht Club. Small craft warning flags
whipped out straight from the staff of the Coast Guard station
at the harbor entrance, and they were still there when we
sailed past next day, although not so rigidly horizontal. In
deference to the wisdom of weather forecasters, a small jib
was set, but outside we found a dying slop of a sea and a
breeze with little heft. Changing to a genoa, *Finisterre* came
alive. For most of our cruise it seemed we had been bucking
the tide; now it was fair. Rail down, we fetched Cross Rip
close reaching. Coming on the wind, the tide set us bodily
forward and we gained on Cape Poge in giant strides. Still on
the final leg into Edgartown, tragedy struck. Gradually the
wind had freshened, but stubbornly we had held on to the
genoa as the distance diminished. Now with Chappaquiddick
Island abeam we were telling ourselves how glorious it was
—glittering water rushing along the lee deck and sloshing

into the cockpit, liferails burying, the quarterwave sucking over the transom—when there was a crash from below. A large platter of leftover swordfish, intended for lunch, had decanted into the port bunk—which happened to be mine.

Perhaps the most sophisticated of the island resorts, with smart shops and a variety of restaurants, Edgartown has a residential area of charm, some of the houses stemming back to whaling fortunes. But I must confess finding the island as a whole a shade too civilized for my taste, with Edgartown too resorty, and the nearby town of Oak Bluffs—reached on a land cruise by car—too much like the gingerbread architecture of the Jersey shore. It is possible my reaction was unfairly colored by a visit to Gay Head, last stand of the Gay Head Indians. The magnificent view from the cliffs, embracing Nantucket, Cuttyhunk, and a whole sweep of the Elizabeth Islands, had been partially obscured by commercial enterprises of the red men: a lunchroom under the banner of Napoleon Madison, Chief Medicine Man; plywood teepees filled with garish pottery and beadwork; a team of oxen, placarded "Take your picture with the oxen 25¢."

Yet my gorge settled and I made peace with Martha's Vineyard on entering Menemsha, final port of call, tucked in behind that same Gay Head. From the water, the entrance is barely visible, just a bell buoy close in under a short stone breakwater. Enter carefully, watching the tide, and be ready to swing sharply to port. There, in a basin, lies a snug working fishing port, picturesque because not consciously so, free of the usual trappings which grow up around quaint places from Portofino to Papeete.

Menemsha shelters an extensive and varied fleet. There are swordfishermen with padded rings atop tall masts, some fitted with seats like children's swings, to make easier long hours of scanning the sea for the sickle fin of a basking broadbill. Over the bows extend almost equally long pulpits, with the ancient tools of the harpooner's trade at hand: barbed lances, tubs of lines, painted floats.

Chocked among these are the offshore trawlers, rugged little vessels, dark green of topside, trimmed in black, with nets drying from orange masts. Like folded wings the iron-studded trawl doors rest on the afterdecks, forming dockside forums for crews mending gear and gossiping with passers-by. In common with similar working boats everywhere, the battered and stained Menemsha trawlers tell the landsman something of the world he never sees: the mincing flight of Mother Carey's chickens before the gale; sullen gray seas rolling out of the murk, insensate and merciless; the anxious run home towards a rock studded coast, pierced by only a few sanctuaries.

Between the larger craft shuttle the lobstermen, looking for space to unload basket after basket of crustaceans fresh from deep caverns, spry battlers showing scant resemblance to the listless creatures expiring among sprigs of parsley in restaurant showcases—lobsters to be bought on the hoof by cruising yachtsmen and cooked aboard snug little ships in salt water scooped from over the side, coming coral red to the table heady with the tang of the sea.

Everything else about Menemsha carries the tang of the sea, too, the piles of traps and floats littering the quayside, the discarded trawl doors, the rusted anchors bedded into the sand and weeds. Boiling tide, wheeling screeching gulls, smell of salt and hint of chill always in the air, Menemsha carries the undiluted essence of the sea—complete to a surf boat poised on rollers at the Coast Guard station, reminder that outside, even in this electronic age, ancient forces exist.

And by way of perfect contrast, *Finisterre* slanted across to Newport in one lazy jump, wind abeam. Cuttyhunk off to starboard, Sakonnet Point also off to starboard, then the panoply of Castle Hill and the inner approaches to Newport, gray

stone mansions and clipped green lawns, flowing down to
encompass a final anchorage in Brenton Cove, the very heart
of American yachting.

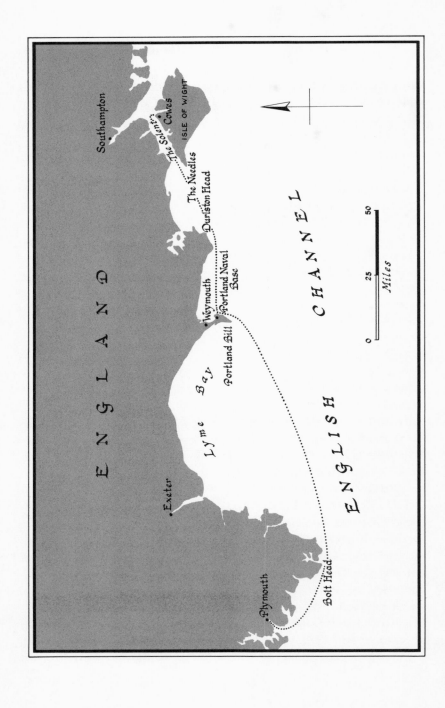

7
Her Majesty's Portland Marina
THE ENGLISH CHANNEL

It says in all the books that the English Channel is a windy place. You can check with any authority on the area, from Admiralty and Hydrographic Office publications to Aunt Emma, who has a vivid recollection of crossing on a steamer from Dover to Calais, and find this is so. Windy, and rough, with the peculiar and disagreeable steepness of sea produced by strong tidal currents.

Yet when we left Plymouth there was still no wind, and the dread Channel lay as smooth as the lake in Central Park. The freak high-pressure system which had kept pace with us for virtually three thousand miles now sat firmly over England. During the final leg of the Trans-Atlantic Race of '52, from Bermuda to Plymouth, we had drifted, crawling the final miles beyond The Lizard as agonizingly as a Sunday afternoon finish on Long Island Sound or the Chesapeake when the sou'wester fails to appear.

I was proceeding on the simple meteorological premise that

it had to blow when it hadn't for so long. We dropped lines from the floating quay, shouted over to *Janabel*, our French competitor, dipped a limp ensign at a corvette anchored in the inner harbor, and powered bravely past the breakwater with almost empty fuel tanks. The marina, that peculiarly American institution where yachtsmen may take aboard the necessities of life afloat—water, ice, gasoline or diesel oil, beer—did not exist. So out we went. After all, *Caribbee* was an ocean racing yawl, an easily driven hull 57 feet overall driven by 1585 square feet of working sail, with plenty more light stuff to hang aloft. And it simply had to blow.

Over the hill where Drake had bowled as the Spanish Armada approached carrying a breeze made famous by history, great cumulus clouds towered; not the clouds of wind, but of a lazy summer day along the shore, with bees droning in gardens and little boys splashing happily in ponds. The warning was plain, but we ignored it on finding a faint breath stirring aloft. According to ship's log, we set main, mizzen, and genoa to make three miles the first half hour. The noon entry read: "Delightful sailing. Devonshire coast lovely." Close hauled under the beach, we slipped through smooth water admiring one of the most magnificent countrysides any of us had ever seen. It smelled as it looked, of green meadows and lazing cows, of wild flowers and mossy dells. Even considering it was the first land we had known for over three weeks, it was beautiful.

Our appreciation of nature began to fade in the afternoon off Bolt Head, a bold promontory. The tide turned foul and the wind trailed off to a whisper, barely enough to bend rising smoke from a cigarette. The genoa sheet sagged. Reluctantly we started the engine, running it slowly to conserve fuel.

At ten a gentle warm breeze and a new moon appeared astern together. Gratefully, thinking of the compensations of a sailor's life, we turned off the engine and set a spinnaker. It was a perfect night: now the breeze is striking in, we assured

ourselves as little ripples began to feather along the track of
the moon, now we will carry this on to Cowes and be in
London in plenty of time. . . . Optimism springs eternal in the
sailor's breast. The log records with what little foundation:

> Midnight. Jibed spinnaker.
> 0100. Becalmed after one hour reaching on port tack.
> 0115. No steerageway. Log line almost vertical.
> 0200. Log line tending aft. Regained bare steerageway.
> 0300. Wind since midnight has come from all directions ex-
> cept ahead. Now ahead. Spinnaker down, genoa up.
> 0420. Sighted Portland Bill light. On engine. Course altered
> for light.
> 0700. Hazy ahead. Mirror calm.

The fearsome English Channel lay as docile as a mountain
pool. Pushed along by the engine, *Caribbee*'s bow wave ran out
to form a perfectly smooth V which trailed far astern, un-
marred. Piled clouds reflected with mirror clarity.

By nine o'clock we had almost had it: sounding revealed a
bare spit of oil in one tank, a thin line scarcely dampening the
stick in the other. Inshore, steep curling waves began to lift
into the Race of Portland. Even with the engine turning, we
were barely holding our own against the ebbing tide.

In desperation I studied the chart. Behind the Bill of Portland, a slim peninsula, I saw there was a buoyed channel into
the fishing village of Weymouth. To reach it we would have
to pass the fortified breakwater of Portland Naval Base, but
I reasoned that as long as we gave the sacrosanct harbor a
good berth we would not be molested. At Weymouth I was
certain we would be able to find fuel. If we could make it.

Caribbee turned the corner and headed north, out of the
worst of the tide. We soon could see the breakwater of the
naval base, and the forts at the entrances which had protected
inner installations from sorties by the Germans. Behind

loomed the silhouettes of large vessels of the Royal Navy. Only a couple of miles to go. . . .

But Gene Nichols, in charge of mechanical problems, who hovered over the tanks like a doctor administering a blood transfusion, suddenly looked up and said, "We won't make it. Getting pretty low."

"Haven't we anything? How about kerosene?"

He considered. "I think there's a little left in the can. I'll see."

While he burrowed into the lazarette I surreptitiously poured into the tank a large tin of salad oil from the galley, having once read how hero saved ship and girl by making port on the cargo of coconut oil. That was in the South Pacific, of course, and was in one of those magazines you buy while waiting for a train, but anyway I thought it worth a try. Gene added the kerosene. A peculiar smell arose, and from under our counter appeared a vapor plume not unlike a jet airplane at low altitude, but the engine didn't miss a beat.

The breakwater came closer, came abeam. Although the outer fortresses were unmanned, there was plenty of activity inside the harbor. A large aircraft carrier swung to a mooring. Nearby were a pair of cruisers and coveys of destroyers and lesser craft. Small boats darted back and forth.

The exhaust changed its steady rhythm. "About empty," announced Gene.

"How about the spare running lights and cabin lamp?"

"Okay," he replied, and decanted a pitiful few drops from the fonts into the starboard tank.

We were exactly opposite the East Ship Channel of Her Majesty's Naval Operating Base. It looked battle scarred and formidable. Having served as lieutenant, junior grade, in a navy on the other side of the world, I knew people didn't go barging into combat establishments with pleasure vessels. It simply isn't done, and damn the reason. In a moment of panic I visualized whistles blowing and loudspeakers blaring if an

admiral looked out of a window at Brooklyn or Norfolk to see
a little boat barging in.

Yet I found myself swinging the wheel hard left. There are
fates worse than a cleanly drilled death, and broiling wind-
less, iceless and beerless in the English Channel seemed one
of them. *Caribbee* passed beyond the sacred portals. Nobody
paid the slightest attention. Diffidently we crept by frowning
turrets and gaping muzzles without a challenge, but then
could find no place to go. Quays were lined solid with ships
in various stages of commission. Between them there were no
gaps. Anchoring seemed unwise. The engine began to miss.
I slipped out the clutch and *Caribbee* drifted to bare steerageway.

We came to a stop off what seemed to be the worst possible
place to pick in a foreign navy yard, the submarine dock.
Sleek grey monsters lay snout to tail, bristling with devices
I was sure were on the top secret list. Aboard the nearest, an
officer in fatigue uniform looked up from supervising a working party. He was the first person who had seemed aware of
our existence. This is it, I thought, sunk without a trace far
from home for illegal entry with intent to spy. . . .

"I say," called the officer. "Would you chaps like to tie
alongside?"

On the last gasp from our fuel we made it. The working
party moved across the submarine's deck to take our lines.
There was not the slightest flicker of curiosity on a single
face. Obviously small yachts flying the American flag appeared out of the haze every hour on the hour at Her Majesty's Portland Marina.

"Hot today, what?" said the officer casually as we tried to
adjust fenders to the rounded topsides.

"Certainly is."

"Calm, too. Very calm lately," said the officer.

"That's our trouble," I answered, sensing an opening. "We
couldn't sail. No wind. We're out of fuel, and have to be in

Cowes this afternoon." I paused, gulped, and took the final plunge. "Any place here where we can buy some diesel oil?"

He shook his head. "I'm afraid not. But come aboard. We'll go see the CO."

Ashore, we plunged into the labyrinth of a large naval shore establishment further complicated by having been part of the front lines. There was still evidence of heavy bombing. Finally we arrived at a small bare building, which had none of the opulent touches of our own lairs of command, and Lt. Squires of H.M.S. *Ambush* disappeared into an inner sanctum. He soon reappeared with a commander in white uniform and rows of campaign ribbons.

"Captain Boord will receive you immediately," he said. "I am Commander Biggs, the Executive Officer."

We walked along a spartan corridor and opened a door.

"Come in," said the officer behind the desk. He moved forward to shake hands. "Have a seat. Cigarette?" We talked. Like everyone I had met since landing, from taxi driver to waitress to customs official, he knew all about the race from Bermuda. The English are still oriented to the sea. I told of *Caribbee* roosting forlornly in the fog off the Grand Banks of Newfoundland, of our heartbreaking drift across a cold empty ocean north of fifty, of our crawling past dread Fastnet Rock in the Irish Sea, past the Scilly Isles, past Land's End; a saga not of storm but of calm, and now we found ourselves again drifting, with urgent business in Cowes, so near and yet so far, all for the lack of twenty gallons of diesel fuel. . . .

The captain became brisk. "Biggs, tell the Supply Officer of *Caribbee*'s requirement. Bring me the forms. Keep them simple. I'll sign whatever necessary." He turned back to me and smiled: "A spot of reverse lend-lease, what?"

The Supply Officer arrived with a sheaf of papers. Captain Boord signed. The Supply Officer signed. They were handed over for me to sign.

Pen poised, I looked up. "Twenty *tons?*" I queried feebly.

"Correct," the Supply Officer said efficiently. "Twenty tons of diesel oil. Present these in triplicate to the fueling depot and they'll pump it aboard." He turned to the captain. "We'll work it in on our generating allowance report. Cut the red tape."

"But twenty tons!"

He looked at me. "Isn't that what you want?"

"No. Twenty gallons."

"Twenty *gallons?*" he repeated in horror. "There is no way I can make out a requisition for twenty *gallons!*"

There was a long pause while the navy tried to conn through a sea of regulations. Lt. Squires saved the day. "Pardon me, captain. But I could let him have it from the ship, with your permission, sir."

We went back to the quay. Two men from the working party undogged a small circular hatch on the after deck of H.M.S. *Ambush* and disappeared. We bent a line on *Caribbee*'s deck bucket and lowered it into the depths of the submarine. A muffled shout arose, the bucket was hauled up, passed across, and poured into our funnel. Slowly we filled one tank.

As we finished, a motor launch approached, brass gleaming, white ensign snapping, officers and men in dress whites. An admiral's barge, I thought, remembering I had seen a command flag on the carrier.

Bells rang. Boathooks whirled through a complicated series of evolutions before laying hold of our rail. A tall young officer stepped aboard. "Good morning and welcome. I am the aide. The admiral sent me over to see if there was anything further we could do. Would you like us to message the Yacht Squadron you are coming?"

The wonderful, wonderful Limeys, I muttered to myself at the wheel as *Caribbee* finally chugged out past the fleet, a couple of hospitable pink gins under my belt: nothing in the world quite like the Royal Navy. Nothing.

But we were not finished. Before *Caribbee* cleared the breakwater another launch sped alongside, and an envelope was handed across. Inside was a signal, typed on a small rectangle of plain white paper. It is before me now, pasted in the log book:

ROUTINE   26IIIOA

FROM CAPT I/C PORTLAND (5)

TO CARIBBEE

GOODBYE, SO GLAD TO HAVE SEEN YOU. BON VOYAGE.

26IIIOA JULY

26/7   HAND I.T.   E.M.C.

Outside, a fresh breeze was blowing.
We didn't need the fuel after all.

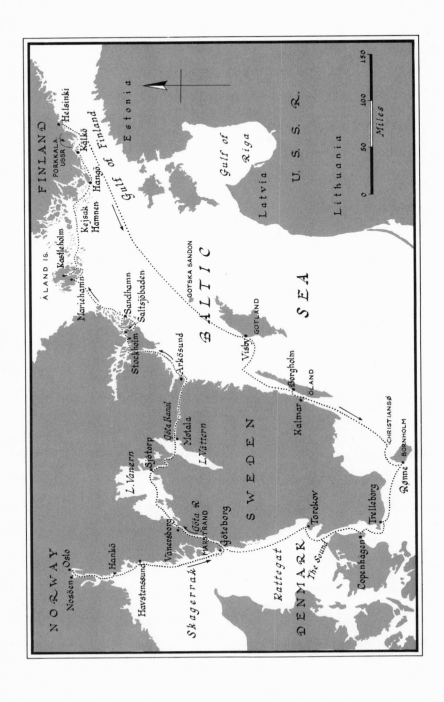

8

Walking in the Garden
THE BALTIC

We left Saltsjöbaden at dawn. It was crisp and clear, a high pressure system drifting down from even higher latitudes, and the wind came in fresh and true over the quarter. Thinking back, we had had westerlies and sunny skies ever since leaving Oslo, nearly a month before. And now we were off for Finland, booming through the Swedish skerries under spinnakers.

Perhaps an inevitability of passing years is the sharpening of memories. For Hemingway's Old Man it was lions roaring on the beach. For me, it is almost total recall of special moments afloat, and there are none which seem to recur so often and with such clarity as my first venture into Scandinavian waters. One reason may be an increasing reluctance to wander more than forty degrees from the equator, putting special emphasis on a near brush with the Arctic Circle, or it may be subconscious framing of an almost perfect slab of life.

But there we were, *Argyll* and *Caribbee*, two yawls 58 feet on deck, *Argyll* destined to win the Bermuda Race the following year, *Caribbee* to go on to assorted successes in the Southern Circuit, both carrying spinnakers and mizzen staysails as we passed Nämdofjärd, not racing any more than is inevitable among sailors, but driving hard through narrow channels in sheer exuberance. As getting closer to the water increases the sensation of speed, so does proximity to the shore. And islands were everywhere. The way led through dots so closely spaced on the chart they resembled scattered grains of pepper; it led toward groups looking from a distance like jutting peninsulas, but which dissolved into pine-clad clumps with glinting passages between; and it led through lanes with pairs of rocks, as gates, at the far end. "Walking in the garden," Nordic yachtsmen call sailing their beloved skerries. Although for the moment we chose to run, none of the fragrance was lost.

By comparison, my original entry onto the garden paths was a timid stroll. After both boats had been lowered into Oslofjord—and making the freighter's scheduled departure date in New York after finishing the Newport to Annapolis race had been somewhat of a saga in itself—*Argyll* took off across the open Skaggerrack to Gothenburg. Bill Moore, as head of a shipping firm serving northern Europe, was familiar with the Bohüslän skerries, and also had business appointments waiting. So *Caribbee* had gone it alone in more leisurely fashion, stopping at Hankö, the focal point of Norwegian yachting, and then had taken to the byways leading to Marstrand. The islands facing the Atlantic were unlike those we were to find in the Baltic, but pilotage was similar. Here the archipelago was almost treeless, each granite outcropping a starkly etched reminder of what lurked below, awaiting the careless keel. And while aids to navigation were plentiful, they took some learning. Buoys, as such, did not exist; channel edges were marked by witch's brooms of twigs tied to a pole: the triangle of the broom pointing up meant one thing, pointing down, another, and there was often a combination of brooms on the same pole. Even more prevalent were lighthouses perched on rocks at the end of fairways, no bigger than privies and not much different in architecture, sometimes hard to spot quickly when rounding a bend with myriad choices opening over the bow.

Historians believe this was the country of the earliest Vikings, whose name stemmed from the word *vik*, meaning a creek or cove, and it would be a perfect base for marauders. It was just as ideal for cruising yachtsmen, I decided on gaining confidence. Contrary to expectations, a warm sun hung over the cockpit, and warm water awaited over the side. The Gulf Stream laves the Bohüslän province of Sweden, bringing true summer to a land at a latitude corresponding to Kamchatka, Siberia, and northern Labrador. *Caribbee* under cruising canvas slid past many islets where golden humans basked in couples or in families, but under the ancient fortress of Marstrand there were hundreds festooning the ledges. "After the long, dark night of winter, spring is like coming out of a cave," explained an acquaintance ashore. "Our bodies crave sunshine, to store it up before the next twilight."

Possibly the Scandinavian approach to summer is the truest indication of the national character. On first meeting, Swedes especially seem formal and distant, perhaps because of an affinity for titles. A man in the shipping business is not the equivalent of plain "mister," but "Mr. Shipowner Carlson," while an associate may be introduced as "Dr. Engineer Hensen." But put them afloat in the skerries, and they go right back to nature. Everywhere we found people enjoying a life that was a combination of cruising and camping, as most of the boats were too small for their crews: bow pulled up on a rind of beach, a log fire or Primus stove on a rock, a tent pitched under a tree, children splashing in the shallows, mama and papa going about housekeeping chores or relaxing with a maximum of simplicity and minimum of clothing.

From Oslo to Stockholm to Helsinki to Copenhagen, the possession of a means of escape to the garden seemed more important than ownership of an automobile.

After rejoining *Argyll* in Gothenburg began a transit of the most beautiful ditch in the world, 240 miles long and punctuated by 64 locks. First came the Göta River, winding from a busy seaport into a placid countryside, with fat cows grazing on lush green fields dotted by haystacks, barns dwarfing farmhouses, the very pattern in which emigrant Swedes cast Wisconsin. Then came modern locks bypassing the falls of Trollhätten, electrically operated and big enough to take small steamers, and we found ourselves on the wide expanse of Lake Vanern, the largest in Europe except for Ladoga and Oneda in Russia. For an entire day we glided across calm waters under balloon jibs. Just at sunset, when a nip came into the air, we passed through the first of the old locks to nest at a pool at Sjötorp.

The Göta Canal was proposed as early as the XVI century, and Gustavus Vasa, a contemporary of Henry VIII of England, took up the plans, but work was not begun until the rise of Napoleon made an exit from the Baltic a matter of national policy. If the French dictator sealed off the narrows facing Denmark, shipping would be trapped. So finally in 1810 construction began, the civilian engineers aided by 60,000 soldiers. There have been virtually no changes in the waterway since the last shovel was cast aside.

Next morning began ditch crawling with a unique twist. At times the banks of the canal were higher than the surrounding land, so we looked down upon the life of rural Sweden. The way meandered between ranks of century-old trees planted to shade the towpaths, sometimes opening onto fields of grain, sometimes passing through quaint villages, sometimes hemmed in by forests of birch and pine. People came out of houses to wave. Bicyclists pedaled from lock to lock, keeping even along the towpaths; at each lock and bridge curious crowds gathered, for ours were the first American ensigns to pass since the war.

Soon we worked out a system to cope with the ancient hand-operated gates. Each lock had its keeper, who walked round one of the capstan-like bars, but the crews of boats going through were required to cope with the other. As each lock was only 97 feet long, and not wide enough to accommodate the two boats abeam, a squeeze play developed: *Caribbee* entered first and went ahead until the bow pulpit almost touched; *Argyll* snuggled into the curve of the counter, when her stern cleared the after gate by inches. Approximately nine feet at a time we hoisted ourselves until emerging at Lake Viken, 278 feet above sea level, and started downhill for the Baltic. Most impressive of all was the final plunge down a stairstep of fifteen locks at Berg, the skerries below like a patterned carpet.

By degrees we worked onward to Stockholm, the Venice of the North, with the magnificent Town Hall soaring over the mainmast as an introduction to the city, and afterward enjoyed the hospitality and competition of the Royal Swedish Yacht Club's annual regatta at Sandhamn. There had been *skåling* and singing in the cockpit in the endless light of midsummer, and tables groaning with *smörgåsboard*: herring with dill, herring with sour cream and chives, herring with onions; sardines, anchovies, tuna; tiny shrimp to be eaten shells and all; smoked salmon, smoked reindeer, smoked eel, smoked sausage; radishes, sliced tomatoes, pickled cucumbers, salads; stuffed eggs, caviar, cold chicken, sliced ham; and platters of cheeses and mounds of dark bread and butter. We washed each dish down with schnapps and afterwards tried to pronounce *sjutusensjuhundrasjuttiosju sjösjuka sjömän*, meaning "7,-777 seasick seamen," which our friends assured us was not only a good test of Swedish pronunciation but of sobriety.

Finally we had torn ourselves away to visit Salsjöbaden, and now were leaving the Swedish skerries, carrying spinnakers. We approached a crossroads old in history. To the north lay the brooding silent forests of the Gulf of Bothnia, to the south the busy Baltic, while over the bow awaited the Gulf of Finland, where a new chapter of conquest was being written. Here had sailed the Goths, restless and aggressive tribes flowing southward to pick the carcass of the Roman Empire; here had crossed the boats of the Swedish Vikings, the *Rus*, who voyaged the rivers of Eastern Europe as their Atlantic cousins roved the open ocean, fighting and trading their way to Constantinople; and here had cruised the fleets of Peter the Great, whose strategy of controlling the maritime approaches to Russia was being implemented by the present rulers.

We glided at 7 knots across an almost smooth sea. Åland Island rose above the horizon. Everything seemed slightly unreal until a very real lighthouse duly appeared ahead. It was Kobbaklintar. As it came abeam we jibed and passed into a new set of skerries, worn smooth by the grinding of winter ice, lying on the dark water like reddish-brown whales. A Finnish couple had joined *Caribbee* for the sail to Helsinki, and Ethel Krogius exclaimed: *"Terve tuloa Suomeen!* Welcome to Finland!"

Nearing the entrance to the harbor of Mariehamn, the spars of a square-rigged ship lifted high above trees and rooftops. It somehow seemed fitting to make our entry at the final home port of the Cape Horners. From this tiny island the late Gustaf Erikson had dispatched ships to load Australian wheat for England, the famed Grain Race, a poignant reminder of the centuries when the world's oceans had been spanned by white wings.

Next morning I went aboard the 4-mast bark *Pommern* with Edgar Erikson, heir to a tradition. Her log showed she had last discharged 46,941 bags of wheat totaling 3,919 gross tons at Falmouth after a passage of 117 days from Port Victoria, Australia, docking on Saturday, July 15, 1939. There had been 25 hands, "including the captain and cook," to struggle with a sail area of approximately 32,400 square feet. Each page of the log bore a neat diagram of the ship, showing what canvas was aloft, and occasional revealing comments in the hand of the mate, such as: "Heavy breaking sea but nothing happened —captain in bed."

The *Pommern*, like her sisters, will sail no more. "It got progressively harder to get cargos, and almost impossible to find crews," Edgar Erikson said regretfully. "Even Finns do not want to sign on, and we no longer have British apprentices needing time in sail to qualify for licenses, such as Thames pilots. But most of all no one can afford modern wages and the cost of food on a ship that can be delayed for weeks by calms or head winds."

As we walked the ghostly deck and looked aloft at the maze of rigging, Edgar Erikson answered a question which had long bothered me—how green crews could cope with the puzzle, when a mistake could be fatal to gear or fellow hands aloft. "One way was to attach playing cards to the braces, lifts, and sheets," he told me. "For the first few days, orders went like: 'haul on the Queen of Diamonds and slack the nine of Clubs,' or 'belay the six of Spades and let go the Ace of Hearts!'" The ultimate role of the *Pommern* was planned as part of a museum commemorating Gustaf Erikson and his vanished fleet.

Fortunately, we had served our own apprenticeship in skerry pilotage before arriving at Mariehamn. Beyond extended a maze. Islands of incredible variety and profusion seemed to stand athwart any possible course, sewn so thickly on detail charts that I gave up trying to count the number in even a small sector. The area was labeled *Saaristomeri Skär-gårdshavet*, which Ragnar Krogius translated as Finnish Sea Archipelago—because "it is a sea of islands and cliffs," the latter his term for rocks and ledges hidden underwater. Added to what was visible, it seemed several decks of cards with a few extra jokers would be required to get us through.

The fair breeze held, so we hoisted mainsail and genoa—my courage did not extend to spinnaker, I confess—and sallied forth. The swept depth of channels were indicated in meters on the chart, and the boundaries were well marked by brooms. The hydrographers had not attempted to show where all the dangers were, but a way to go where there were none. Soon my misgivings evaporated. *Caribbee*'s log carols: "Wind southwest force 2–3. At Falkarna light eased sheets and set mizzen staysail. Speed better than 6 knots. Sky almost cloudless and sun hot. Passed through a bottleneck between islands so narrow had to trim the main boom, and only the upper part of sails felt breeze, where a small boy called from ashore: "*Dom kör med motor?* Do you go with a motor?"

The outer skerries were barren rounded humps, as we had found approaching Mariehamn, but as we penetrated farther into the archipelago they became wooded, until finally we sailed between pines massed to the waterline. No houses intruded, and no other boats were astir. We glided along listening to the voices of the forest, not the sea: the swish of wind in the treetops, not the purl of wavelets on rocks. There is a somber haunting quality to the innermost Finnish skerries, even on a brilliant sunny day. They have a singular compelling beauty, yet somehow remain outposts of the lonely snow-mantled Arctic wastes. The comparison is inevitable: they look like the music of Sibelius sounds, variations of the theme of *Finlandia*.

Vivid in my memory is an anchorage called Kejsar Hamnen, meaning the Czar's Harbor. According to Ragnar, it had been a favorite retreat of Alexander II, Emperor of Russia and Grand Duke of Finland. Ringed by islets reflecting in the placid water, it was indeed a royal gunk-hole. But it is especially remembered by Finnish yachtsmen because of an humble fisherwoman named Stina, and sometimes goes by her name. One day she came alongside the imperial yacht in a decrepit skiff, towing a fish float astern. The Czar descended the gangway and asked jokingly if she had any fish to sell. In reply, she handed him the line to the float, while she dipped inside. The officers of the yacht and the czar's bemedaled entourage were horrified, but His Majesty was amused. The old lady became famous as Kejsar Stina, and the royal yacht bought fish from no one else.

By contrast, our next harbor was Hangö, on the southwestern tip of the mainland. Buildings were paintless and pocked by shrapnel and bullets. The letter "o" had been shot away from the sign at the entrance to the *Societethuset Hotel,* and some windows were still boarded over. The Russians had captured Hangö during the "Winter War" despite stubborn resistance. Now the Finns were rebuilding. Continued Russian occupation of the fortified zone of Porkkala had closed the skerry route to Helsinki; as heavy drift ice made it impossible to keep the Gulf of Finland open to shipping during the winter, Hangö was being expanded as a port. Here, as elsewhere, the Finns were striving to rebuild and repay, without asking for outside aid. First things had been put first: houses were allowed to remain drab, but the delivery of trawlers and other reparations demanded by the Soviets went on apace. As a military attaché stationed in the capital of another Baltic country had remarked, "The Finns do not recoil from human sweat. They work."

We were soon to encounter even more tangible evidence of Finland's giant and inscrutable neighbor. Beyond Kälkö it was necessary to leave the skerries to skirt the 15-square-mile zone still garrisoned by the Russians. No one knew what was going on inside Porkkala. Finns living on the perimeter heard almost incessant blasting, but even the locomotives on Finnish trains were replaced by Russian at the border, and passengers passed through with the curtains tightly drawn. Many were the tales Ragnar had to tell of yachts and fishing vessels being apprehended by patrol craft well offshore, and remaining interned under unpleasant conditions for long periods.

To thwart claims that territorial waters were being violated, the dauntless Finns set out and maintained a semicircle of buoys, but there were reports Soviet patrols had passed through to force victims inside.

On the opposite side of the gulf, little more than 15 miles away, the Estonian island of Nargö bristled with guns. Thus Soviet batteries commanded all traffic. Peter the Great had conceived the plan to thus "cork the bottle," and *Caribbee* approached the bottle's neck with some trepidation. It was a day when the sou'wester was smoky, so the land was enveloped in haze. Only the tops of a few lookout towers were visible, but we were sure that we formed neat pips on the radar screens, and that there was no doubt intelligence reports made clear to the operators who was running the gauntlet.

Caribbee happened to be in the lead as we approached. Binoculars finally picked up the beginning of the line of buoys through the mist, inshore, but as we drew abeam we saw something else—a patrol craft coming out on an intercepting course. A steep quartering sea was rolling us rail down, so it was hard to focus on details,˙ especially as the stranger was wreathed in the spray of the bow wave. At a distance of a couple of hundred yards she swung broadside, a gray ghost with guns pointing skyward, and for the first time we could distinguish the flag at her stern—not the hammer and sickle, but the blue-cross-on-a-white-field of Finland. We dipped our ensign, flying from the leech of the mizzen. Faintly across the water came the sound of a whistle, and her crew turned out to man the rail, standing rigidly at attention as the narrow hull appeared to roll through ninety degrees, until her own flag was dipped in answer.

The fearless Finns, I thought from the wheel, especially as the patrol hovered within the circle of visibility until we had cleared Porkkala. The dauntless Finns! I still thought as we sailed away from a mooring off the Nyländska Jaktklubben a week later. Helsinki seemed to personify the spirit of the nation. In 1940, the Olympic Games had been cancelled because of the attack by Russia; during our visit, preparations were again going forward for the reception of athletes and visitors, as a matter of civic pride, even though the presidential palace lacked paint. Everywhere the crews of both boats had found hospitality, but here it was almost overwhelming. We had happened upon the *kraftör* season, when the northern Baltic countries go slightly mad over fresh water crayfish, brought cardinal-red to the tables on heaped platters. Homes and restaurants blossomed with *kraftör* tablecloths and decorations, and the rafters rang with *skåls* and gay songs. Before we departed, gone was the impression of a somber people in a somber land.

And when we were ready to leave, the wind swung right round; after a rainy spell the westerlies which had brought us reaching all the way from Norway shifted to the opposite quadrants of the compass. *"Skål!"* toasted a Finnish friend in farewell. "You have luck! A dry easterly, the only good thing to come out of Russia!" So we set spinnakers to go driving through the Soviet slot, and after the markers of Porkkala fell astern at sunset, began ticking off the lighthouses on the Finnish coast: Jussarö, Russarö, Utö. The wind blew harder, backing into the north, so on *Caribbee* we shifted from spinnaker to high-cut reaching jib, and with the passing hours added more layers of sweaters under the oilskins. "If this is August, I wonder what it would be like in December," commented Bill Moore at midnight. For this 270-mile leg to Gotland, our longest single run of the summer, we had set a radio schedule, knowing no eavesdropper would be able to spot our positions by the way we pronounced the place names, especially when off Estonian and Latvian shores.

Mid-day found *Caribbee* near Gotska Sandön, *Argyll* out of sight over the horizon ahead. The log remarks, "Sliding along lazily. Back to Bermuda shorts and a Nassau straw hat. A brilliant day, clear except for a fat little cumulus cloud hovering over Gotland like a fat cherub in a medieval painting." Perhaps it was more than symbolism, for Visby was a landfall going backward through time. Original capital of the Goths, its men roved far before history was recorded. Iron Age graves have yielded Chinese pottery and shells from the Indian Ocean. In other areas, ancient Greek and Arabian coins have been unearthed. During the Middle Ages it flourished as a trading center until it rivaled London in size and importance. Its merchants wrote the earliest known maritime codes.

But the clock stopped for Visby one July day in 1361, when King Waldemar of Denmark landed from the mightiest fleet to sail the Baltic. Grim souvenirs of the invasion remain in the museum: breastplates pierced by lances and arrows; steel helmets cloven by swords, shattered skulls still inside. The Danes crushed resistance, burned, pillaged, and exacted tribute. Visby never recovered, never rebuilt, but as a town fell into a slumber as deep as the warriors buried in the surrounding fields.

And so we found it as we crept slowly along the limestone cliffs of Gotland in the golden light of late afternoon, the weathered defensive walls looking from a distance almost as King Waldemar must have seen them. After the Danes departed, the people of the island were too poor to make changes. They lived in the same old houses generation after generation; there was no incentive to pull down the churches, the battlements, or other remnants of the earlier civilization. The medieval character remained almost intact. Curiously, its ancient misfortune was the basis of present prosperity. Visby draws tourists from all over the world. Yet ashore we found no jarring notes. New buildings harmonized with the old. In the narrow streets it was possible to feel something of bygone days, men-at-arms moving past shuttered houses by torchlight, the town quiet behind its thick walls and deep moat, every approach sealed except the "Lover's Gate," where young couples were permitted to stroll out into the country-side.

Gotland lies some fifty miles off the Swedish coast. We sailed through the breakwaters of Visby just as a fiery sun disappeared below the horizon, on course to enter Kalmar-sund by the northern end of Öland Island. The breeze was fresh and the night dark, so the profusion of navigation lights on rounding into the sound was both dazzling and confusing. Much coastwise shipping passes through the rock-strewn channel, preferring the shorter distance and sheltered water to the open Baltic outside.

Two memorable fortress-castles faced Kalmarsund, one on Öland Island at Borgholm, the other at Kalmar, on the mainland a few miles to the south. A German yachtsman years ago wrote of Borgholm as "a magnificent frame for an ennobled version of communal life . . . not founded on southern ideas of show, but upon the ideal of combining human beings and not dead stones to form a magnificent pageant." A huge una-dorned edifice surrounding a courtyard where troops of cavalry could deploy, Borgholm evoked the thunder of hoofs and trumpets, indeed "one of the most impressive buildings in all Northern Europe," as Hans Domizlaff said in *Cruises of Dirk III*.

Quite different was the castle of Kalmar, although it, too, was a fortress, known for centuries as the "Lock and Key of the Swedish Kingdom." The dictum was that whoever con-trolled Kalmar Nyckel, or Key, was master of the remainder of the country. Yet Kalmar was poetry in stone, almost femi-nine in its delicacy and grace, giving no hint of the twenty-four sieges it had withstood. Despite the dynasties of warriors who held sway since King Magnus Ladulås began construc-tion in the XIII century, perhaps a woman was its most fa-mous occupant. In 1397 gifted Queen Margaret brought Nor-way, Denmark, and Sweden together in the Kalmar Union, a federation which did not manage to survive after her death.

Leafing through a log whose pages are beginning to turn yellow, I find a recurrent entry: "Maybe *this* the best sail yet!" It is there again after our departure, followed by: "Almost rail breeze reaching with big genoa, sea smooth, 8 knots plus." We seemed to have a private high pressure system of fair winds and smiling skies entangled in the upper rigging, towing it along wherever we went while the radio reported other parts of Scandanavia suffering the normal quota of chill overcast. Only twice since Oslo had rain fallen while we were underway, and the only tack recorded after leaving Lake Vattern came shortly before leaving Kalmarsund. Today the pointed turrets of Kalmar Nyckel—almost like minarets—stood out with cameo clarity against the unforgettable blue of a high in high latitudes.

Yet on this leg conditions were almost our undoing. A late afternoon start was timed to put us off the tiny Danish island of Christiansø at daylight, which came early so far north. But it was only 25 minutes past midnight when we ran out the distance. Gradually the wind had freshened and the sea built, while a veil of cirrus slid under the stars. The Baltic had decided to show its teeth. Crests lifted us high before bursting into eerie radiance. Otherwise the night was utterly dark except for a light atop an abandoned fortress guarding our goal. As I strained my eyes to pick up a lesser leading light promised by the chart, suddenly *Argyll* appeared close ahead. Bill Moore had turned on spreader lights as he ran off to drop the genoa. *Caribbee* followed suit.

Careful seamanship undoubtedly dictated heaving-to until dawn, or continuing to the neighboring island of Bornholm, whose commercial port of Rønne could be entered without hazard. However, I don't believe it occurred to either skipper to do either. *Argyll* and *Caribbee* bore off for the dim loom of Christiansø, which was punctuated by only a few feeble glimmers, one of which must be the white-green-red light at the entrance to the harbor. Honesty prompts me to confess that it wasn't until the next morning I fully realized what we had done.

There was no harbor in Christiansø, really, only a narrow lane of water where a past geological upheaval had split one large rock large enough to qualify as an island into two. The same freak of nature had opened a channel through myriad lesser rocks at both ends. Men later built a small stone structure on a low promontory, and installed a kerosene lamp inside. They left a rectangular opening toward the sea, which was covered by panes of glass. The center was clear, then came flanking strips of green, and finally panes tinted red. The white sector beamed down the middle, the green defined the limits of the channel, and the red shown over shallows strewn with boulders.

Standing by the miniature lighthouse, whose top I could touch with outstretched arm, I realized why I had been unable to keep *Caribbee* from sheering out of the white sector each time a sea slid under the counter. It covered a ribbon not much wider than our beam! There was some cushion in the green, of course, but nowhere did the gap between rocks with seas breaking over appear much greater than our overall length. Turning my head, I could see *Argyll* and *Caribbee* snug alongside the quay. To wind round to head the other way would be a maneuver requiring some planning. Our point of no return had arrived the instant we entered the channel.

Fortunately, the seas had quickly smoothed as we came under the lee, so *Argyll* had been able to land a man short of a hand-operated bridge spanning the twin islands of Christiansø, which we closed behind *Caribbee*. So we had moored in the center of a sleeping town, and never did schnapps taste better. Coming on deck in the morning we found astonished villagers staring down. We also found we had made fast to huge iron rings set into the stone blocks of the quay, whose purpose was to breast off local vessels in heavy weather. During winter gale swells sometimes broke a meter deep the whole length of the port, and the entire population turned out to tend lines.

Only 160 people lived on the island, mostly fishermen and their families, occupying barracks dated from 1685 to 1736. They seemed people out of another country, like their dwellings. Each man spoke and stood aside when we met, raising his hand in a gesture of respect making me remember the old English phrase, "touching the forelock." Fortifications bristled everywhere, but, like so many places with a martial past, Christiansø now lay peaceful and forgotten. Airfields on Bornholm had annulled any lingering strategic importance. Its German garrison during World War II consisted of three soldiers. But the dangers of the conflict had not ended for the fishermen. Their rugged existence was complicated by the dumping of 200,000 tons of poison gas 15 miles to the eastward. Occasionally canisters were caught in the nets.

After resting quietly until a summer semi-gale blew itself out, we cleared the other end of the Christiansø slot to find our old traveling companions, clear skies and a warm fair breeze, awaiting us. Rapidly Bornholm lifted above the horizon. The first impression was a rolling pattern of green and brown fields, broken by the red roofs of the towns of Sandvig and Allinge; on rounding a point, the shore rose steeply in heavily wooded cliffs, surmounted by the imposing ruins of Hammershus fortress. It seemed very Caribbean, especially as we smoothed our water and lost speed as we came into the wind shadow.

There was nothing of the West Indies ashore. Instead, the flat farm land, neatly spaced haystacks, and sleek cattle, were a Danish version of Holland, complete to windmills dotting the landscape. Rønne was a busy port, crowded with small freighters and trawlers, final visual confirmation that the age of commercial sail had ended on the Baltic. The masts of a few schooners lifted above the pack, but closer inspection revealed wheelhouses and diesel exhausts aft, and no sails on the booms. Curiously, though, even the newer steel coasters were fitted with long bowsprits, with nary sign of a jib.

Between Bornholm and Copenhagen extended a last reminder of the agony Europe had recently endured. Southern Baltic waters were still thickly sewn with mines. Our Bible became a joint British Admiralty-U.S. Navy publication entitled *Nemredi*, replete with such cautions as: "Mariners are warned to keep a sharp look-out for drifting mines . . . the temptation to cut corners must be resisted . . . in areas considered free of mines a risk may remain for years." Not only had the opposing navies planted fields in every direction, but aircraft had jettisoned untold tonnage of high explosives. And while we were reasonably sure wooden sailing vessels were safe, Bill and I agreed without debate to follow the swept channel from Rønne to Trelleborg, at the tip of Sweden.

Before the war, Trelleborg had been an entry port for Polish coal, and a terminus for ferries commuting to the picturesque towns rimming the southern Baltic. The Russians had stopped such traffic. Trelleborg was as dead as if it had come under the bombs. Coal chutes stood gaunt and rusty along deserted quays, the ferry slips lay empty. But adversity had resulted in one gain. For the same strategic reasons the Göta Canal had been dug, the rise of another dictator required the cutting of a canal through the Falsterbo peninsula. It was neither imposing nor lovely, but saved the passage outside, where shoals forced the channel close to the Danish shore, controlled by the Nazis.

For us, it cut off a long trek by the paths laid down in *Nemredi*. Leaving, we found ourselves in Öresund with a direct approach to Copenhagen. There are three exits from the Baltic: Öresund, so important it is referred to in all languages bordering the Baltic simply as *The* Sound; and the Great and Little Belts, winding passages between Danish islands. Even on The Sound navigable waters were limited to lanes which had been swept and re-swept, but soon the towers and trees of Copenhagen lifted over the bow.

Although the Danes had endured invasion and occupation, there were few reminders of the grim past in Copenhagen. Its gracious life had blossomed again. Couples strolled the wide and shaded streets, or lingered over aperitifs in sidewalk cafes, or sunned on benches in the parks. Copenhagen seemed more than ever like Paris. Restaurants were crowded and the meals marvelous; there was no shortage of food, but rationing remained as Denmark voluntarily tightened its belt to export meat and dairy products to less fortunate neighbors.

When not ashore, we readied *Caribbee* for the last passage of the summer. Signed on for the run to Gothenburg were Bent Silfverberg, a Danish friend who had been aboard for the Miami-Nassau race earlier in the year, and Carl Kanow, better known to yachtsmen on both sides of the Altantic as "The Leaping Dane"—"Leapy" for short. Hospitality made it hard to slip our mooring off the Royal Danish Yacht Club, but finally we turned the bow toward Helsingför, where The Sound pinched to the width of a river. At the narrowest point stood the fortress of Kronborg, better known as "Hamlet's Castle." A few days before, we had looked from the battlements to the coast of Sweden, less than two miles away. Now we stared up at the frowning walls, seeing them as earlier sailors had when the cannon forced passing ships to heave-to and pay toll. Shakespeare chose an appropriate setting for his drama of dark deeds. The huge pile itself seemed to brood, a somber shape full of threat.

The wind was light on the Kattegat, after we had cleared The Sound, and progress was limited to bare steerageway. A check of the chart showed the nearest haven a breakwater at the tiny fishing village of Torekov, so at sunset we crept behind its sheltering arm. Again we were in Sweden. Inside, the harbor was hardly bigger than we were long. The crew of a trawler helped us warp around, then make fast alongside.

We brought a fine turbot flapping from her hold, and dined upon it after a first course of North Sea shrimp—shrimp so small that a dozen or more could be served in a single teaspoon, with a delicacy of flavor to match.

Morning brought thick fog. The leading light on the breakwater, a boatlength away, was invisible. But as soon as the mist began to turn silver, indicating the sun had lifted above the horizon, we were underway. Cautiously we crept from buoy to buoy until we were in the open Kattegat. Within an hour the fog lifted, as a breeze struck in. Then began "the best sail" of the summer. At least the log calls it that, once again. As the sun climbed, the wind freshened, until the rail scooped dollops from the crests racing past. An almost polished clarity of the atmosphere intensified the colors of the sky and sea, and the Swedish shore.

The wind freshened further, raising white horses which began to kick up more than flying spray. Occasional solid water burst on deck to roll heavily aft. But just as the moment of decision to shorten sail was inevitable, *Caribbee* came to the light at Nidingen. Our luck still held, for Nidingen marked the beginning of the west coast skerries. We ducked into their shelter. The sea smoothed magically, and the extra edge was taken from the wind. Once more we walked in the garden.

Ahead, that September afternoon, we saw the rooftops of Gothenburg rising as we wound our way along paths of glittering blue, until we picked up the same mooring we had dropped nearly two months before. We had not only closed a loop around southern Sweden, but added a few extra curlicues to the track chart. Now, these later cruising years, I prefer to swing at anchor off palm fringed beaches, rather than rocky coves girt by pines. These lines are written with the trade wind streaming through the hatch. Yet my lions on the beach remain pale Nordic beauties basking in the *skärgården*, and I still say *"skål!"* as I raise my glass in memory of the Baltic.

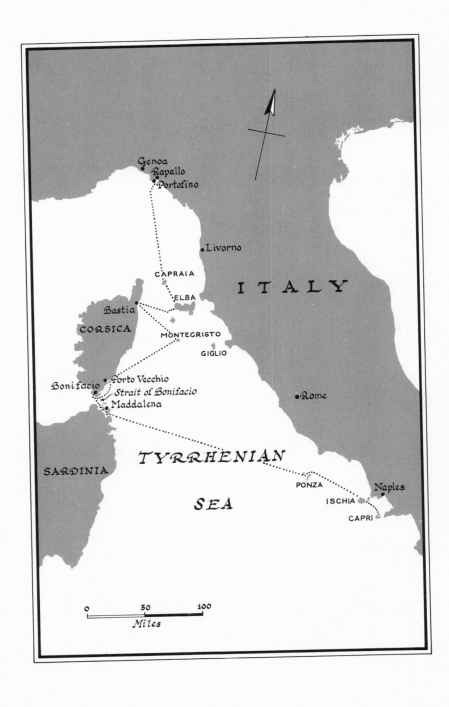

9
The Lovely, Lazy Sea
of Piu Tarde
THE MEDITERRANEAN

Only on the Mediterranean can many people be whole. Something about it is like music. Tell me the comparison is impossible, and I agree. Occasional bursts of song and random guitar chords from arbored garden and waterfront *trattoria* cannot swell into a vast celestial symphonic background, sensed rather than heard. Yet, for me, it is so. Music creates mood, a receptiveness to beauty, and along the borders of this enchanted sea always there are vistas which affect me the same way: colors flowing down mountainsides to spill into the water, play of dawn and sunset, mist over valleys, breakers against granite, birds crossing a sky bluer than Dufy's palette, a distant headland coming closer, and the village waiting beyond. Call it mood, call it awareness, call it inner peace or beatitude or sheer joy in being alive, another day ahead to enjoy, but there it is, that feeling for the Mediterranean and the shores it washes.

There was no wind at all as *Oliana V* crept out of the harbor of Portofino on a brilliant Sunday morning. It was early. I lounged against the mizzen rigging watching the town recede, guarded by the absurd ramparts of Castello Brown, perched on the crest of the hill above. At this hour, the cobbled waterfront piazza was empty, as it had been in June, when I arrived. The daily hordes of August trippers had not begun to swarm down from busses parked at the end of the road, tourists of every shape and nationality, serpents in shorts and Tyrolian hats despoiling Eden.

As I looked back, there were the empty tables of Il Pitisforo, home of *capelli da prete* and *scampi ai ferrai* beyond compare; and the other tables of the other restaurants rimming the piazza, facing fishing boats drawn up on rollers as they had been for generations. There was my favorite spot to sip a Negroni while engaged in the difficult evening task of wondering what to have for dinner, when everything was so good; and there over the cross-trees of a voyaging British cutter was the very window of my room at the Hotel Nazionale, so recently abandoned that the little maid who always bobbed and murmured *grazie* to anything said in my halting Italian probably had not even arrived to make the bed.

It was hard to leave, hard to leave. The moored fleet of yachts along the quay was reflected and doubled in the mirror of the harbor; each boat met a phantom counterpart at the waterline, inverted, masts poking down as far as up. Two sets of pastel houses stood on each other's heads, like a circus balancing act, duplicated to the last piece of laundry drying from windowsills and the three-dimensional rococco paintings on the walls, more improbable than any stage setting.

The rich dark green of pines, patterned by purple bougainvillaea and candy box villas, ran up a steep hillside to the Church of Saint George, looking down on the harbor on one side, the open Mediterranean on the other. The same Saint George who slayed dragons to protect the maidens of Merrie England is the patron saint of local sailors. Legend has it

Portofinese manned the ships carrying Richard the Lion-Hearted to the Crusades, and they brought back a relic of the saint, which is paraded on feast days. Inside the church paintings testifying to Saint George's saving grace hang in dim recesses: brigantines and top's'l schooners and paddle-wheel steamers, beset by towering foam-capped seas. In each picture, Saint George sits astride a white charger limned in the darkest storm cloud, lance at the ready, protecting the seaman who commissioned the painting in gratitude that his prayers were answered.

It was hard to leave, hard to leave, but somehow the deck of a small boat bound for other ports makes any departure less painful. People ask where you go when places get too crowded, especially in mid-summer now that Europeans compete for the sun and sights with peripatetic Americans. San' Tropez. Palma de Mallorca. Antibes. Portofino, Monte Carlo. Cannes. Automobiles bumper to bumper and barely room along the beaches to dry a bikini—the whole perimeter known as the Costa Brava and the Cote d'Azur and the Italian Riviera. The answer is simple, if practical: you put forth into the open Mediterranean, to visit the lesser ports, the villages and the beaches harder to reach, not yet discovered by the road-bound tripper, perhaps to find among them your spiritual home for the future.

Outside was as smooth as the harbor. I walked forward to look into the cove of Piaggia and the entire Gulf of Tigullio lay over the bow: Santa Margherita and Rapallo and Chiavari, towns and isolated villas rising from the shore to the heights, tier on tier of man's colors in a vast natural amphitheater, surely one of the most breathtaking unions of land and sea on our planet. In the vastness, *Oliana* moved like a wind-up toy boat. Rhythmically the engine pushed us across the liquid mirror, bubbles in the wake tiny bits of shattered glass breaking the otherwise perfect reflection. "It is always here the same," had said Lippo Riva a few days before, wise in the way

of Mediterranean waters. "Either the wind blows too hard—
pouf!—or there is no wind at all."

For all its virtues, the Mediterranean cannot be called ideal
for yachting. During most of the season, there is not enough
wind for the sailing sailor; yet, when it does come, there is
likely to be too much, especially for small power vessels.
Consequently, *Oliana V* was designed and built as a compro-
mise by the firm of Sangermani at nearby Lavanga, amply
powered for the calms, but with sail enough in her ketch rig
to be smart in a breeze, a fine Italian representative of the
modern breed known as motor-sailers.

Only four days previously I had gone with Lippo to the
launching, to find *Oliana V* sitting in a cradle on an exposed
sand beach. Not a shred of protection lay to the westward,
whence come mistrals and other fierce winds. Vessels built by
Sangermani can only be launched during a calm, and once
launched, they must be ready to go. Somewhat dubiously I
watched her enter the water after being blessed by a barefoot
monk from the monastery on the hillside above. I was assured
she was fully found and ready to swim away like a newly
hatched duck. Sails were furled on the booms, and the motor
purred on the first touch of the starter. Almost without pause
our launching momentum had been a departure for Portofino. There had been two days of stowing personal gear, and
now on this morning of bright promise we were off to the
south with Capri as a final destination. *"Come il dolce alla fine
d'un pranzo,"* as Olli Riva put it: "Like the sweet to end the
dinner."

The antipasto was destined to be the island of Capraia,
some 85 miles to the southward. First there had to be a pause
off the waterfront villa of the Rivas, at Rapallo, to say goodbye
to their children and take aboard a few last minute delicacies.
An early start had been planned to arrive at Capraia before
dark. Right here it is necessary to make a distinction about
Mediterranean cruising, which, like all cruising, is not only

a way of life, but reflects the philosophy along the shores. For an Italian, the *mañana* of Spain becomes *piu tarde*, not tomorrow, just "later." Translated into practice, it means never hurry to do something else so long as you are enjoying what you are doing at the moment. Meals are timed by the flow of wine and conversation, not the hands of a watch. So after the Riva children paddled out in a rubber raft, we swam. An awning was rigged over the cockpit. Friends abandoned waterskiing to come alongside and see the new *Oliana*. Champagne appeared. More friends arrived. Cheese and grapes were added to the deckhouse table. Lippo was not the harried skipper, being delayed; having experienced Italian energy and hard driving in the Giraglia Rock ocean race, recently finished, I was under no illusions about lethargy either: it was to be a *piu tarde* cruise. So happily I turned off for the duration the time-clock built into the Anglo-Saxon brain, and filled a glass.

Eventually, children and friends went ashore; anchor up, *Oliana*'s bow swung towards the open sea. Soon we left astern the criss-crossing wakes of skiers, and the water stretched ahead like moire silk, incredibly blue, but only a few shades darker than the sky. When Portofino was abeam, a faint breeze struck in around the end of the Camogli peninsula, encouraging us to set sail. It dwindled away, and we went back to powering. Sunlight shafting into the depths alongside like a gigantic star sapphire, last glimpse of Castello Brown, purple light on distant headlands. Gradually my eyes closed, and I dozed, to awaken to lunch set on the folding cockpit table. A tall bottle of Rhine wine in the center, sides dewy. Chilled glasses. A bowl of dark Spanish tuna overlaid by thinly sliced onions, a salad of tomatoes and diced green peppers, a cold roast of veal, a Danish ham, a basket of fruit, and a platter of cheese. We dined, and somehow the entire afternoon had vanished astern, along with the land and recent memories, and faint on the horizon ahead was a new island, full of promise.

It was dark when *Oliana* crept behind an unseen breakwater. Above, silhouetted against the stars, I had the impression of a cliff crowned by battlements, a somber fortress still standing guard against invading fleets long vanished. For a sailor, it is difficult to say which landfalls are most intriguing. It is exciting to watch by day an unfamiliar shore rise from the sea, taking on detail; and there is an especial feeling about making port at dawn or sunset. Yet somehow there is the fascination of mystery in closing the land in utter darkness, steering towards a winking pinpoint of light that gradually becomes brighter, finally to drop anchor without knowing what day will reveal.

With morning, it was plain that Capraia still drowsed in the past. Only the first wave of the new discoverers had arrived, sun seekers living in tents along the beach. A few skin divers basing on inflated rubber boats explored offshore rocks, while girls in bikinis watched from ledges. The town on the hill above was almost empty. Lippo explained: "The young people go to find work in Turino, or Milano, or elsewhere in the north. Here there is no cinema, no TV, no football." Houses of squared stones built to last through the centuries lined deserted streets, narrow in the medieval fashion, yet each with a glimpse of blue water at the end.

An ancient fortress entered through a nail-studded door, commanded by arrow slots in flanking towers, seemed capable of resisting any invasion of modernity. Looking down the sheer granite precipice below the walls, then to the horizon, it was easy to recapture bygone scenes: sentries in armor peering towards an approaching fleet, pennons flying above ram bows, oar-blades flashing in the sun; trumpets sounding the alarm, and villagers driving livestock towards the shelter of the walls; fires lighted under cauldrons of pitch, quivers filled with arrows, stones balanced on the edge. Yet I was wrong. Even here the past is capitulating to the pressures of the present. An *albergo*—a small hotel—had been fashioned from the old chambers, and guests lolled in deckchairs on the highest battlements.

Capraia possesses few beaches, but many rocky coves where the water lies still and clear. Because most of its trees were cut when the ruling city-state of Pisa needed ships to counter the fleets of rival Genoa, it has the clear-etched starkness of an Aegean island, a resemblance extending to the *trattoria* on the quay a few feet from *Oliana*'s stern. As in a harborside Greek *taverna* we sat at bare board tables under hanging grapes, sun filtering through the leaves, and sipped a tart *vino rosso* from the volcanic soil of Elba that almost had the lingering aftertaste of *retsina*. Yet there the similarity ended, with heaped plates of spaghetti and Italian vivacity.

From Capraia, Elba is a short run. Barely had we cleared the harbor before we could see our next destination high and solid above the horizon. A warm breeze touched our shoulders in gentle reminder that we were supposed to be sailing sailors, and we hoisted main, mizzen and balloon jib to steal quietly across the calm sea. The Mediterranean carries an inescapable sense of men and ships which have passed before, and I thought it might have been just this way when Napoleon made the same landfall, his spirit to flare into the Hundred Days and the final fulfillment of destiny at Waterloo in a defeat so complete as to make the word a part of the language.

Elba is a green island, yet not tree clad; its color stems from verdant fields terraced up the hillsides like a giant's stairsteps, and foliage around scattered villas. As we approached Marina di Marciana in the soft light of sunset we saw a town of pale stone cubes and red tile roofs, with lesser villages receding into haze on the heights behind, shadowed valleys between.

Elba is beautiful on first impression, a feeling not dispelled by later acquaintance. The next morning we powered from the port to a beach resort at Biodiola, dropping anchor off a crescent of pure white sand reminiscent of the Caribbean. While "discovered," Elba had not yet been invaded: two hotels looked from one end of the cove, over the sea, and tents clustered at the other, but there was no sense of crowding. We swam, and waterskied behind boats hired from the shore, and then set sail to the westward, intending to spend the night at the fishing village of Marina Campo. The wind seemed to be coming from behind each headland, forcing us to tack the length of the north coast. In sailing, there are always compensations, and ours was the reward of island vignettes: tiny coves scooped deep into the rocky shore, a crescent of gleaming sand at the end; boats and drying nets below lone houses, terraced vineyards surrounding villages high above.

Marina Campo had none of the charms we had come to expect. Large trawlers puffed diesel fumes. Waste oil glazed the harbor. There was a smell of fish and the blare of cha-chas from a juke box in a waterfront restaurant bearing in garish neon the name Kon-Tiki. Yet away from the quay we explored a charming little town, with winding narrow streets and houses from another century. We dined, and moved into the outer bay for the night, beyond range of Kon-Tiki.

In the morning the water lay under us as clear as a mountain pool. Near the anchor chain a small octopus was going through setting-up exercises, all eight arms flexing and unflexing—good for biceps and shoulders—and I thought I detected a few deep knee bends. Donning mask and flippers I lazily swam down for a closer look, only to find that the water was deeper than it seemed from deck. The octopus continued his workout, and I returned to the cockpit to munch grapes and *pignoli*—dried pine nuts, the unsuspected yet vital ingredient of sauce *al pesto*, which Gino the Genoese sailor-cook began to make as we powered towards Bastia.

Al pesto may be the finest of the pasta sauces, as visitors to the northern seacoast towns of Italy will remember. Dark green in color, delicate in flavor, the name stems from a pestle, sometimes used with a mortar for crushing the herbs. But this is how Gino went about the operation as I stood watching: on a clean board chop a large handfull of the washed leaves of fresh basil, together with one or more cloves of garlic, depending on your tolerance. Cut, cut, cut, working back together with the blade of the knife until finely minced. Chop in about one-third the amount of *pignoli* (which may be bought at most metropolitan Italian groceries, along with the other ingredients). Add freshly grated parmesan cheese, and one other, also grated: either sardo or pecorino, the latter easier to find. Blend thoroughly, then douse with olive oil and work in a generous amount of softened butter. Salt. Taste, and add more of anything to achieve a subtle balance of all: when perfect the result should be a thick paste, glistening with richness; there should come through the blended flavors of basil, garlic, both cheeses, olive oil, butter, and an intangible background note of *pignoli*. The sauce may be used immediately over lasagna or any other pasta, or it may be kept refrigerated for several days in a covered jar.

When I came on deck most of the 32 miles to Bastia lay astern, and the mountains of Corsica rose steeply from sea to sky. As a reward for my time in the galley, Lippo brought forth a dewy bottle of Zeltinger Langerback '59, proving his opinion that "Nothing is so cool and fresh in hot weather as a Rhine or Moselle wine." Lippo Riva was not only a sailor —(in his last *Oliana*, a small Sparkman and Stephens centerboard yawl "almost like *Finisterre*," he had dominated the Mediterranean ocean racing circuit)—and a big game hunter (nine extended safaris to Africa, with a bag including some of the rarest trophies on the continent), but he was also a linguist and connoisseur of good living. Part of the reason for our visit to Bastia was to effect what Lippo jokingly called a *"coup de main du vin,"* stocking French wines for the rest of the cruise at French prices. Like most Europeans, Lippo had not lost an appreciation of basic things, despite his complexity as a highly civilized individual: the pleasure of a chilled glass of wine on a hot morning, the ages-old taste of olives, bread, cheese, and fruit, under the open sky.

We sipped, and swam almost below the ramparts of Bastia, then powered into the ancient harbor in the center of the old town, as opposed to a large modern breakwatered port slightly to the north. Awnings were rigged, and a faint breeze blew through. The harbormaster came to the foot of the stern boarding plank to give clearance. Bastia dozed in the sun. Around the quay stone buildings leaned against each other, hunched and gray, like men tired by a weight of years. The present seemed dominated by a memory. Through every street strode the ghost of the island's famous son, The Little Corporal from Corsica. Endless souvenirs of Napoleon filled the shops: bronze busts and statues, crockery and glassware adorned by portraits, coins and dishes of copper—everywhere reminders of the brooding eyes under the forelock and cocked hat, the hand thrust into the coat and booted foot aggressively forward.

Yet in the late afternoon Bastia came very much alive. As the sun lowered the park along the waterfront filled with people, the evening promenade dear to the Latin heart. Girls dressed in their finery pretended not to notice admiring swains, couples at small round tables dawdled over cloudy glasses of *pastis*, families strolled under the palms, while the sky paled and a cool breath stole in from the sea. Suddenly it was dark, when the sun dropped below the mountain range behind the city, the towering central spine running the length of the island. Lights winked on, and restaurants began to fill.

Corsica is French, but with typical Mediterranean overtones, probably stemming from the *Mare Nostrum* of the Romans, Our Sea, a common heritage which influences all life on its shores. A large island, it combines a wild and rugged interior with an infinitely varied seacoast, deeply indented by bays and coves on the west side, bold and yet sand fringed on the east. Later we were to cruise past miles of beaches, deserted except for an occasional tent or fisherman's hut. In many ways Corsica had a primitive feel, but tucked in the medieval waterfront streets of Bastia—streets so narrow that the houses above almost touch, streets so unaccustomed to wheeled vehicles that they become flights of steps—is a little bit of Paris, the market-place. Under awnings were stalls with good things necessary to *la bonne cuisine:* mounds of cheeses, sausages, fruits, fish; salad greens and carefully arranged vegetables; while in one section a golden bull's head surrounded by carved ears of golden corn surveyed cuts of beef and veal. We trudged through with baskets, cheerfully poking and squeezing and bargaining, part of a ritual, finally to march back to *Oliana* with long loaves of French bread carried over the shoulders like rifles.

For my benefit, Lippo planned to make a detour to include an island with one of the world's most romantic names, Monte Cristo. Lying by itself almost midway between Corsica and the Italian coast above Rome, it is rarely visited, a game sanctuary not open to the public. As *Oliana* bucked a fresh sirocco—the southeast wind off the Syrian deserts—there was plenty of time to wonder what it would be like. The first impression was of a single rock pinnacle, hazy and unreal, a fragment broken from the moon. Earlier, I had had difficulty persuading myself that an island of Monte Cristo actually existed, and was not part of childhood fantasy, like the mythical Count himself. Now as I watched it come closer—watched the craggy peaks compound, saw the carelessly strewn detached boulders—I thought it strange that chance should have directed a novelist to choose such a perfect background for a story which had captured the imagination of generations of readers. For Alexandre Dumas never saw the island he made famous, but picked Monte Cristo from a map because he liked the name.

There is a single valley slashed down the center, a narrow vertical band of vegetation dividing the stark granite mass. The valley terminates in a small cove, gripped between two rocky arms. Smooth enough to form a harbor in easterly winds, it becomes a seething inferno during a mistral, so any vessel entering must always be ready to put forth at the first sign of a shift.

There is a single house ashore, among the trees above the cove, and a keeper to protect the game on the crags from Ponza fishermen who shelter during strong siroccos. But after a swim Lippo told a story of jolly bygone men who leapt from crag to crag, where now only wild goats disport, which somehow made Monte Cristo seem more part of the human world. High above *Oliana* he pointed out the walls of an ancient building, almost indistinguishable from the towering cliff it crowned. Once it had been a monastery. For many years the inmates lived blamelessly, walking barefoot to tend meager gardens and vineyards, chanting prayers from dawn to sunset. But the gaiety that swept Italy after the Middle Ages, the upsurge of spirit flowering into the Renaissance, infected Monte Cristo. Rumors reached the Pope of full barrels of wine being rolled up the paths, to come down empty; of songs other than hymns lifting to the sky; of merry monks pursuing bucolic maidens among the peaks. As a mark of Papal displeasure, the monastery was closed and the monks scattered, no doubt to secretly remember the good old days on Monte Cristo.

With dawn, the wind came in fresh, not the dread northwest mistral, but a southerly, a mezzogiorno. Squalls rifled down the valley to snatch our stern, secured ashore by a loop of line over a boulder. The sky was pale lavender, although *Oliana* still lay in deep shadow. Thick clouds touched by the sun flowed across the culminating peak of Monte Cristo, writhing and tortured, putting forth icy white tentacles, which slithered down the valley to be suddenly snatched into nothingness by another savage gust. When it blows on the Mediterranean, it can blow hard. Yet I had the feeling that it was a harbor like Great Salt Pond on far away Block Island, where terrain funnels a wind into more velocity than outside on the open sea.

And so we found. Setting main, mizzen, forestaysail, and Yankee—large jibtopsail to sailors on the Yankee side of the Atlantic—*Oliana* rounded the point to meet only a moderate breeze, which soon trailed away. By nine o'clock we sat in a row along the top of the deckhouse, sipping wine and eating hunks of bread and a nameless cheese from the market in Bastia, looking out over unruffled water.

It was afternoon when the engine brought us back to Corsica. Passing the deep and almost landlocked bay of Porto Vecchio, *Oliana* swung south to skirt Point di Chiappa and cut inside the Cerbicales islands. Behind long sweeping beaches we could count five distinct ranges of mountains lifting tier on tier to the central spine, white sand perimeter and green heartland, wholly unexploited, happy reminder that there is always somewhere else to go when old haunts get too crowded. Every point was topped by the conical stone lookout towers which have become to me the hallmarks of the northern Mediterranean littoral, relics of the last wave of invaders, the roving corsairs of the Barbary coast.

It had been our intention to anchor for the night in the Golfo de Santa Manza, just short of the southern tip of the island, lured by a lyrical description in a French cruising guide. On entering, we found a rather shabby bay of cloudy water and grey beaches, plus an ominous vanguard of tents and parked Volkswagons, the covered wagons of the modern pioneers. Muttering an opinion of travel writers, *Oliana* presented her stern, and soon we neared the Strait of Bonifacio, for me almost as rich in associations as Monte Cristo. While not so conclusive a portal of commerce and conquest as Gibraltar or the Skagerrak, the narrow gateway between French Corsica and Italian Sardinia has been one of the vital passages of maritime history. In the days of sail, it was the scene of some dramatic—and many tragic—incidents, being famed as a graveyard of ships and crews. Nearing, we could see why. Huge boulders lay singly and in clusters, some barely breaking the surface, a patternless rockpile scattered by the mischievous children of some super race. Passing through, the course was not direct, but a dog-leg, while swirling currents tugged at our bow. It would be a passage of terror in the darkness of a winter gale, as it had been for the poor souls aboard the French frigate *La Semillante*. They had sailed from Toulon on February 14th, 1855, to be caught by a mistral the following day. That night the ship struck Ile Lavezzi, a rock like the back of a surfaced whale on the north side of the Strait, and 773 passengers and crew perished in the boiling cauldron.

But now it was calm, and from the bow I stared curiously ahead. Every important trade lane had its iron door and lock in the old days, not only to control passage for political reasons, but to exact tribute from hapless merchants. I felt that a strait which had been important since the dawn of civilization must have a rather special guardian, nor was I disappointed.

Nature and the labors of men long dead have combined to make the fortress town of Bonifacio one of the most impressive ruins in the world, something like Visby in the Baltic, from a distance a medieval stronghold preserved intact through the intervening centuries. Built atop a sheer rock promontory rising perhaps 300 feet above the surf creaming at the base, the town walls are almost a continuation of the cliff itself, altered only by narrow windows and arrow slits. Unbroken the battlements run inland, to the end of the peninsula, curving towards the harbor in a wall that hardly dips as

the elevation lowers, the most impressive masonry I had ever
seen.

The present town was begun about 300 A.D., although previously Phoenicians, Greeks, and Romans, had established garrisons. In 833 a Pisan count undertook to improve the fortifications as a barrier against Saracen invaders. Between 1091 and
1283 it was fought over by Pisa and Genoa, to finally become
a colony of the Genoese. In 1397 it underwent the first of a
series of major assaults, this by Spaniards. During 1528 it was
ravaged by the plague, reducing the population from 5,000 to
700; recovering, it was subjected to a French-Corsican siege
by land, while being assailed from the sea by a Turkish fleet.
Women fought on the walls along with the men, until a sur-
render was finally arranged, but the Turks broke their word
and massacred the garrison. And so it went, century after
century: war, famine, pestilence, death—the grim riders of
the Apocalypse over the battlements, below ordinary men
and women trying to live their lives. There were a few reliev-
ing periods of grace among the turbulence. In 1215 St. Francis
of Assisi arrived to take refuge in a grotto, and in 1625 the town
with great pomp and ceremony received the bones of its patron and namesake, the martyred St. Boniface, which still
repose in the central church.

As *Oliana* crept under the walls, a narrow entrance opened,
once commanded by batteries on either side of the channel.
Really fine natural harbors are rare on the Mediterranean:
this is one of the best, winding like a narrow fjord deep into
the land, beyond the reach of any sea or tempest. And at the
end we found a village much like what Portofino must have
been years ago. Fishing families lived above dim shops along
the single cobbled street forming the quay. Portly matrons
leaned on windowsills to gossip with neighbors. Men in blue
jackets mended nets, or unloaded baskets of fish and crustacea
—both clawed and clawless lobsters, unusual to take from the
same waters, together with giant spider crabs. Except for a

tobacco shop which also sold postcards, the stores were still oriented to local needs: inexpensive wine sold by the pitcher instead of the bottle; twine, hooks and sinkers; plain work clothes backed by musty shelves of thick sweaters and underwear, testimony to bitter winters.

Moored stern-to along the quay was a small but impressive fleet of Italian yachts from the Gulf of Tigullio, recent finishers in the Sete to Ajaccio ocean race, keeping rendezvous with *Oliana*. While we had drifted windless or used an engine on the east side of Corsica, they had been finding strong breezes to the west, and even promised us a mistral the next day. Soon we were progressing from deck to deck, one of the best aspects of boating, finally to end in a body at the outdoor tables of La Caravelle, a hotel and restaurant in the best French provincial tradition. While papa supervised the kitchen, mama presided over the wines and the till, and the elder son brought to the tables such delicacies as salad Nicoise, *soupe du poisson*, and grilled lobster.

The next day a mistral was blowing, as promised, but it made little difference in the snug toe of our sock, especially as we had planned to explore the old town on the heights. After panting to the top of a cobbled road so steep that even the donkeys tacked uphill, we found something of a ghost city, just being rediscovered and perhaps repopulated, as the Volkswagons had infiltrated by a less precipitous route. Before Columbus sailed on his first voyage of discovery, 8,000 people lived in Bonifacio; now there are less than 2,000. Streets of ancient houses still stand, empty and gutted, although the thick stone walls could shelter men for more centuries to come. Yet unfortunately, through poverty and neglect—perhaps compounded by notions of sanitation which have changed little since the Middle Ages—Bonifacio lacks charm away from the waterfront.

But on leaving the battlements crowning the cliffs were as impressive as before. The minstral had tapered off during the night. Astern the mountains of Corsica lifted through successive stages of green to purple distances, while over the bow Sardinia seemed almost a mirror copy. Long seas swept in from the open reaches to the northwest, breaking on meeting currents in the Strait, until the whole surface was a pattern of deep blue and creaming white. For once sailing the Mediterranean was just right: not too much wind, not too little, and from the desired direction. Happily we tasted salt spray as *Oliana* drove through under full sail.

Small islands cluster off the north coast of Sardinia, an archipelago of winding passages and sheltered coves, not unlike the skerries of Sweden. Together with our friends of *la flotta di Tigullio* we anchored for lunch and a swim, then like a flight of seabirds proceeded into the harbor of Maddalena. It had begun to blow again, and we were content to moor in a row along the quay and visit. An ineradicable memory of Mediterranean cruising is the sandals on the stern of every boat, lined up like shoes outside a mosque. The well dressed yachtsman is almost invariably barefoot aboard; the richer the owner and the more opulent the vessel, the more informally clad he is likely to be. The true Mediterranean look is built around fishermen's blouses, faded slacks, work shirts, and bikinis, although caviar and *Blanc de Blanc* may be served by uniformed stewards.

While we lounged, freshening wind sang a deeper note in the rigging. Product of a frontal system sweeping across the Atlantic Ocean to be compressed by the Pyrenees and the Alps as it funnels down the Rhone River valley, the mistral has earned the respect of seafarers through the ages. A characteristic is clarity; every vestige of haze is driven from the sky, leaving it a great inverted cerulean bowl. Against it our burgee of Yacht Club Italiano—the red cross of St. George on a white field—stood as solid as a shield. Mounting seas assailed the stone breakwater, crests blowing to leeward like horizontal rain.

And what does one do weatherbound in a Mediterranean fishing village? You sit at a sidewalk table out of the wind, blinking in the brilliant sunshine, drinking coffee and eating little cakes; or watch nets being dipped in vats which seem to contain wine, staining hands and feet red, before running in dark channels along the cobbles; you lazily address postcards and read weeks-old London newspapers and study Italian, until it is apertif time aboard *Xingu* or one of the other boats. Afterwards you walk up one of the narrow streets to a trattoria, and consume proscuitto and salami and linguini and salad and cheese and fruit, filling your glass from bottles of *vino del paese*, product of neighboring vineyards, and discuss music and art and politics and boats, and perhaps love and the atomic bomb, all with great intensity and feeling.

Radio Grasse in the morning forecast predicted a *tempête*, so I took a taxi to look over the Strait of Bonifacio from the heights. It was a fearsome sight. A northwest wind of Force 8 to 9, gusting higher, was meeting a current. Towering steep seas dashed against the rocky shore at my feet, and the open channel was a smother of white. Any sailor under the rather prevalent delusion that the Mediterranean is always docile would have a rude awakening. In the days when Venice set the rules for maritime traffic, navigation was forbidden during the winter months, so numerous were shipwrecks and founderings. While during the summer the winds are generally mild, an occasional mistral may pounce from the Gulf of Lyon.

Summer blows rarely last long, so it was no surprise to awaken to silence on the third day. We went early on deck, to find that although the sky remained clear, the wind had abated—but only for a lull, warned Radio Grasse: within 24 hours the mistral was to resume, fresher than before. Thus for once the slogan of the fleet was not *piu tarde*. Everyone was trying to get under way as soon as possible. The barefoot harbormaster raced from boat to boat, gold shoulder boards flapping like wings, while the donkey pulling the ice cart almost broke into a gallop.

Our next run was the longest of the cruise, 160 miles southward to Ponza, so we wasted no time in dropping our lines to the quay. Passing Cape Ferro, we had a glimpse of the archipelago beyond Caprera, small islands and peninsulas looking like small islands, scalloped by bays and beaches, a garden spot to explore some other day. Waving farewell to *Niña* and *Xingu*, *Oliana* stood forth into the open sea. Only a light northerly wind and a surprisingly small sea remained from the minstral, and both diminished as we dropped Sardinia astern. Later, a mild sirocco riffled the dying swells. The sun set dark red, not bright to the eyes, but like the stylized sun in a Japanese painting. Stars flared while the sky was still blue, becoming ever more brilliant. The sea! So capricious, so unpredictable, so fascinating! Tonight smooth under a making new moon, the starpaths long shimmering spears of silver; last night the battering ram, the rending jaws, the implacable tireless destroyer.

After midnight, a light no brighter than a star appeared on the horizon ahead, separated from its fellows by twinkling in a timed pattern. Gradually it lifted to be abeam with the soft paling of the night into pre-sunrise colors. Ponza in silhouette resembled a crouching antediluvian monster, the lighthouse a weird blinking eye atop a horn, a long low neck rising to an arched spiny back, the rest of the island curving away into a tail raised at the tip. As we slowly rounded the point, stars faded and the land took on color and detail in the recurrent miracle of dawn, a moment when everything looks and feels differently, the greatest loss of urban man, sequestered from nature by towering buildings and an artificial rhythm of existence.

The port of Ponza opens at the head of a tapering bay, behind a small inner lighthouse and a church faintly Moorish in outline. Detached villas dot the outer approaches, some perched like osprey's nests atop cliffs that drop sheer to the sea. Rounding a breakwater, the town comes suddenly into view, square houses of stone, painted in pale shades of yellow and pink, accented by green shutters and tiny wrought iron balconies. Below, in a long horseshoe around the quay, warehouses and small shops are almost like caves dug from rock, as their roofs form the central street. Yachts moor along one side of the harbor, fishing boats on the other. Tables under striped umbrellas look down on both, and pedestrians may amble in indolent ease, because automobiles are not allowed to invade the waterfront. As a backdrop, terraced vineyards run up the mountainsides, green against the granite peaks.

I had been told to notice the dogs of Ponza, and a representative waited on the quay to greet us as we ran ashore the stern boarding plank. Descendants of animals imported for hunting, as the island is on a famous flyway for migratory birds, they roam freely with a fine proprietary air, and attach themselves to visitors much like guides. Our friend seemed to be mostly pointer, a well groomed and jaunty type who spoke Italian. After conducting us the length of the waterfront street, he gravely led the way to a shaded trattoria table in gentle hint.

Charm—that indefinable but tangible quality—reaches to claim a visitor even before he steps ashore. Desmond Molins of the English yacht *Blue Sapphire*, met while weatherbound in Maddelena, called Ponza his favorite island. Less accessible to swarming hordes than Ischia or Capri as it is too far from Naples to be reached on a day's excursion, it remains relatively uncrowded. True, there are shops calling themselves boutiques, stocked with the usual tighter than skin slacks, mad hats, and bedizened bikinis, and there could not be so many restaurants if there were no visitors, but there was not yet the commercialism that most cruisers despise. Coupled with clear water and a good beach not too far from the center of the town, I felt it my discovery of the summer.

Quite the reverse was Ischia. After the small quiet harbors lying in *Oliana*'s wake, it was a rude return to civilization. Always before I had thought of it as midway on the discovery scale between Capri and Ponza, but the first impression was like the Riviera of Nice or Cannes: noise, cars, neons, and people. Yet, in fairness, there is a cult of visitors devoted to Ischia, and deservedly so. It is a big island, with plenty of room to be most things to most travelers. Perhaps it is the greenest of the southern Italian islands; there are wonderful stands of pines cheek by jowl with the flowers of the tropics, and beautiful views of the sea from the heights.

But the best views include Capri, and how can any island within sight fail to suffer by comparison? Capri, gem through the centuries, so enspelling that it could lure an Emperor away from Rome at the pinnacle of the Eternal City's glory; Capri, each vista more lovely than the last, never to be wholly forgotten. Have you ever stood on the heights at sunset of a full moon, watching the luminous disk rise over a mountain above while looking down a valley to the sea? Although there is the first touch of mystery and magic softness of the night, day lingers in the overhead sky, and in the water far below. Flowers are still purple and red and yellow, the pale pastels of the hillside villas are not lost, and the green of the pines remains rich. Bats fly against a sky that is pink and lavender on the horizon, while crickets chirp. There is a faint smell of smoke and flowers, and a caressing softness in the breeze. And always there is the real or imagined sound of distant music, an indefinable thread binding all senses together.

As *Oliana* approached Capri from the west, Vesuvius was to port, dominating the curving Bay of Naples, while the hump of Sorrento was almost in line with the corner of the island. A fresh mezzogiorno had blown during the morning, and we rose and fell on a long beam sea. Closer, and we could see the houses of Anacapri like a white epaulet balanced on a shoulder of granite; beyond, dwarfed by the majestic scale of the peaks, perched Hotel Caesar Augusto, looking out over the sea; while still beyond, in a saddle of the mountains above the harbor, rode the central village.

Only once since my original visit to Capri years ago had I wavered from my conviction that it is the most beautiful single place in the world. Then I had sailed aboard *Staghound* into Papetoai Bay of far-away Moorea, one of the enchanted suburbs of Tahiti, and felt that the magic quality of Capri had been surpassed. Now, seeing it again in the soft light of late afternoon, my first love returned. Capri *is* the most favored creation of nature on this planet.

Yet alas! in almost equal proportion to its loveliness, Capri has been desecrated by man—not the ancients, although it has been lived in since the dawn of history, but by the modern tripper and heedlessly rapacious shopkeeper. There is a change from year to year, accelerated rather than diminished: garish pottery, neon signs, shoddy souvenirs spilling into the cobbled streets; plodding sightseers, music boxes blaring "Isle of Capri," no space to sit at the tables in the piazza, once like a doll's stage set: noise and bustle and hurry, daily excursion steamers during August flooding in fifteen times the population of the island each morning, to drain it away each night, leaving behind enough to fill the hotels and nightclubs.

So what do you do when the discovered places get too crowded in mid-summer? You go back aboard and sail away, perhaps to Corsica, or to Elba, or to Ponza—especially Ponza. Or perhaps you up anchor and begin a new cruise, around the corner of the Sorrento Peninsula to Positano, and start again from there.

10
Rift in the Curtain
THE DALMATIAN COAST

The ancient battlements of Dubrovnik lifted with the sun. Earlier, golden rays had outlined the crests of the mountain range beyond, like surf strongly backlighted, while the shore remained in shadow. There was a brief moment of transition as the incandescent disk appeared and vaulted clear, then the sudden brilliance of an Adriatic day. The sky was blue, the sea bluer. The gentle *maestral* wind of summer, which had dropped off during the night, stirred again, blowing away a gauzy haze over the land. Walking forward, I could see through binoculars the red tile roofs of villas framed by pines and the dark spears of Lebanon cedars, and a scattering of modern buildings at the water's edge, and—dominating all—the towering walls of the medieval city, topped by fortresses and church steeples, weathered stone rosy in the early light.

It was a landfall holding a special promise. After the Iron Curtain clanged down at the end of World War II, the Dalmatian Coast assumed some of the mythical quality of a modern

Atlantis. An earlier generation of yachtsmen, who had known it during the final days of the Austro-Hungarian Empire, sang praises sounding suspiciously like nostalgic dreams of a never-never land, combining the islands of Greece, the dramatic slopes of Italy, and the charm of an unspoiled French Riviera. A study of charts seemed to verify all these things. Yet it remained out of reach until the Communist government decided to open Yugoslavia to tourism. Roads were built, hostels and hotels blossomed, and restrictions eased for that arch symbol of capitalism, the cruising yacht.

"When I came in during 1957 the officials couldn't understand what you could want, going around in a boat," Hod Fuller told me. "I was only allowed to anchor where police were stationed. As we sailed along the coast, look-outs signaled each other with mirrors. Boarding parties armed with tommy-guns came aboard, usually around midnight, to demand our 'papiera.' When I came back in '62, they were friendly, but not well organized. Since they have improved. Now we'll see."

Our immediate goal bore the unromantic name of Gruž, the modern port of Dubrovnik, tucked in behind a peninsula to the west of the ancient city. As *Velila* approached the quay, uniformed men waved us to the spot to drop the anchor, then took our lines when we backed in the stern. The leader stepped aboard. "Good morning," he said in English. "I am Captain Edi Bulić, at your service. If you will let me have your papers I will have them processed. You are at liberty to cruise as you wish. Meanwhile, is there anything you need? Fuel, water, provisions, laundry, theater tickets, guides?"

Marina Dubrovnik lingers in my mind as a model of the species, even though a hint of iron remains within the velvet glove of welcome. The booklet given us to outline services available also included a page of "regulations," which forbid water-skiing or dumping refuse, or disturbing "your neighbors by shouting, singing or playing your radios too loud," or even "charging the batteries, which causes vibration and noise," except at certain specified hours. Remembering nights made hideous by neighbors in marinas elsewhere, I was intrigued to read farther and find "the excuse of not knowing our rules cannot be accepted," so "to ensure that all of our visitors have a most pleasant stay, the Harbour Authorities have instructions to enforce all heretofore mentioned rulings."

We arrived on July 4th, a familiar date in American revolutionary history, to find it a national holiday of Yugoslavia, for similar reasons. Shops were closed, and flags were everywhere. It was a bad day to get anything done, thus a good day for sight-seeing. The taxi stand across the street from the marina office was deserted, and no street cars appeared on the tracks. We began walking toward the city. Soon a clanking sounded from behind, and a vintage Toonerville Trolley appeared. We were caught between stops, but I jokingly made a hitchhiker's gesture of thumbing a ride. The motorman smiled and applied the brakes.

Dubrovnik is entered over a drawbridge, whose iron counterweights are still in place. Fate placed the small Roman outpost of Ragusium on a strategic island, which was destined to become a frontier between east and west. Its later name stemmed from the Slav word for a grove of oak trees, *dubrava*. By the tenth century there were extensive fortifications, but the system of ramparts and flanking fortresses did not reach full flower until the end of the sixteenth century. As it stands today, the wall is 6,342 feet in length—more than a nautical mile—reaches a height of 72 feet, and in places is over 16 feet thick.

Climbing to the battlements commanding the Pile Gate was an undertaking, but then we were rewarded by a promenade along the top of the wall, looking down on a crazy-quilt pattern of medieval houses, each roof tile formed of wet clay pressed against a man's thigh, until finally we stood above the

Old Port. Richard the Lion-Hearted had sheltered there in 1192 when homeward bound from the Third Crusade. The Old Port had known the swift feluccas of the Saracen pirates, as well as the gilded galleys of the Venetian doges, for it had been under seige by both. As a portcullis protected the shore approach, a heavy chain stretched from the Fortress of Sveti Ivan to the opposite shore barred ingress by sea.

Within its ring of stone, Dubrovnik remains largely unchanged. The Pile Gate leads to a broad, lance-straight avenue called the Placa. Token of continuity during shifting fortunes and political regimes is the Well of Onofrio, still the meeting place for young lovers as it was when it formed the setting for a famous Renaissance comedy, and still a source of fresh drinking water. Palaces rivaling the magnificence of Venice face narrow side streets. Recent are Diners Club and American Express placards in the windows of boutiques selling Yugoslav handicrafts, and current issues of Western newspapers and magazines displayed in kiosks along the Placa.

Recent also are luxury hotels like the Argentina, where we lunched. It flowed down the side of a hill, a few kilometers out of Dubrovnik. Every room had a private balcony looking over the Adriatic. From the terrace of the restaurant on top, we could see back to the Old Port. Descending to sea level, we found a swimming pool, surrounded by gay umbrellas. We had hardly relaxed in beach chairs before a waiter arrived to take our order for drinks. "While the hotels were building, the staffs were sent to Switzerland, France and Italy for training," explained Hod, "so ever since they were opened, the service has been impeccable."

Dubrovnik's location at the end of an archipelago extending to the head of the Adriatic had much to do with its importance as a port city throughout its history. It also makes it the ideal place to start a cruise. After visiting a small but hospitable yacht club, and taking on fuel—choice of two grades of diesel oil, two octane ratings of gasoline, plus ready-mixed

outboard fuel—*Velila* headed slightly north of west to enter
the K, 안 Kanal. All channels between islands, or between offlying islands and the mainland, are "kanals." They
take their name from the most important bordering shore.
Contributing to the unique character of Dalmatian cruising
is the shape of the islands. Instead of being free-form, but
tending toward the round, as most places, they are long and
narrow, and oriented almost exactly parallel to the mainland.
Thus the "kanals" are in reality watery highways, straight
stretches protected from the open sea, virtually free of unmarked dangers, with harbors on either hand. The greatest
problem facing a voyager is likely to be one of choice, when
so many variations in course are possible—extending almost
50 miles offshore from the city of Split are four layers of
islands, each with an enticing kanal between!

Fortunately, making the decisions for me was a skipper
probably more familiar with the waters of the eastern Mediterranean basin than any other American. Horace W. "Hod"
Fuller had settled in Athens after our Caribbean cruises in
Carib. He soon acquired a boat, and was beseiged by former
shipmates wanting to go along as charterers. Through the
years Hod had poked into nearly every anchorage from Venice to the Turkish coasts. We had last cruised the Greek isles
together aboard his schooner *Aegean*; now he had acquired
Velila, a 77-foot Rhodes designed motor-sailer, and extended
an invitation to visit the Dalmatian coast which could not be
refused. I had joined at Brindisi, on the heel of the Italian
boot, and an overnight passage had brought us to Dubrovnik.

So there we were powering over the mirror smooth water
of the Koločepski Kanal, harbor awnings still shielding the
cockpit. Unlike the western Mediterranean, where there is
usually no wind or too much for comfort, or the Aegean,
where for days on end the *meltemi* can rage at gale force, the
Adriatic in summer is normally blessed with pleasant sailing
conditions. The *maestral* is a breeze from the northwest that

begins to blow in the morning, most days. It rises with the sun to moderate strength during the afternoon, and falls away again as the sun lowers. But today it was off duty. To port a string of small islets were green to the water's edge, then reflected in a perfect double image. Tents blossomed in clearings, and sunbathers festooned rock ledges. To starboard, the lower slopes of the mainland were wooded, broken only by the roofs of villas and gardens, but the higher peaks had much of the austere majesty of the Italian coast, rugged cliffs showing through a frieze of scattered pines. Tucked into coves were fishing villages, and ruins stood on headlands.

It was hot, and a swim seemed in order before lunch. *Velila* was nearing the tip of Šipan Island, with a choice of three exits into the next kanal. Hod chose to let them wait. Instead, he headed for a gap between two tiny dots off the shore of Jakljan, where one of the excellent Yugoslav charts bought at Marina Dubrovnik showed a 6-meter bridge. The standard pilotage problem is not hitting bottom, but finding some within reach of the anchor chain. Here the water shoaled, as promised, so we came to rest in a pine-lined bower, to the sound of cicadas. The water was warm—Hod put over a thermometer and it registered 72 degrees—and so clear that through a mask I could make out details where the chart showed 25 meters.

Lunch was eaten under awnings after entering Mljetski Kanal, and by mid-afternoon we crept past a small lighthouse atop a conical rock. Here began a narrow lane extending far into Mljet Island. Cupped by hills at the end lay the village of Polače, no more than a dozen houses. When we dropped anchor I was content to sit on deck and soak up perfection, but Hod put over the dinghy for a shore expedition. For on the other side of Mljet, separated from our harbor by only a pine-clad spur, awaited Veliko Jezero, a drowned valley with an island in the center. After walking across, a boat took us to a twelfth-century Benedictine monastery, which had been made into a hotel. The restoration had not spoiled its charm, nor the beauty of the sunset from its terrace.

An even stronger feeling of the living past gripped us next day at the port of Korčula, on the island of the same name. After coming stern to quay we climbed cobbled streets to a house once occupied by Marco Polo. The view from a square tower on the roof was limited to nearby islands rimming the horizon. Yet it was the accounts of Marco Polo which sent Columbus and Vasco de Gama and Magellan forth in search of the riches of Cathay and The Indies. Others followed in their wakes until there were no more horizons uncrossed. Thus, in a sense, the little lookout tower of Korčula opened upon the whole world.

The oldest part of town lay behind a defensive wall, and at every turn were souvenirs of Venetian influence: the Lions of St. Mark reproduced over the town gates and cathedral doors, and exquisite carvings around the fireplaces of ruined houses. Some medieval streets were lined by *kućišta,* homes which were burned after the occupants died in the great plague of 1529. Through the centuries they have remained as they were after the purging torch had passed. Looking in through the gaping doors and windows, we saw in skeleton form the construction techniques of the day. The sixteenth century looms large in the annals of Korčula, for in 1571 the Moorish pirate Uluz Ali captured and sacked the town, and carried many of the survivors off into slavery.

Outside, Hod let *Velila* drift while we swam, hoping to wait in a breeze. Suddenly ripples appeared from astern, opposite the expected *maestral,* but we scrambled aboard grateful for any slant. "Wait," counseled Hod as I attacked the mainsail cover. "Let's see what we have in the next kanal." At Point Kneža the narrow channel we were in would open into the Korčulanski Kanal, ten miles wide. Hod was right. When the lighthouse on the point came abeam, *Velila* crossed a visible line of demarcation: her stern was lapped by whitecaps while her bow was mirrored in calm. "I've seen it happen before when these high narrow islands taper into a funnel, with open water beyond," commented Hod as he handed me a glass of Greek *ouzo* in consolation.

Hvar brought a touch of modernity. As we entered the harbor, a Russian built hydrofoil of gleaming aluminum and stainless steel styled like a space craft was pulling out. Hvar seemed a center of the tourist influx. Germans and Scandinavians appeared to predominate, scantily clad blond types highly visible against the stolid Slavs. I left the quay to climb a hill above the town, following ramparts running from the sea to a fortress on the summit, but it was unimpressive after Dubrovnik.

When I returned to *Velila* my skipper was ready to go. Hod does not lie to a dock in the center of a town if it can be avoided. So off we went to pass the night in Luka Palmežana, an arm of the sea winding into a nearby islet. When we came to the inner sanctum, Hod exclaimed in dismay. A small sloop flying the Yugoslav flag was already there. After some hesitation, Hod dropped anchor on the opposite side of the cove and our Greek sailor, Phillipo, rowed a stern line ashore to make fast to a pine tree. It was almost sunset, so we settled in the cockpit for a drink. As he was lifting his glass, I saw Hod's expression change. Another boat was coming in! So with the last light we departed, to grope our way into another sheltered sanctuary around the corner. "I guess I'm spoiled," remarked Hod after we had re-moored, "but I don't like to share an anchorage."

It was a luxury doubly appreciated after the moon rose over the surrounding hills. Sitting on deck we scooped out morsels of *oursin*, edible sea-urchins Phillipo had gathered around the boulders, and drank the slightly acid Yugoslav wine, and listened to music recorded in Tahiti. In the morning we swam in water so clear *Velila* seemed suspended as we looked back, and discussed the probable origin of a mysterious hole in the rock where our stern line was made fast. Obviously it had been cut by men, and long ago: was it a primitive mooring bollard, and, if so, from what epoch, and what types of craft had used it before *Velila?*

Our speculations put us in the right frame of mind for trying to visualize Diocletian's Palace in the days of greatest glory. The Roman emperor built an immense residence on the site of an earlier Illyrian-Greek settlement, which is now the city of Split. Like Tiberius on Capri, the master of most of the known world was content to spend the last years of his life away from Rome, and on his death in 313 was buried on the shore of the Adriatic. Even though during the early Middle Ages the town of Split developed within the walls of Diocletian's Palace, some of its past magnificence is visible. Split is a city which has emerged into the stream of modern life without wholly sacrificing its ancient character: although it is Yugoslavia's second busiest port, and a terminus of railway lines and burgeoning industrial center, Split is adorned by jewels of sculpture and architecture.

The harbor is protected from the open Adriatic by four distinct layers of islands, with sea lanes between, thereby offering a choice of four sheltered routes for our return passage. But Hod decided to round the outermost bastion, in hope of finding a breeze offshore. A stagnant high sitting over northern Italy was stifling the normal flow of thermal winds along the coast. We were not very optimistic as we skirted the lighthouse on the western tip of Hvar, and set a course for Lastovo, but felt we had nothing to lose.

To starboard lay Vis, which had played a key role in the struggle of the Yugoslav Partisans against the Germans in the closing months of World War II. Arms and supplies had been ferried to the islands by boats running the gauntlet from Italy, and wounded evacuated. From June 1944, until the capture of Belgrade late that fall, Vis had been the headquarters of the "Supreme Command of the National Liberation Army and the National Committee for the Liberation of Yugo-slavia." It must remain an important military base, as our chart showed virtually the entire island to be *zabranjena*—prohibited. It was forbidden to approach within 300 meters of the coast except at the port of Komiža.

But nothing was said about a passage on the back side of Lastovo being *zabranjena*, thereby precipitating in international incident fraught with grave diplomatic possibilities. *Velila* plowed over a sea breathlessly calm. Not a vagrant cat's-paw, not a suggestion of swell, not even the wake of a distant steamer, broke the bright metallic sheen of a surface which ran on to make an invisible weld with the sky where the horizon should have been. The happiest member of the crew was the cook, who came on deck to tell Hod he would produce a fish soufflé for luncheon if given a precise moment when we would be ready to appreciate a culinary master-piece.

Hod studied the chart and predicted the minute we could drop anchor between two islets off Lastovo, and allowed time for a swim. Exactly on schedule *Velila*'s anchor plummeted down, we went over the side, and gathered round the festive board as Phillipo tweeted the bos'n's whistle signaling lunch. The soufflé was produced with a flourish, floating cloud-like above its dish. The cook hovered expectantly as Hod poised a spoon over the center, and—a boatload of soldiers bearing stubby machine pistols bumped into our topsides, unintelligibly but unmistakably saying we had to get out. And fast. We did. Too late we noticed signs posted along the shore. Unfortunately, Hod had chosen the spot as the only place shallow enough to find bottom, and for awhile the passage beyond was too narrow to drift while lunching, so the soufflé was not eaten until it had reverted to the consistency of yesterday's mashed potatoes. "If the cook quits, we shall demand reparations," declared Hod.

Otherwise, Lastovo was a charming island. Little more

than a mile beyond the scene of disaster opened a beautiful sheltered bay with the village of Ubil snugged at the end. The tents of campers showed it was not restricted territory. Still farther, behind Cape Struga, a peninsula jutting into the open Adriatic, we found another sheltered bay shown as Port Rosso on a British Admiralty chart, although it was not given a name on the Yugoslav edition. Anchored in the center was a small ketch, painted a brilliant canary yellow. She flew the French flag. "It must be George, who spent the last two years moored next to us in Athens," exclaimed Hod. "I wonder what he is doing here."

We came alongside and shouted. George was under awnings aft, having a siesta, but he roused to report he had been in the bay for four days, and didn't know when he would leave. The Yugoslav wine was "*pas mal*" and cheap, and he could get lobsters—not just *langouste*, but the real ones with claws—from local fishermen in trade for cigarettes and a few centimes. So far as the protracted calm was concerned, he liked it, having quit the Aegean because he was "tired of the meltemi never stopping to blow." Before the autumn *boras* began—the northerly Adriatic storms which frequently attain hurricane force—he would be snug in Marina Dubrovnik, which offered winter rates and services to yachts laid-up. Meanwhile, how could you beat this?

Hod opined it would be hard, but he wanted to show me a special spot farther along. *Velila* continued while George again relaxed on the cushions. Outside, we rounded the ultimate point of land without finding a breath of breeze. The Adriatic lay like a vast mirror except for the V's at our bow and stern. A string of islets and rocks on our port hand looked slightly unreal, even though guarded by an impressive lighthouse, shown on the chart to have a visibility of 18 miles. It is a well marked coast.

As the sun touched the water astern *Velila* crept into a pool on the western end of Mljet. Phillipo had barely made the stern line fast ashore and returned aboard when we found we were again *zabranjena*. This time we were evicted by a personable young officer who spoke excellent English. Every phrase began and ended with the phrase "I'm so sorry," but move we must. We departed with some reluctance, as Uvala Lokva was almost the snuggest snuggery of the cruise. Also, it was dark. Enough light remained in the upper sky and was reflected by the water to make out the contours of the coast, so soon we were in another cove, almost back-to-back with our outward bound anchorage of Polače.

In the morning we re-entered Mljetski Kanal, keeping close to the Mljet shore to look at the port town of Sovra, then passed on to enter Luka Okuklje. In Yugoslav *Luka* means "haven," and this was one: a deep fissure into the land behind a rocky peninsula protecting the entrance from the north, whence blew the most dangerous winds, and beyond a fish-hook curve toward the toe of the sock to damp out any curling swells. "Take a good look," said Hod as we went in. "I want to show you something later."

We moored *Velila* in a basin which would qualify anywhere as a true hurricane hole. After launching the dinghy, Phillipo lowered in a Johnson Air-Buoy. I began to get the idea. We went back to the entrance, and once in the water the picture was clear. The ship—probably Roman—must have been driving for Luka Okuklje. Visibility might have been bad: perhaps night, or perhaps the helmsman was blinded by squalls of rain or snow. Or maybe a flaw of wind coming off the cliffs had made it impossible to fetch the opening into the land. In any case, the vessel had driven into a wedge of submerged rocks, no more than a boat-length from safety.

As I swam down, supplied by air from the buoy, I came upon the cargo in an almost perfect state of preservation. The ship must have been loaded with oil or wine—or perhaps grain, as the Romans carried almost every commodity requiring packaging in the narrow-neck, pointed-bottom clay jars called *amphorae*. The uppermost began at a depth of about 15 feet. Below the bottom fell away rapidly, but, as far as I could see through the crystal water—perhaps to 90 feet—amphorae were scattered on the sand. They formed a clearly discernible outline of a hull. Descending to the limit of my tether, I tried to get one free, but the sand had filtered inside and impacted outside until it was as though the amphora had been imbedded in cement. My struggles resulted in a few fragments, but I stopped because it seemed vandalism to disturb such an extraordinary glimpse into antiquity. The wreck had been discovered by chance by a spearfisherman among Hod's crew on a previous visit.

After Luka Okuklje our island hopping ended. Going behind the archipelago off Dubrovnik would mean a detour, while a course of 118 degrees—either compass or true, as this is a part of the world where navigation is made even easier by lying on an isogonic line of zero variation—took us 40 miles down the coast to Molunat. When Dubrovnik came abeam it looked as inviting as before, but we resolutely pressed on, following a mountain range that seemed ever higher and more rugged.

Molunat is a peninsula with two arms extending like the flukes of an old-fashioned anchor. Behind each lies a cove, Donji to the northwest and Gornji to the southeast. Gornji is further protected by scattered islets, but as *Velila* came to rest, we had a wide expanse of open sea in view for the first time. "It will probably blow a gale from the south, after all the calm, now that we're exposed," said Hod. "But if it should come in from this side, all we have to do is to run round the peninsula."

The night stayed peaceful, utterly still after the lights had been extinguished in a small fishing village over the bow, and early we were away for the culminating passage of the cruise. Long had I heard tales of the Gulf of Kotor, a fjord-like complex of salt water lakes extending far back into the mountains. For once anticipation was matched by reality. It began by passing under the fortified point of Oštri, a lock on the door through the centuries, giving the waters within a feeling of complete protection and detachment.

What is generally called the Gulf of Kotor is not a single *Zaliv*, or Gulf, but three—actually four, according to the nomenclature on our Yugoslav chart. The first was named Hercegnovski Zaliv from a town near the sea. Then came a pinching in of land on both sides, widening again to form the second zaliv. This terminated in a passage almost 2 miles long, as narrow as a river. Emerging, we suddenly found ourselves rimmed by towering mountains, the lower slopes a varigated palette of cultivation, the distant peaks purple in the summer haze. The water under us was not blue, but milky green, the shade and texture of old glass. Weathered stone walls, red tile roofs, flowering trees, church spires, ancient fortresses, soft white clouds against a very blue sky—the inner Gulf of Kotor was as perfect as a travel poster blown up to life size.

We could plainly see the twin islets which are the most spectacular feature, but we were saving them for later. Hod swung to starboard, toward the city of Kotor, at the very end of the complex. The body of water opening off to port was charted under the name of a lesser settlement, a zaliv which even the Yugoslavs do not seem to remember. Nearing Kotor, it was easy to see why it had given its name to the merging gulfs. Battlements ran far up the mountainside, culminating in a fortified castle which might have been a stage setting for Camelot. Kotor has been important throughout recorded history, beginning as a Greek outpost. After mooring to the quay, we entered thick defensive walls by the *Vrata od Mora*, the Sea-Gate, to find a busy city combining the old and the new.

It was in the soft light of late afternoon that *Velila* approached the islets of Gospa od Škrpjela and Sveti Dorde, both crowned by small churches, otherwise totally different.

A Benedictine abbey stood on the latter as early as the twelfth century. But Gospa od Škrpjela came into being during the Middle Ages as an act of faith. Seamen from the nearby port of Perast, a center of shipbuilding and shipping during many centuries, were inspired to create an artificial island. Before sailing, they rowed boulders out from Perast to a shallow bank about a mile offshore, and dropped them with prayers for a safe passage; on returning, they brought out more stones in thanksgiving. When an island appeared above the surface, work on the construction of a church began in 1630, and continued for over one hundred years.

Hod positioned *Velila* precisely between the two before dropping anchor. We went ashore first on Gospa od Škrpjela, and found mementos of a seafaring history, as might be expected. The church was a jewel, decorated by masters from Venice, Genoa, and Perast, but we were most interested when the nun who acted as guide showed us enormous rope-strapped blocks, wormed, parcelled and served by a long-gone master bos'n, and contemporary paintings of ships in violent storms executed by sailors whose prayers for protection from the elements were answered. There were also hundreds of silver votive tablets likewise bestowed in thanksgiving—perhaps after it was no longer possible to haul out stones as an act of devotion. The whole island was as neat as a ship's deck, not a tree, hardly a blade of grass.

We visited the second island by invitation, after thinking it was deserted. A boat rowed out from Sventi Dorde. In the stern was a Hungarian priest, who told us he was in charge of 20 divinity students holding a summer seminar. They would be honored to show us their island. Going ashore, we found the old abbey cells forming a dormitory. Two barefoot nuns presided over cooking pots in the courtyard, and a tent with bare planks for a table formed the mess hall. No medieval friars could have lived more simply. As the priest escorted us to a garden shaded by pines and cedars, the students followed, hanging on every word, smiling and nodding. Dosia Fuller passed around a package of cigarettes. Golden nuggets could not have been more gratefully received. When we left, the entire group gathered on the little stone quay. At a signal from the leader, they sent us off with a song.

It was the night of the full moon, and after sunset the Gulf of Kotor became a sheet of burnished silver, lying in a jewel case of mountains. Our flanking islets were at once silhouetted and touched by an unreal light. We were sitting in the cockpit, saying little, when suddenly the night was filled with music. Our friends of the afternoon had gathered on the tip of Sveti Dorde, and were serenading *Velila*. For over an hour they sang, but even after the last note music seemed to linger in the night.

It might be expected anything else would be anticlimax, but the next evening we swung off the peninsula of Sveti Stefan. We were to be treated to still another aspect of cruising the Dalmatian coast. As part of its program to accommodate visitors, the government had converted into a hotel an entire sixteenth-century village which had retained its original character. A causeway joining the former islet to the mainland had been provided with sand to form a beach. We landed and walked towards an ancient gate through a double lane of flags—Yugoslav and American. Beyond, we found something rather perfect in its own way. The feeling of a *vieille ville* was nearly intact. Crooked narrow streets led past houses whose interiors had been modernized by plumbing and electricity, but which stayed the same outside. We finally climbed to a candlelit terrace high above the Adriatic, and dined with the moonlight fingering the weathered rooftops, as it had through the centuries, while under us *Velila* swung at anchor.

There remained one side of Yugoslavia we had not seen, but we found it the next day. The port of Bar was an industrial and shipping center mushrooming by state decree. *Velila* crept behind an immense concrete breakwater sprouting cargo loading cranes. Railway engines puffed busily. Trucks and bulldozers rumbled. A facade of modern buildings rimmed the waterfront, but beyond unpaved streets were dusty and pitted, where the pace of construction had not caught up. Bar was still a frontier settlement, being carved from sparsely settled countryside, strangely at variance with the walled medieval towns and tranquil anchorages astern.

Bar is almost on the southern border of Yugoslavia. After clearing, we took a departure for Corfu, the uppermost of the Greek Ionian islands. Between lies Albania, which all shipping gives a wide berth. We had barely come on course after leaving the breakwater when we were shut off from the coast by fog. Or maybe it was the Iron Curtain closing, once again.

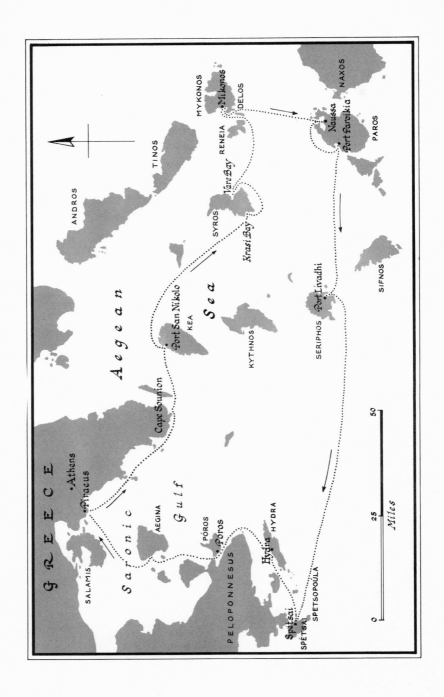

11

Cruising the Wine-dark Sea

THE AEGEAN

What sets the Greek Isles off by themselves is perhaps a quality which exists as much in the mind as in reality.

The Cyclades are closely spaced, so on rounding the point of one island you see the next, and the one beyond, and others marching over the horizon to port and starboard—but many archipelagos are the same. The sea is very blue, and tends to be rough in the channels; and frequently distant peaks are overhung by clouds which never seem to detach themselves to drift overhead: that, too, is fairly common. There is the usual wind which visiting sailors are warned about in advance, and picturesque vessels evolved by local conditions, and ports ranging from the snug to the uncertain.

But throughout there is a certain simplicity that has its own appeal, not only as expressed in the classic ruins which somehow seem an extension of the landscape, but in the faces and actions of living inhabitants who wrestle from the earth and sea the necessities of life. Among the Cyclades are no subtleties of color and texture, no green of woodland bounded by meadow and field, no flower gardens and gay-painted houses glimpsed through foliage. Here is only the clear-etched line of barren hill and mountainside against the blistering blue of sea and sky, clusters of houses white-washed into brilliance as blinding as the spume on offshore ledges. Goats browse where the eye cannot spot a single spear of grass, bees produce honey from unshaded rock, wheat manages to find crevices to survive.

Transcending all, there is a sense of the flowering of the human spirit. The humble lives of the people away from the centers of wealth have a dignity worthy of their distinguished past. They are proud of the imposing marble reminders that here western civilization first flowered, and they remain proud of their islands. Perhaps a key to their attitude lies in the simple word *xenos*. It not only means stranger, but guest. Implicit is the thought that a visitor must be made welcome.

My sense of belonging began as I stepped aboard the 60-foot schooner *Aegean* in Passa Limani, the Pasha's Harbor, on the Athens waterfront. Almost a quarter-century before, in the Bahamas, I had a part in her inception; she was the dream ship of my first deepwater skipper, Cy Strong, and many nights we sat around the cabin lamp discussing details on paper. She had later taken form as *Centurian*, solidly put together with natural crook frames of horseflesh and madiera from Abaco, and planking of Florida long leaf pine. Cy never lived to sail her to the South Seas, as he planned, but she roved the Atlantic. I had last seen her in Bermuda after weathering a severe hurricane.

Aegean had come into the ownership of my old friend and shipmate Hod Fuller, after he had settled in Athens. Hod had married a Greek girl, spoke Greek, felt Greek, was knowledgable and enthusiastic about everything Greek, past and present, so wanted to show me some of his favorite Greek isles on a postman's holiday. His charter season was over for the year, and I was making my way home westward from Honolulu with cruising stopovers after a Transpacific Race.

We had barely cleared the centuries-old breakwater of Passa Limani before *Aegean* heeled to a wind whistling down the slopes of Mount Hymettas. I was getting my introduction of things typically Greek in a rush, as now we were in the grip of a late season *meltem*, or *meltemi*, a wind as characteristic of the region as the trades in the tropics. Lingering on my palate from lunch was the strong flavor of *ouzo*, the smoky, licorice-flavored brew which is the national drink of Greece. And looking astern as we drew far enough away to see the city in perspective, I was treated to still another unique characteristic of Attica—the quality of the light.

Clear in the afternoon sun was the Acropolis, crowned by the Parthenon. Somehow it was as though I was not looking at it through several miles of intervening atmosphere, but up close, as in a reversed telescope. There was the perspective of distance, without the haze of distance. This clarity serves to underline the stark simplicity of the Cyclades, lending to the noon sun a merciless harshness, etching sharply each line of the islands. Yet the same clarity melts into many-shaded sunsets, and softly luminous nights.

On a nearby hill, nearly twenty-five centuries before, the Persian invader Xerxes sat in a golden chair looking down on Salamis Bay, across which we sailed, prepared to watch his fleet overwhelm the ships of Athens. But the Persians were defeated, so in 447 B.C. the Parthenon was begun in honor of the Goddess Athena, beloved protector of the flourishing city-state which bore her name. In its days of greatest glory, a statue of Athena capped by a golden helmet and brandishing a golden spear would have been visible from far at sea. For then, as now, the crowning achievement of a civilization also formed a handy mark for a navigator.

Our course carried us southeastward, close under the shore. Even here whitecaps marched in close ranks, for the *meltemi* blew fresh. As we passed Point Vouliasmeni the wind chopped from almost dead aft to forward of the beam. Standing amidships, I lamented the passing of old time ships as Xerxes had wept for his legions. Three headsails lifted from the sharply steeved bowsprit over a gilded figurehead, three more sails strained from masts set up with deadeyes and lanyards, all mementos of another vanished age. *Aegean*, with her tanned sails of canvas, clipper bow, lubber's net, 'midships bulwark and raised poop complete with rail, was herself an anachronism, a Cape Horner in miniature.

Spindrift plumed to leeward like smoke, while the light slowly faded. Phoebus Apollo was nearing the end of his daily trek across the heavens in the sun chariot. Astern, a new quality came over Athens, a soft glow, faintly rose, touching Mount Hymettos and the clouds above. The glow tinted the columns of the Parthenon, and then came the sunset miracle which caused the ancient inhabitants to call Athens the "City of the Violet Crown." A corona seemed like a halo above the weathered marble.

As Athens disappeared Cape Sounion lifted, last bastion before the open Aegean. According to the *Sailing Directions*, "This cape, well known to navigators, often delayed by difficulty in doubting it, was dedicated to Poseidon." At the summit stood a ruined temple to the God of the Sea, and in the sheltered cove at its base huddled a fleet of caiques, the high-bowed, slab-sided ships of burden that have remained almost unchanged for two thousand years. They were waiting, as had their predecessors through the centuries, for Aeolus to deal better winds from his bag.

Clusters of tourists near parked busses gaped down as *Aegean* surged bravely past, a great white bone in her teeth, ignoring the warning of the anchored caiques. Sounion is one of those capes which separate the seagoing goats from the harbor-bound sheep. We were no sheep, we told ourselves, standing resolutely forth into the wine-dark sea of Ulysses.

Soon the full weight of the *meltemi* caught us, funneling down the Mandri Channel between the narrow island of Makronisi and the shore of Attica. Short steep seas began coming aboard in solid sheets, cold. They poured off the tacks of sails and sloshed deep in the scuppers, slowing us to bare steerageway. Phoebus Apollo called it a day. So did we. With the last light we were back in the fold behind Cape Sounion with the other sheep, sipping *ouzo* in tiny glasses, listening to the whine in the rigging as *Aegean* rolled gently to swells from her namesake sea, glad to be warm, cozy sheep rather than frozen goats.

We were awake and away from an empty anchorage at 6:30 next morning. The caiques had taken off like a covey of quail at the first light. The October air was nippy, but the *meltemi* was a whisper instead of a shout, barely enough wind to fill sails against the sea still running. Powering into the path of the sun, we rounded the cape. The lower slopes were still deep in purple shadow while the pillars of the temple at the crest were golden shafts reaching for the heavens.

The Greek isles are divided both by geography and nomenclature into four main groups. The Ionian Islands are to the west, at the mouth of the Adriatic Sea, between the peninsulas of Italy and Greece. In the Aegean are the Cyclades, closest to the mainland; the Dodecanese, farther out; and the Sporades, still farther, an outer perimeter scattered carelessly by nature from the shore of Turkey to far north along the Greek mainland. All, of course, are the tops of mountains which did not sink in the prehistoric convulsions. Lying on a submerged base, they reflect the rugged contours of the southern Balkans. From a pilotage standpoint, the Greek islands are easy cruising. Deep water runs close to shore, with few outlying dangers, these well charted, and there are numerous harbors.

There is only one difficulty in sailing the Aegean, and it is atmospheric, rather than geographic, except in origin. As the

Red Sea and the surrounding deserts heat in the sun, a low pressure area forms. Far to the north, the Black Sea and southern Russia are cool, creating a high. Air flows down this pressure gradient to spill out of the Dardanelles and sweep across the Aegean as the *meltemi*, a wind which at times can attain gale velocities.

According to Hod Fuller, the ideal schedule would be to visit the easternmost islands of the Aegean in May and June. The *meltemi* does not begin until summer, and then blows hardest and most regularly during July and August. This early start would allow a passage along the Turkish coast from Lesbos to Rhodes, the Dodecanese, and from Rhodes a slant to Crete if desired, followed by a sail through the Cyclades to Spetsai and the Gulf of Athens. When the *meltemi* began, the cruiser would pass through the Corinth Canal into the Adriatic, touching the Ionian Islands, ending at Corfu. Beyond lies the Dalmatian coast, Venice, and other delights of the Adriatic. Then, if time was unlimited, the cruise could continue around the tip of Italy, before the Adriatic *bora* winds begin in September, with the whole Mediterranean ahead.

For those who must be governed by the calendar, the best cruising time in the Aegean is spring, when winter rains have touched the islands with wild flowers and patches of green. The second best period is late August, September, and into October, when the *meltemi* slacks off but winter cold has not arrived. If only July and August are possible, stay behind Cape Sounion, or spend your time cruising the Ionian group; but, if your heart is set on the Aegean, regardless of the season, be prepared for occcasional hard sails plus days pinned down in harbor, when it would be unwise to sail at all.

As we dropped Cape Sounion astern the *meltemi* did not come up with the sun, as is frequently its wont. Instead, the sea, first in the Mandri and then in the more exposed Zea

Channel, lay surprisingly flat, dimpled by occasional crests
and flaws from the surrounding mountain heights. Lazily we
rolled along, *Aegean* as comfortable as an old mother hen.
Gradually Zea lifted, called Keos by the ancients, the first of
the Cyclades. And gradually a harbor opened on the northwest corner, Port San Nicolo, toward which Hod had laid a
course.

We slid into the embrace of the land, a whitewashed lighthouse to port, a whitewashed village to starboard. Dark
brown nets dried above the cobbled foreshore, fishing caiques
were moored in water deep blue and pond smooth, a peasant
rode a donkey down a rocky path, a tiny chapel perched on
a hill. It was Greece as I had imagined it. *Aegean* passed
another point into another cove, a veritable thimble of a harbor, with yet another and tinier village, even whiterwashed.
The anchor chain rattled through the hawsepipes, and there
was suddenly the stillness following harsh sound when lesser
sounds are magnified. We could hear goats and chickens, and
from afar the rumbling of an unseen cart. A few pale trees
stood near the water at either end of the village, but all else
was barren, the hillside a pattern of boulders. The sun blazed
down, as it had when Keos boasted six temples to Apollo and
two to his sister Diana; or during the earlier era when a huge
stone lion had been hewn from the rock of the island even
before the dawn of the Athenian civilization by Minoan rov-
ers from Crete, who controlled the sea and its traffic—papy-
rus and gold from Egypt, copper from Cyprus, ivory from
Syria, cedar from Lebanon, dye from Tyre.

We swam, and allowed the past to enhance the pleasure of
the present. Barba Costa, *Aegean*'s Greek cook, brought us
retsina as we sunned in the cockpit, a wine whose resin flavor
pre-dates man's knowledge of how to preserve the fermented
juice of grapes. Like pepper and spices introduced during the
Middle Ages to disguise tainted meat, the use of resin has
continued as a matter of taste: Greek peasants and fishermen

enjoy their wine no other way. While I confess the first few sips suggested Costa might have mistaken the paint locker for the cellerette, *retsina* soon seemed as much part of the ambiance as passing caiques.

That afternoon we ghosted out of the harbor and along the coast to the north point of Zea, where an increasing breeze took us in charge for Syros, 30 miles to the southeast. To port lay Andros, to starboard Kythnos and Seriphos. It was a sparkling day, and gradually we added every piece of canvas in *Aegean*'s wardrobe, so the wake lay white and wide astern. It brought to mind a passage in the *Odyssey*, when Ulysses must have experienced just such a mild *meltemi* on his return to Ithaca: "The wind was fair, a fresh northerly, and we speeded along as if we were running downstream in a river."

It was nearly dark when we crept close to the shore of Krasi Bay on Syros, so it was not until next morning that I looked down through water as clear as in the Bahamas or Tahiti to grass on the bottom three fathoms below, and watched little fish nose the anchor chain. Ashore, fishermen spread nets to dry after their night of work while we swam to begin our day.

When we left, and came over deep water outside, I decided the Aegean actually is a darker, richer blue than water elsewhere, in certain light truly the "wine-dark sea" of Homer, which suggests purple overtones. As I stared fascinated, the bow swung toward Vare Bay, on the far side of Syros. Having thought we were going directly to Delos, I walked aft to ask why. "We need bread," Hod explained. "We might be able to get some from the monastery there on the hilltop."

At the splash of our anchor, a group of fishermen squatting in the shade of a beached caique looked up. Hod called in Greek, pointed, and after a long exchange one of the men began to climb a path. Finally he returned with two large round loaves. With the help of the fishermen he launched a boat and rowed alongside. When he handed the loaves to Hod, an argument began. Barba Costa poked his head through the galley scuttle to join. Voices raised and hands waved before money was passed and the man rowed smilingly back to his friends. Robber, I thought, not having understood a word, but remembering experiences in various parts of the world: rapacious taxi-drivers, piratical waterfront bums, and cut-throat characters who demanded large sums for petty favors. "How much did he want, Hod?" I demanded.

"Nothing," said Hod, looking at the humble little cottages on the treeless waterfront, as impoverished as the boulder-strewn hillside beyond. "Nothing. He took money to pay for the bread, but he wouldn't take anything for himself—said we were *xenos* and he was glad to help."

Outside again, we sunbathed under a cloudless and wind-less sky, the diesel kicking us along over a calm sea. Lazily on our way to fabled Delos we talked and read, until suddenly Rhenea was alongside, once an island knowing only the beginning and end of life. In 426 B.C., the government of Athens, in order to halt the increasing power and influence of Delos, had decreed it forbidden to be born or to die in the rival city-state. Thus expectant mothers and the ill and aged were transported to nearby Rhenea. Mortality was high, home-life and civic progress disrupted, but the stratagem succeeded, a savage footnote to the exalted culture of Athens.

Delos comes closest of the Greek islands to recreating the look and feel of the past. Since 1873 excavations have gone on without cease, until much has been restored of a Golden Age city. Here are shrines, as Delos was a Holy Isle, sacred to Apollo; here are shops along stone-paved streets, and the ruins of houses; and quays for ships, with warehouses and taverns behind; and even "foreign colonies," for among the ruins archeologists have discovered the gods and household furnishings of Egyptians, Syrians, and later, Romans.

It must have been a gracious and spacious dwelling place of man, beautifully situated, looking out over water on three sides, with gleaming temples crowning the hilltops behind.

During the days of glory there were trees and other greenery —according to mythology Apollo was born under the shade of a palm tree—and the life which flowered in such a setting must have been leisured, intellectual, and lusty, as in the restored central square huge phallic symbols alternate with marble benches set out for philosophers.

Delos in many ways is a summation of the tragedy of Greece. The Cyclades group takes its name from being arranged in a cycle, or circle, around Delos, and in ancient times it was a religious and commercial center. Through its history it was preyed upon by successive waves of jealous and covetous outsiders; first the Egyptians; then Athens in the days of rival city-states; then the Romans, followed in turn by barbarians from the north; the Knights Hospitaliers of St. John during the crusade of 1333; the Venetians; the roving sea-pirates in every age; and finally the Turks—all pillaging and stripping and carrying away, until Delos was reduced to the level of a goat pasture. Everywhere relics of the great era— the marble columns, the ruined temples, the walls patterning the hillsides and the terraced stone platforms of forgotten fields—are as stark as skeletons in the desert. Not so much as a blade of grass softens the desolation.

Silently we walked the silent streets. Beside us strode the togaed past, while offshore *Aegean* swung in waters that had borne every successive marine vehicle since the dawn of time. Yet if Delos is an island of ghosts, before dark we had arrived at a place very much alive—Mikonas, the Capri of the Aegean, less than ten miles away.

Even from the sea Mikonas looks gay. Beyond a breakwater the town rises tier on tier, ivory-white, dotted by the red and blue domes of churches, while tiny chapels perch on every prominent hilltop. Newcomers are told there are 365 places of worship on the island, "one for every day of the year," many built by sailors who had taken vows during storms.

Tiny tables like those of Parisian sidewalk cafés rim the

waterfront, and natives and visitors sip *ouzo* or thick black coffee in tiny cups while watching the harbor pageant and passing throngs. Behind, narrow streets and alleyways twist up a natural amphitheater of hillside, nowhere a straight line, donkey trails lined by houses. Each turn brings an architectural delight, a flight of steps and a doorway, chimneys and dove-cotes like carved cameos against the sky, a glimpse into a courtyard. By sunlight or moonlight all is dazzlingly white; in Mikonas not only are the houses whitewashed, but the cobbled streets as well.

But Mikonas has been discovered. Boatloads of trippers arrived regularly, shops were consciously quaint, arty characters in baggy slacks and sandals lounged at the waterfront tables with girls whose hair matched their beards.

Yet the artificial seemed to fade away as Hod related the story of Petros, Peter the Pelican, who had been brought back from Florida by a returning sailor. At first a great curiosity as the only pelican on the Aegean, Petros soon became the town pet. Fishermen gave him fish, until he became so fat and lazy he could barely rise from the water. As Hod told me his saga, Petros was lifted by hand from the cobbled beach and perched on the stern of a dinghy by a villager, who then tossed him scraps. But the idyll of Petros once was interrupted when he was kidnapped by fishermen from the nearby island of Tinos, who declined to give him back. Enraged, the town fathers of Mikonas sent a telegram to the Prime Minister of Greece, refusing to vote in the coming national elections unless redress was made. Without waiting for a reply, fishermen armed with antique hammer shotguns piled aboard caiques, surrounded the house of the mayor Tinos, forced the liberation of Petros, and returned triumphant to Mikonas.

Mikonas was the most northerly and easterly port of the cruise, as I wanted to visit Spetsai and other islands fringing Peloponnesus, and see something of the Gulf of Athens. So after a morning ashore, prowling narrow streets and peeking into courtyards blindingly white, we got underway for the 20-mile run to Paros. But not before Barba Costa served us a lunch typical of the fare of a Greek fisherman at home or in a waterfront taverna. The pìece de résistance was octopus. The tentacles had been cut into chunks and pounded, like Bahamian conch, then simmered with herbs in olive oil, red wine and the ink of the octopus. The thick dark sauce was poured over mounds of rice. Greek cuisine still recalls man's progress away from the crude diet of the cave. It is based on products of the olive, the grape, the cereals, among the earliest plants cultivated, suplemented by other staples whose origins are lost in antiquity.

We lingered over the dessert Costa brought us, a pastry of paper-thin layers sweetened with honey, so it was sunset when the hook was dropped in the landlocked harbor of Naussa. It was a good place to spend the night, but early the next day we were away for Port Paroekia, the principal town of Paros. Even from the water I was enchanted: a long crescent of beach, nets drying on the sand between gay-painted boats pulled up on rollers, a centuries-old circular marble lighthouse on the quay. It was Sunday, and ashore we found the town crowded with peasants dressed in their best. Across from Hotel Meltemi at the edge of the sea was a donkey parking lot. As each group came down the path from the hills, the donkeys were driven into a shaded enclosure by an attendant, while papa and mama and the children walked the rest of the way.

We found simple and friendly people sauntering the streets. Stores, barbershops and tavernas were busy. As in Mikonas, each turn of every narrow cobbled lane brought a new vista, but here all was softened by foliage. Bunches of grapes hung from balconies, and there were purple splashes of morning glories and red blazes of hibiscus against the whitewashed walls. Palms could be glimpsed through arched gateways. Of the Cyclades, Paros was the greenest. Although perhaps less picturesque than Mikonas—the whitewash is not so dazzlingly bright, there is less up-and-down and twist to the streets, and fewer architectural gems—I found Paros less self-conscious and less touristy.

By late afternoon we were away. Hod and I both preferred to visit the towns by day, but to anchor in deserted coves for the night. Thus the sun had set when *Aegean* ghosted into Port Levadhi on Siphnos. Only a few cottages rimmed the beach. We rowed ashore in the dusk to have a drink at the taverna. Typically, it was a plain bare room with a few tables and chairs on a cement floor, lighted by kerosene lamps. Two fishermen playing backgammon in a corner murmured a greeting as we entered, and the proprietor and his wife saluted Hod as an old friend, putting out the best *ouzo* and a bowl of Amfissia olives, purple as grapes and wrinkled as prunes.

Later, back aboard *Aegean,* we sat in the cockpit while the moon lifted above the encircling peaks. Softly over the water came a voice singing a lament in the thin high monotone of the East, a sad sound, yet lovely. Unable to locate the source of the music, we lifted our heads to look at the village on the hillside above. It had suddenly been illuminated by the rising moon, tiers of houses clinging to a slope so steep it seemed to hang like a painted backdrop.

Hod had warned me Aegean weather could change swiftly, yet my last look at the serene sky did not prepare me for awakening to rain pattering on deck or gusts whistling through the rigging. At 6:30, when we got underway for the longest open-water passage of the cruise, leaden clouds were masking the sunrise. Clad in oilskins, we poked around the sheltering point into a small but lumpy sea, wondering what Poseidon might have in store.

We found only a moderate southerly. Sails were added one after another until *Aegean* romped along. Astern the dropping Cyclades merged with distant rain squalls, and the 65-mile passage vanished in water tumbling under the broad quarter. By mid-afternoon *Aegean* slid into the snug harbor of Spetsai, and I was introduced to a wholly different type of Greek island.

Spetsai is reminiscent of the Mediterranean, perhaps a French Riviera town on an Italian island. It is much greener than anything in the off-lying Aegean archipelago, and much more sophisticated. From the deck, as we approached, could be seen tall Lebanon cedars, dark against the paler green of palms, pines and olive trees. The houses, in a long crescent facing the sea, were shuttered and imposing, obviously the part-time residences of people who worked elsewhere and came to Spetsai to enjoy a leisured life. Seeing the town up close did not dispel my impression. Spetsai is a resort, the summer home of wealthy Athenians. Sidewalks and approaches to the villas are intricate mosaics of black and white pebbles, usually nautical in motif—anchors, crossed cannon, compass roses, even full-rigged ships. Yachts cluster in the inner harbor, and fishing boats nestle behind a protecting breakwater off the central square, overlooked by the outdoor tables of the tavernas.

Separated by only a narrow strait is Spetsai Pulo, the private domain of Stavros Niarchos, Greek shipping magnate. Going ashore by invitation, we were overwhelmed by a gigantic works program. Dredges, divers and barges were busy on a breakwater forming a harbor for *Creole*, at 190 feet overall the largest sailing yacht afloat, and lesser vessels of a private fleet; bulldozers and grading equipment constructed roads; a small army of craftsmen transformed and enlarged a villa. Gamekeepers supervised a battery of pheasant breeding pens, and at adjoining kennels trainers exercised dogs.

Awed, Hod and I were content to anchor for the night in a deserted cove at the western end of Spetsai called Zogeria. Cannon buried at the water's edge to take the hawsers of vanished ships testified to departed importance. Around us grew olive trees, pale and silvery, and spears of sisal, almost tropic in aspect, but above on the hillside sighed the heavy dark pines of temperate latitudes. We seemed a thousand miles from the stark Cyclades. Rain drummed on deck during the night as the wind swung, but *Aegean* lay snug in her rock nest.

We awakened to a fresh *meltemi* which had swept the sky clear of cobwebs. It was a crisp morning of dancing whitecaps and glittering spray as *Aegean* beat through Petasi Strait. To port extended the shores of the Peloponnesian peninsula, to starboard Hydra Island. Looking at the chart and at the shore, nowhere was a straight line, reminder that the coastline of Greece is one of the longest in the world in proportion to the area of the land, 18 times that of France, and 4½ times longer than England's. partially explaining its seafaring tradition.

Behind the stone breakwater of Port Hydra was a log jam of caiques being made ready for winter, dinghys wedged like kindling wherever there was a gap. Villagers sat placidly sipping coffee at waterfront tables, descendants of sturdy fighting men who had a major part in the battle against Turkish occupation, a struggle that was fiercely waged during the nineteenth century. In 1821 Hydra boasted a population of 40,000 and a fleet of 150 ships. It was a base of marine guerilla warfare which not only raided commerce but launched hit-and-run attacks against the sprawling Ottoman Empire. The leading families made great fortunes in plunder but put them back into the war of liberation. Nothing now remains but a village of less than 3,000, drowsing in its memories.

Lingering, we sipped *ouzo* until after sunset, when the moon shone as a burnished silver disk over the mountains. Dinner was leisurely. We were giving the *meltemi* time to drop, as it does most nights. Outside, *Aegean* drove through a short steep sea to Poros, again wholly different from anything we had visited. Behind a headland extended a long narrow inlet. At the far end was the port, caiques moored bow to stern along the quay. Across a narrow cobbled street stood shuttered houses, looking like miniature fortresses, but relieved of grimness by the Christmas-tree effect of streetlights running up the hillside to a single narrow peak.

Instead of stopping off the town, Hod passed through another gap into an inner harbor. I had been told it resembled an Italian lake, and it did, even in moonlight. In bright sunshine the next morning it did not take too much imagination to see a resemblance to Lago Maggiore or even Lago di Como: the same blue water, the same green hills lifting to high mountains, the same dark spears of cedars, white villas with red-tile roofs, patterns of villages in the distance, and lace handkerchief clouds, much softer textured than those which hang over oceans.

There is always a reluctance to come to the end of a cruise. This time the gods tried to compensate by providing perfect conditions. We hoisted sail in the salt lake and sailed for the pure joy of sailing before passing out through a rock bound cut into the Gulf of Athens. A steep little sea greeted us, but within two hours the anchor was down inside the harbor of Aegina. After the quiet ports astern, it seemed active as an anthill. Caiques awaited turn to unload at the quays. Small commuting steamers laden with passengers maneuvered off the central square, listing precariously as their human cargo rushed to alternate rails calling greetings or farewells.

We rowed ashore. Some fishermen mended nets on the cobbles, fingers and toes following the intricate pattern, while others daubed paint on scarred caiques. There was a feeling of fall in the air. The tavernas had taken in their awnings, houses and shops stood shuttered.

In the afternoon we were away to a dying *meltemi*. By the time we neared Athens the sun was low over Salamis Island. A full moon lifted over the slopes of Mount Hymettus. Lights winked from naval vessels offshore, and began to ripple in tiny points up the hillsides. And as *Aegean* moved through the breakwater in the wake of so many ghostly ships, there was suddenly the purple afterglow, the violet crown, miracle of beauty to returning sailors through the centuries. Then it was night, and in the moonlight gleamed the Acropolis, loveliest creation of man.

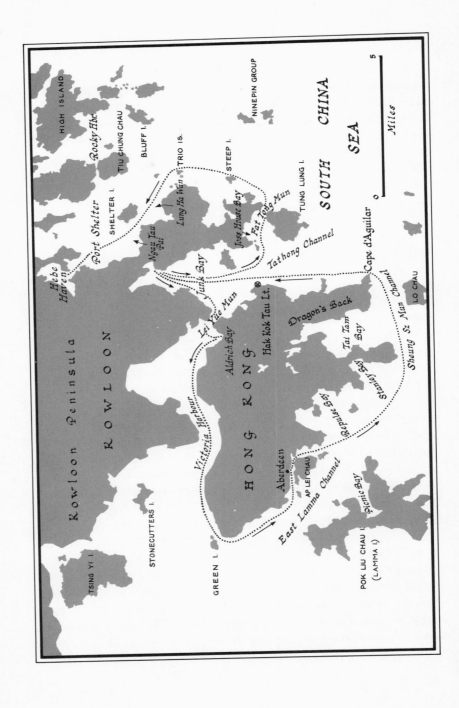

12
Oriental Shakedown
HONG KONG

As *Sans Terre* neared the narrows of Lei Yue Mun I lifted my head to look around. Close aboard, the water was the green of pale jade, but in the distance it took on a metallic sheen under the wet sky of the southeast monsoon. A faint haze muted colors and outlines. Four junks on our port quarter seemed to be materializing out of an ancient scroll, mysterious and unreal. Full length battens in their sails made them look like huge butterflies. Nearer, two motorized sampans rolled to an invisible swell, or perhaps to the burden of humanity they carried. From the Tathong Channel, steamers converged on the narrows, but were too far away to be a problem.

Glancing astern, I followed the furrow of our wake. Beyond the end of the pale tracery, on the far shore of Junk Bay, I could still see the sheds where *Sans Terre* had been transmuted from a concept into reality. Already I had the confidence that stems from good, meaty materials and careful workmanship. Unconsciously my concentration on such mundane matters as water temperature and oil pressure gauges had lessened.

Feeling the tug of a swirl of current, I looked ahead. Over the bow was opening an extraordinary sight. Hong Kong is a name to evoke images. For me, it had always conjured up visions of East meeting West: skyscrapers towering over teeming alleyways; fabulous bargains; rickshaws; suits tailor made in twenty-four hours; Susie Wongs wearing high-collared but slit-skirted *cheongsams;* coolies in black pajamas; conical hats; and Chinese food to satisfy a gourmet's dreams.

I had come to build a boat. When not in the shipyard, I had found all these things. But now, atop my flying bridge, I was finding something more: Hong Kong is perhaps the most interesting place in the world for a lover of the sea. In every respect it is oriented to its waterborne trade, from the hold-over of a noon cannon fired so square-rig skippers could set their chronometers before the days of radio, to a prohibition of flashing neon signs ashore, which might be confused with navigation lights. Nowhere else have I encountered so many arts of the sailor being practiced in so many forms—and on such a variety of craft.

Or against such a dramatic backdrop. Combine the natural beauty of the harbors of Rio or San Francisco with the impact of Manhattan's skyline, add a little of the majesty of London, pinch a bit of color from Naples, mix with the darting traffic of Rotterdam, and you have something of Hong Kong—but only a little, because Hong Kong is also in part a city where a substantial percentage of a population of 4,000,000 lives on the water, and through the centuries have evolved vessels as picturesque as they are practical.

Our first goal was fuel, and although the brand name on the pump was familiar, the method of serving it up was not. Beyond the narrows opened Aldrich Bay—but perhaps opened was not the right word. Like every other cove on the perimeter of the metropolis offering shelter, junks and sampans had clustered into a village. The lane leading to the fuel barge was the equivalent of a busy street back home. The trucks were cargo junks, steered by tiller from a poop built high to see over merchandise piled amidships. In the immemorial manner of truckers, they held the middle of the road until the last possible moment, then grudgingly yielded a minimum of room as catastrophe seemed inevitable. The busses were smaller and leaner junks, some as laden as their dry land counterparts at rush hours. The taxis were the walla-wallas and sampans were the Volkswagons, weaving through the other traffic as though it didn't exist. There were even delivery vans: boats selling food and clothing, plus every household item which could be required, from baby medicine to coffins, for many of the Hoklo people go ashore only once, and then forever.

It hardly seemed possible that less than three months before I had gone to Miami to plan modifications on a Grand Banks 42 with John Newton, of American Marine, Ltd. Previously, much thinking had gone into the transition from *Finisterre* to *Sans Terre*, from a wind driven ocean cruiser/racer to a diesel powered ocean cruiser/home afloat. I had made sketches of an interior layout adapted to my needs, including space for files and a writing desk, and a list of extras to make life aboard easier and more pleasant. A hi-fi center with remote speakers was placed in the main cabin, along with a coal burning fireplace to take the chill off nights at sea, and an air conditioner to temper sweltering tropic harbors. But as the name *Sans Terre* means "free from the land," additional fuel tanks were tucked in, and space allotted for a fresh water maker and deep freeze, to extend the comfortable cruising range.

Five weeks earlier, when I had flown to Hong Kong, *Sans Terre* was a hollow shell. She changed so fast during the early stages that more than once I suspected hulls had been switched while my back was turned. Many items were prefabricated. When assembled at the boat, an astonishing number of jobs could be going forward at once, because an unbelievable number of Chinese could work in a small space at the same time. One day, when the lunch gong sounded, I counted 36 coming down the ladders, and felt I had missed a few: certainly when I was aboard earlier there had been at least a man for every foot of overall length! Modifications discussed one morning were usually completed the next, and I was as satisfied with the craftsmanship as the progress. Now, as *Sans Terre* responded to my touch on the helm, I felt the same kinship and trust I had enjoyed with my previous boats.

After having run the gauntlet to the fuel barge both ways with topsides intact, I felt easier about venturing forth into the busy harbor. Off to port appeared the Royal Hong Kong Yacht Club, the masts of its sailing fleet protruding over a typhoon proof breakwater. Since my visit of ten years before, I had forgotten to think of the colony as a yachting center, with weekly processions of small classes 'round the buoys, and distance events for its ocean racers culminating annually in a 600-mile passage across the South China Sea to Manila. Nor had I remembered the environs of the city as a cruising area of charm and variety. "Hong Kong is only one island," my old friend Bill Hancock had reminded me over a gimlet on the yacht club veranda on my arrival. "There are nearly two hundred others. We're short on dimensions but long on coastline."

Perhaps it was because I was mentally projecting a cruise that I failed to note *Sans Terre* had arrived off the Star Ferry terminals. Here the spacious harbor pinches in to a waist. Suddenly unidentified floating objects seemed to be hurtling towards us from all directions, for we were at the marine cross-roads of the Far East.

The Star Ferry Line, shuttling between the sister cities of Hong Kong and Kowloon, carries over 100,000,000 passengers a year. Normally, a half dozen of their swift vessels are under way at the same time; in addition, several competing lines running ferries to different points pass through the same narrows. Traffic. The previous year 6,775 ocean going ships arrived and departed via the same channel. More traffic. They discharged over 22,000,000 tons of cargo, almost all of which was offloaded into huge junk-lighters, which then made for the narrows. Still more traffic. And while no exact figure is available on the number of fishing junks, water taxis, supply barges, patrol vessels, bum boats, tugs, pleasure craft, sampans and other craft in the colony, it must be astronomic— and that day all seemed to arrive in the slot at the same moment as *Sans Terre*, hooting and tooting. Bedlam.

Timidly I applied the rules of the road in the fashion of Chinese writing, backwards and upside down, which resulted in a proverb worthy of Confucius: "Biggest boat pass first." Sampans and walla-wallas gave way for us, I dodged the ferries, ferries kept clear of shipping. Finally we were past, able to admire the scenery. Off the port side Hong Kong Island rose steeply to Victoria Peak, 1,800 feet high; ahead was a scattering of small islets off Lan Tao, an island larger than Hong Kong, whose western tip projected into the forbidden waters of the Canton River; and to starboard loomed Kowloon Peninsula, outpost of the great bulk of China. I had thought I would feel like a bug on the bottom of a boulder, waiting to be crushed should the mass move. It was an apprehension forgotten the first day. The confidence of my Hong Kong friends that it wouldn't happen—yet—bred confidence, so I had relegated the Red menace to the status of another navigational hazard.

In honor of the occasion, Jim Hoffman, a shipmate on cruises as widely separated as the waters of Japan and the Bahamas, had flown down from his law office in Tokyo. Tony Fleming, an English aircraft engineer who had turned boatbuilder, and whose attention to detail made the construction of *Sans Terre* a pleasure, had come along to make sure nothing had been overlooked. Nothing had, and we were in a holiday mood as we left the island of Pok Liu Chau to starboard to run the East Lamma Channel towards the port of Aberdeen. The admixture of the Oriental and Anglo-Saxon which gives Hong Kong its unique character extends through place names.

Aberdeen could happen nowhere else. A channel between two islands, with a pocket at the end sheltered from typhoons, it is in reality a floating town. Or, to be more accurate, as the population living aboard boats has been estimated as high as 100,000, a floating city. We entered through another narrow lane, this time between rafted fishing junks lying in ranks twenty to thirty deep. Looming over the forest of rigging was a vessel out of the Arabian nights, Cantonese version. Despite my attention to sampans criss-crossing our bows I watched it take form: three tiled pagodas on the upper deck, surrounded by carved dragons and denizens of the sea; below, two more decks supported by scarlet pillars. Large letters proclaimed: TAI PAK—SEA FOOD. Not a square inch of the huge floating restaurant lacked a design in gold leaf or in colors to make a rainbow fade away in despair.

Waiters scurried out to take lines, and after we were made fast, escorted us to look down into pens where lunch awaited on the fin. Swimming lazily were snapper, grouper, sole, parrot fish, and dozens of others I did not recognize; langouste and crabs roamed the bottom; and countless prawns flitted across the middle depths. A high-hatted chef came out of the adjoining galley carrying a dip net and scooped up our choices.

For the ship's log I scribbled down that first trial run menu, in the hope it would shape a proper gastronomic course for future cruising: braised shark's fin soup with crab flakes; boiled prawns in their shells; stuffed crab claws; fried prawns in chili sauce; langouste with black bean sauce; and a magnificent snapper which had been split down the backbone, one side poached and the other fried, both served with sweet and sour sauce. Naturally, there was Wantun soup with noodles, and rice, either steamed or fried; and vegetables, including black mushrooms, bamboo shoots, and *choy sum*, a green looking like kale but with a flavor all of its own. Plus oversize bottles of the local San Miguel beer and endless pots of pale tea, tapering down to quartered oranges and almond cakes when the other dishes had run out.

As we dined, a parade passed beneath our table. Row after row of junks dropped their lines to head for the offshore fishing grounds. Finally we followed, easing *Sans Terre* between a stern that towered high above our flying bridge and a bluff bow looking as relentless as an oncoming bulldozer. I hoped the eyes painted above the waterline had 20/20 vision in case our engines quit. In fact, I wished *Sans Terre* had a pair of eyes, too, because the mist which had hung over the hillsides all morning was now thickening into fog. The fleet which had left harbor earlier was gradually being swallowed, and even junks a few ranks ahead of us in line were growing indistinct.

Hong Kong, although within the bounds of the tropics, partakes of the weather of the bleak Asian landmass rather than the sunny South Pacific. Since my arrival in mid-February, the breezes had been strictly breaths from Siberia, tempered just enough to bear torrents of rain instead of blizzards of snow. Recently the warmer southeast winds of the spring monsoon had set in, and the result had been fog, ranging from light to opaque, but never wholly disappearing. Fall is the best season, according to local hands, after the end of the typhoon season, which corresponds to the hurricane period in the Caribbean. Then the days are usually warm and the nights crisp, with clear skies around the clock. Summer is hot and muggy, and winter likely to be as I found it—adding up to the fact that the climate of Hong Kong does not measure up to its other charms.

Visibility remained fairly good as we passed inside Ngan-chau Island, permitting a veiled view into Repulse and Stanley Bays, and a count of 67 big—therefore potentially dangerous—junks in sight on the other beam. Then everything vanished just as I finished taking a bearing on Cape D'Aguilar, the tip of a mountainous peninsula shown on the chart as the Dragon's Back. So far as I was concerned, dragon's mouth would have been more accurate. To port, rocks and ledges; to starboard, the limits of British territorial waters, where heavily armed Red Chinese junks patrolled; ahead, a detached islet surrounded by more rocks; and, if we missed that, Tathong Channel, the main thoroughfare for shipping. Our compass was borrowed, put aboard at the last moment and casually checked between only a few buoys, and our speed in terms of rpm's was unknown.

Jim took the wheel, Tony acted as bow lookout, Marge Hoffman and Mary Fleming were stationed on either beam, while I shuttled between chart and compass, muttering to myself an opinion of skippers who put gastronomy ahead of navigational nicety. When land finally loomed over the bow, I confess at first not being sure whether it was our goal, or Lo Chau Island, to the south, as the Pilot Book described both in similar terms. Carefully skirting a line of rocks awash, as much by sound as by sight, we groped our way to a positive identification, and thus had the consolation of knowing that neither compass nor estimate of speed had been far wrong.

With more confidence I laid down a course for the next headland, and when we hit it on the button as our estimated arrival time ran out, the rest was routine: on to the lighthouse of Hak Kok Tau, visible at a distance of 70 yards, and then across Tathong Channel as the fog thinned. Soon we were able to see into Junk Bay, and it was only a short run to the dock of American Marine, where Whit Newton, John's brother and director of building operations, took our lines.

The monsoon weather continued. Pinned to a mooring, I spent several days learning about the care and feeding of a pair of 120 hp. Ford diesels with Lehman conversions, an Onan 6 kw generator, and such previously unfamiliar luxuries as a water pressure pump, hot water heater, and refrigeration compressors. Under the supervision of Tony Fleming or a Chinese mechanic, I tightened and loosened stuffing boxes, traced out systems leading to sea cocks, took apart bilge pumps for cleaning, changed filters, and learned how to restart a diesel engine if it developed an air-lock from running short of fuel. It was all necessary homework for the type of cruising I hoped to do, but still I kept watching the sky and the track of the barograph pen.

Time was running short. Yet I was determined to see what lay beyond the horizon, near as it was. "All told in real estate and 'British waters' the colony is roughly 40 miles wide and 30 deep," I read in *Hong Kong: Borrowed Place, Borrowed Time*, by Richard Hughes, the most informative book I have found. The quote continued: "It is virtually surrounded by Chinese Communist islands with watchful garrisons." Local sailors added warnings on outlying areas theoretically within territorial boundaries, but impossible for British authorities to patrol, where every junk was potentially dangerous, as there was no telling when fanatic Red Guards might be aboard. Thus lowered visibility brought dangers other than navigational.

Still, within safe reach the chart showed an area which combined the characteristics of the whole—if I could only see to reach it, and then see something of the countryside after I got there. As I was abandoning hope, a day arrived when the sun was almost visible. Our own Junk Bay sampan village reappeared, dripping clothing festooning the rigging, and even the serrated peaks of the Dragon's Back loomed through the mist. Despite a lingering memory of some bad moments in the jaws of the beast, I started the engines after lunch and dropped the line to the buoy.

At the exit of Junk Bay, a turn to starboard would have taken us back through Lei Yue Mun into the bustling harbor. Instead, a turn to port brought *Sans Terre* into Joss House Bay. Almost symbolically, two junks from Red China were ghosting in the same direction. Plastered along their topsides were streamers proclaiming the thoughts of Mao, and as I came close for photographs the gestures of some crew members made plain what they thought of capitalists who rode around in yachts. When we left them astern, I was happy the blessings of the communist state did not run to engines: as a rule of thumb, junks under sail came from China, while those under power belonged to Hong Kong, where the government subsidized the fishermen.

The mountains surrounding Joss House Bay were like the hides of some vanished monster, brown skin hanging in folds, with a pattern of green in the deeper creases. The temple from which the bay took its name perched atop Tung Lung Island, but there was no need to stop to make an offering to the gods, as *Sans Terre* had slid down the launching ways wreathed in the smoke of joss sticks lighted by the workmen. We were further protected by a Laughing Budda and an image of T'ien Hou, Queen of Heaven, venerated by the boat people of Hong Kong.

At the far side of Joss House Bay lay Fat Tong Mun, a narrow channel much like Lei Yue Mun, but a gateway to a different world. Swirling tidal currents gripped the keel as we entered, and swells rolling in from the South China Sea met us as we cleared. Seaward, there was no defined horizon. Seabirds swooped over stark rock cliffs, where slate grey waves splintered into pale fragments. Not a house could I see, not any other reminder of the teeming metropolis astern: only scattered barren islands.

The course took us outside aptly named Steep Island, but inside the group equally appropriately called the Ninepins. Here the southeast wind was stronger, putting peaks on the swells. I thought I heard thunder, and swiveled around in the helmsman's seat to search for squall clouds. Everywhere the sky was the same, a uniform lead grey, looking as wet as a dripping sponge. Yet in the distance I could see Bluff Island, at the entrance of Rocky Harbour, where on the morrow I expected to raft up with part of the yacht club fleet off the tiny village in Snake Bay. Beyond, if visibility held, came Mirs Bay and a run deep into Tolo Channel.

Nearing Trio Islands, the thunder sounded again, louder. Again no sign of a gathering squall, so I turned back to the land-seascape ahead. Almost always, on approaching a new cruising area, I am reminded of some place already visited. But here nothing came to mind. There were many islands, but there was none of the blend of woods and rocks found in Maine or the Baltic skerries; neither were these islands stark and sculptured, as in parts of the Aegean. If anything, the deeply indented bay opening over the bow was like the seacoast of Japan, combining majestic and forbidding approaches with sheltered inner passages, and lovely vistas in miniature. Somehow—and this I find difficult to define—it was as I had expected the mainland of China to be, away from the grafted glitter of Hong Kong: austere, mysterious, and conveying the impression of being incredibly ancient.

The thunder sounded again, and this time I realized it was not thunder, but cannon fire. I had forgotten Whit Newton had once mentioned that periodically the Hong Kong garrison conducted target practice, sealing off Port Shelter. I pulled back the throttles, in a quandary. It was growing late, and with the lowering sun visibility would swiftly decrease. The course to Hebe Haven, at the far end of Port Shelter, where I planned to spend the night, was intricate and devoid of aids to navigation. There was still time to return to Junk Bay, but this I was reluctant to do. As an alternative, perhaps it would be possible to go into Rocky Harbour. I looked at the chart. Another salvo made me lift my head. Bright yellow flashes blossomed as shells exploded on the slopes of Tiu Chung Chau and Bluff Islands. The targets bracketed the channel to Rocky Harbour!

On the point of giving up, I wondered what had happened to the sampan which had crossed our bows earlier, on course for Port Shelter. Through the glasses, I could see it well inside, not far from where the guns must be, plugging along close to the shore. Another sampan was passing ahead, headed in the same direction. They must know the local ground rules, I reasoned, and we have T'ien Hou looking out for us, too. So *Sans Terre* swung to follow in the wake.

As we neared the elevated point of Lung Ha Wan, the muzzles of a battery of howitzers bristled against the sky. Trying to look inconspicuous, and hoping our gray topsides were something of a camouflage, we crept along as close to the rocks as I dared. Nothing happened. We came out on the other side without even a shouted warning from the battery command post, fifty feet overhead. As I breathed a sigh of relief, thunder from ahead: another battery was firing from Ngau Tau Pai, a mile away. This time we were not so lucky. Just as *Sans Terre* passed under, Her Majesty's Twentieth Lancashire Fusiliers let go with everything they had. The muzzle blast nearly blew us out of the water, but the bite was almost worse than the bark: great *car-rum-ping* shocks coming back from the explosions on the other side.

As though on signal, the mist began to thicken. When Shelter Island came abeam, it was only a ghostly outline. We glided on over water lying as smoothly textured and silky gray as a gunbarrel while our world contracted to the Cruising Club burgee on the bow staff. The chart showed 7 fathoms, so it was possible to anchor anywhere in sheltered Port Shelter, but I was willing to settle for no less than Hebe Haven, a harbor within a harbor. Dead slow we stole ahead, eyes straining into nothingness, giving a dream quality to the shore which finally appeared to port. Swinging to starboard, another faint outline evolved. We had hit the ribbon of water leading into Hebe Haven.

Inside, the fog had not yet penetrated. With startling clarity surrounding details were reflected inverted in the mirror of a perfect anchorage: the cup of hills, trees along the beach, a little village, small sailing yachts and sampans. I picked up an empty typhoon mooring and went below to a hot shower, stereo music, and coals glowing in the fireplace. Familiar books were in the shelves, nostalgic photographs on the bulkheads. I filled a tall glass and looked outside. Rain had begun to fall, not the familiar light drizzle, but huge scattered drops throwing up geysers which bloomed and vanished like blossoms in an enchanted garden. The incomparable snugness of a small boat's cabin enveloped me. I was content with the Hong Kong debut of *Sans Terre*. But as fog moved in to replace the rain, I made a vow. Our next front yard would bloom with sunshine and cactus, not monsoon raindrops.

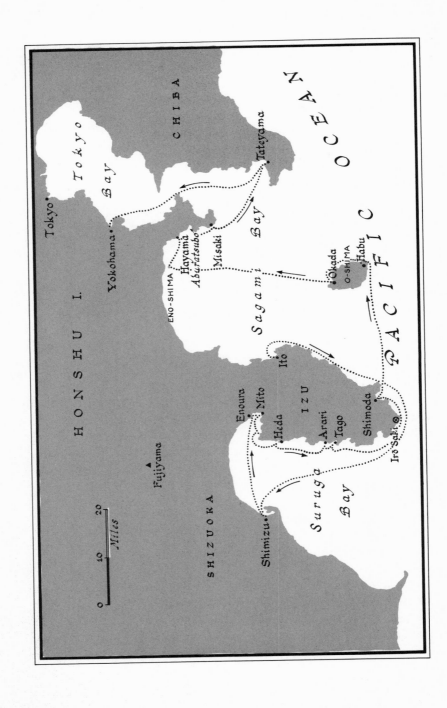

13

The Heritage
of Hiroshige

JAPAN

Mists shrouded the peaks and trapped night shadows in the valleys as *Andrea Gail* crept between the sheltering arms of the breakwater of Itō. In the strange light the sea was almost the color of eggplant, purple overtones against gray granite offshore rocks and the subdued dark green of pines flowing down to the water's edge. Sampans, seen as though through gauze, tended nets buoyed by logs, while seabirds fluttered above. As the bow began to rise to a southerly swell, I felt suspended in time and place.

Beneath the overcast, the hands of the clock advanced but the morning did not. The Izu Peninsula remained elusive, withdrawn. Then, as we neared Tsumeki Saki, a rip appeared in the cloud cover. Suddenly a freshening breeze had torn away the mist, a celestial unveiling of Japan, staged, it seemed, for my special benefit. Now the sea was jade green, paler near the crests. Near the shore it was no longer lazy, crashing down to spout geysers white against the forested slopes.

Wedging myself between mast and shrouds to see better, my first thought was that the coast looked like an ancient woodblock print by Hiroshige come to life. Row on row of mountains marched to the sea from the central inland spine, as abruptly contoured as crumpled balls of paper, each separate, each somehow asserting individuality. Here a lone pine stood sharply etched on a point, inviting the eye to put a frame around it; there trees ran down a cleft in a sweeping green avalanche of forest. Apparent immediately were the textures and shapes in nature which have inspired generations of Japanese artists.

Ahead loomed another point, Irō Saki, magnificently bold, a white lighthouse dwarfed by the cliff below. "Rounding the Horn," an acquaintance in Tokyo had jokingly called the passage past Irō, and I was soon to see why. Compressed between the tip of the Izu Peninsula and the offlying islet of Mikomoto Jima, the current rushes and boils, 2.5 knots under normal conditions, according to the chart, more according to local navigators. Open to the whole sweep of the Pacific and with a rocky shoal bank stretching out to add to the turbulence, the sea takes on something of the form and substance of the conical dragon's-tooth boulders strewn along the shore.

In the time-honored fashion of sailing vessels confronted by head winds and steep head seas, *Andrea Gail* slowed to let her crew admire the scenery. A 45-foot sloop designed by lifelong resident John Laffin, *Andrea Gail* was part of a small but growing ocean racing fleet. She had been chartered for my cruise from Michael Sodano, ex-Marine Corps Colonel, now president of General Electric Japan. Mike had been prevented by business from being aboard for the first day's run. With John Laffin, Mike Junior, and Tokyo attorney Jim Hoffman, plus Sato and Hoshi, the *Gail's* boat boys— "boy" in the Orient can cover a vast range of ages—we were making the 78-mile run from Itō on Sagami Bay, around the Izu Peninsula to Shimizu on Suruga Bay, where Mike was to join us.

For awhile it looked as though we would stay right off Irō Saki. Spray drove aft in sheets, the wake lay as a serpentine trail across the seas astern, but *Andrea Gail* seemed to be making no progress. Further offshore a parade of coasters drove through the slot inside Mikomoto Jima, cascades of white water tossing like manes above the plunging bows. Slowly, however, bearings began to change. Now we were sighting around the corner of Izu, along a coast rugged and bleak, with offlying islets and surf thundering even in the coves. Finally we rounded the outermost point and eased sheets. The coast began to unroll like a painted screen as *Gail* swooped over the crests, Sato and Hoshi tending a fishing line astern.

The wind we had been fighting all morning and now rode so swiftly was the tail end of a summer typhoon. A week earlier the full fury of the storm had threatened, delaying our departure. Rather than waste part of his arranged vacation, Jim Hoffman suggested we take a land cruise by hiring a car and driving part of the Tokaido Road, the ancient highway linking Tokyo with the former capital of Kyoto. Jim had become fascinated by the Orient while in the army, and settled in Japan after the Korean War. He not only spoke enough of the language to smooth the way, but had made a study of local customs and rituals. It would have been difficult to find a better guide.

Through the centuries the Tokaido has been the principal artery of Japan, not only the scene of continuing pageanty, but of history itself. So Jim and I had set forth with a bound folio of Hiroshige's famous *Fifty-three Stages of Tokaido* across our knees, wood-block prints depicting the road as the artist saw it in the 1830's. We dined only in Japanese restaurants and slept on the *tatami* mat floors of Japanese inns; I ate raw octopus, rice and seaweed for breakfast, and began to speak a few recognizable phrases. I learned the ritual of the honorable bath, managed to sustain life with chopsticks, and easily fell in with the custom of chain drinking pale green tea from an endless succession of handleless cups. Hot saké became as natural as a chilled *vin blanc.* Thus sitting in the cockpit of *Andrea Gail,* I felt I had come to know something of the Japan not seen by casual visitors. And the more I had seen of Japan, the more I liked it.

As we entered farther into Surgura Bay the seas diminished, and so did the wind. The boys stopped fishing to help set a jibtopsail, while the headlands and villages of Izu unfolded with delightful variety in form and name. Gradually our course for Shimizu took us into open water, and the land was swallowed in the summer haze. Through the afternoon we glided along. Ship's routine was disturbed only by a succession of fish being taken on the feather lure trailing astern: small tuna, mackeral, and dolphin, perfect for the frying pan or *sashimi,* thin slices cut across the filleted strip, eaten raw after dipping in soya sauce and grated horseradish. Having watched fishing lines fruitlessly trolled behind sailing boats in many parts of the world, it was a pleasant contrast to terminate operations through surfeit.

Toward sunset, *Andrea Gail* neared a long low point called Mino, scene of a legend typically Japanese. The classical name of the sandspit is actually Mino-no-matsubara, which means "Mino, Pine-clad Seashore." A lovely avenue of pines does indeed grow behind the beach. One is especially famous. In distant times a fisherman found the feather robe of a fairy hanging from a branch. He would not give it back until she had danced for him to music which drifted down from the heavens. The incident became the theme of a Noh play, and visitors are shown the very tree, known, quite naturally, as "The Pine Tree of the Feather Robe."

Under the spell of my daylong reverie, I was prepared for merging of the real and the dream when Jim Hoffman glanced off to starboard and commented casually, "There is Fuji." By a trick of haze and lighting, the symmetric volcanic cone had been hidden earlier. Now a towering cloud behind was tinted delicate rose, gold at the edges, an odd effect almost like a halo. And against the cloud was silhouetted the ethereal perfection of Fujiyama, Fuji-*san*, to early Japanese the meeting place of heaven and earth, the home of the gods.

Strangely, as the sun dropped below the horizon and the sky darkened into night, the illumination of Fuji became more brilliant, until it completely dominated the land to the north. I stood braced at the main shrouds to see better, in the grip of poignant beauty which did not entirely fade when we entered the harbor of Shimizu, redolent of fish from the moored fleet and petroleum from the huge refinery nearby. Always in Japan a contrast: between ancient and modern, east and west, the subtle and the crude, beauty and raw commercialism.

After one look at the busy port, Jim and I decided to seek solace in a totally different facet of oriental culture, the Japanese inn. Now, as a sailor unabashed in his appreciation of the finer things of the shore, let me go on record as classifying an *inchiban*—a "No. 1", a first quality—inn as among the more civilized works of man. In a typical Japanese hostelry a wave of solicitude sweeps out and engulfs the guest at the entrance. Kimonoed maids bow deeply, flutter, and bow deeply again. Somehow you are divested of your baggage, down to the smallest item. You have changed from shoes to slippers to walk the halls, are guided through a labyrinth of passages offering a succession of lovely but miniscule views of shrubbery, running water, and rock. Finally you halt to remove the slippers, and step onto the mat of your room. More bows, more flutter, and the *shoji*, the paper screen that serves as a door, slides shut.

Underfoot the *tatami* is softer than any carpet, for beneath the visible woven cover is a thick pad of rice husks. There is no clutter of furniture, only a low lacquer table flanked by cushions and perhaps backrests. In an alcove will be a painting, or a scroll, and a flower arrangement. Every Japanese room has a focal point, a place of honor for the honored guest. Beyond is a smaller room, opening upon a garden, a tiny planted area that contrives to lend an air of spaciousness, as though you were looking out on all outdoors. Caging walls fade away.

Soundlessly the *shoji* opens, and a maid appears with a damp towel tightly rolled and presented in a little wicker basket, plus tea—both likely to be hot in winter, chilled in summer. You get out your Japanese dictionary, muster your scant vocabulary, and convey the idea that you will enjoy the *o-furo*, the honorable bath, immediately, and dine afterwards. Kneeling on the *tatami* and bowing head to floor, the maid withdraws.

Depending on the establishment, the *o-furo* may be private, or shared with others, although the custom of mixed public bathing has almost completely ended since post-war occupation forces introduced western curiosity in nudity. Use of a bath requires rigid observance of one rule: you get yourself clean before entering the tub. This is accomplished by sitting on a tiny stool and sluicing pails of water over the body, soaping vigorously, and sluicing down again. The tub is filled with very hot water, and is a place to relax before sluicing again with pails of cold water.

After the bath, you don a *yukata*, a cotton robe provided every guest on arrival, rendering negligible the usual traveler's problem of what to wear. You wear the *yukata* bearing the inn's device as long as you are a guest. Dinner will be served in your room. Public gathering places such as bars, lounges, and restaurants, simply do not exist. In Japan the traveler is given the right of privacy, or to choose his own companions. Trays will be brought by maids, an arrangement of porcelain or lacquer dishes and bowls which are subtly complimentary in color and texture. Each meal is a delight to the eye as well as the palate. Table d'hôte is the rule, but this is ideal for the gastronomic adventurer as it provides a cross-section of the Japanese cuisine which could never be selected from a menu by a stranger.

After dinner there is another barrage of bowing and fluttering. Somehow the dining table has disappeared and in its place a *futon* has been spread, thick quilted mattresses laid directly on the *tatami*. And a very comfortable bed it is, too. Close at hand on the floor are placed a night-light, an ash-tray with matches, a carafe of water, and a slow-burning insect repellent if you insist on keeping the garden *shoji* open. Already a tea service and thermos of hot water has been put on a table in the smaller room.

By this time I must confess to having attained a peace and beatitude rare in my experience as a nomad, woefully accustomed to a series of dismal rooms bearing an unmistakable hotel aura regardless of the language being spoken in the lobby. I felt cared for, pampered, and spoiled—and without any thought of the outstretched palm, as tipping beyond the percentage added to the bill is a blight that has not reached these shores.

Breakfast is the hardest hurdle for a *gaijin*, a foreigner, a less elaborate version of the previous night's dinner, including always seaweed, soup, raw fish, sour pickles, and rice. Once I rebelled, and the night before managed to convey the idea that I would like a pair of fried eggs for breakfast. They arrived, cold, as a dessert to the usual *asa gohan*. The Japanese phrase for breakfast means literally "morning rice," which indicates the difficulties in achieving a break with custom. It was an experiment not repeated. Have you ever tried to manage a soft fried egg with chopsticks?

Back at the dock after our night at the inn, Jim and I found Mike aboard and *Andrea Gail* ready to go. Extricating ourselves from a web of lines to surrounding fishing boats, we powered past the breakwater to hoist sails. It was a clear morning, with a light southerly breeze fanning the long southerly swells which still persisted. The course was east, a lazy beam reach. I sprawled on the deckhouse and scanned the shore through binoculars.

Soon I identified the Satta Mountains, running down into the sea, a difficult barricade in the earliest days of the Tokaido Road. Here travelers had to leave the shore and enter the ocean, battling seas and undertow, until in 1655 the government drove a path over a high gorge to facilitate the journey for visiting Korean envoys. Then, for long years in the turbulent history of the road, the danger changed to brigands lurking in the dense forests, ready to pounce at lonely Satta Pass. Through glasses I could follow the modern highway winding down from the mountains and along the Coast to Okitsu. On my land cruise I had savored the hospitality of the Minaguchi-ya, the hostelry where for twenty generations the same family has catered to those passing along the Tokaido, a saga described in the best-seller *Japanese Inn*, by Oliver Statler—must reading before a visit. And on a nearby hillside I could make out the lonely, lovely 1,400-year old Buddish temple of Seiken-ji, where I had walked among apricot trees put down by the hand of Tokugawa Ieyasu, sixteenth-century founder of the Tokugawa Shogunate. Seiken-ji is not only officially named by the government as "a Place of Scenic Beauty," but also qualifies as a "Moon-viewing Resort," a rare accolade.

The 18 miles across the northern end of Suruga Bay spun astern. Fuji gradually appeared as sun burned away the early haze. Then over the bow materialized a cone-shaped little island called Awa, which divides the largish bay of Eno Ura into two smaller segments, Sizuura Kō with the town of Enoura to the north, Omosu Kō (Kō means harbor) and the town of Mito Hakuti at the opposite end. Still carrying genoa we stole past Enoura, scanning boats building along the beach, and passed behind Awa to fetch up in a wooded nook beyond Mito.

Approaching, we were startled to be hailed in English, and

soon came alongside *Tankenka,* "Explorer" in Japanese, a power cruiser owned by Jim Phillips, an American resident of Tokyo who is an inveterate sport fisherman. At sunset we observed that most pleasant of cruising customs, getting together for a gam and the tall, cool glass. Under us the water lay flat, reflecting the changes in the sky above. And just at dusk there boomed across the silent harbor the measured strokes of a temple bell, so deep in tone and so resonant that the vibrations hung in the ears long after the strokes had ceased.

When we came out next morning Fuji was standing guard to the north, almost clear of clouds. There was no wind. Under awnings we powered close along the shore. Behind a miniature Sandy Hook called Osē Saki fishermen were handling nets from old-fashion sampans, rowing standing erect with oars having a curious cross-bar at the butt, a T-grip, which allowed a feathering action almost like sculling. Offshore, power draggers were returning to Mito, practically awash. Always, in Japan, fish and fishermen: nets, bait cages, oyster floats, traps; tiny boats anchored in the shallows, medium size vessels disappearing over the horizon, huge electronic-studded ships docking after far-flung voyages—to the Polar Seas, to the Caribbean, to the Indian Ocean, to the Mediterranean—with fish cascading out of refrigerated holds on conveyor belts to support a population too great for the land to feed. It is impossible to understand Japan without thinking of fishing as a necessity, perhaps the key to national survival. Some 100 million people are compressed into four islands having a total area of less than several American states —and because of the rugged terrain, only 15.5 per cent of the land is arable, despite efforts inconceivable elsewhere.

Rounding Osē Saki, the coast fell away almost due south. Strong currents formed peaked ripples and swirls, strong enough to swing the bow sharply. Sampans and gulls patrolled the edges of the rips. A few miles farther *Andrea Gail* poked into the sheltered harbor of Heda for a look, then came out to find breeze enough to fill the sails. Ghosting along, we passed a series of tiny villages, perhaps a dozen houses rimming a beach flat enough to permit pulling up boats beyond the surf line, each settlement separated from its neighbors by bold headlands, living lives little changed through the centuries.

The west coast of the Izu Peninsula compares in beauty with any I have ever cruised: points, crags, valleys; sheer cliffs; cones of rock, detached islets, boiling ledges. The forests stand thick and rich against the granite. It is impossible not to be impressed by their magnificence in a land where wood—including paper products—has for centuries been the basis of the whole civilization: houses, temples, boats, as well as perhaps the greatest variety of everyday articles fashioned by any nation. The Japanese use their forests, but despite the awesome press of population they have not destroyed them.

Off an especially bold cliff in our path bobbed four small sampans, barely clear of the surf and the backwash. In each was two men and a girl, the men tending ship, the girl awaiting her turn to go below. At regular intervals a small basket was lifted through ten fathoms of water. Not even John Laffin or Sato could guess its contents: not pearl oysters, for they are farmed in guarded pens, and surely not abalone. Then, as *Andrea Gail* came close abeam, a man in one of the boats tossed across a shell like a small conch. I immediately recognized it from a memorable dinner in a Japanese inn as *sazae*, part of the ritual of *tzuboyaki*, "cooking in the shell." Vividly I could picture a maid keeping her kimono sleeves away from a brown eathernware dish as she applied a lighted match. The *sazae* rested on a bed of rock salt. Flame burst from alcohol-soaked cotton buried under the salt. Soon the liquid in the opening of the shell began to bubble—a quail egg floating in a broth of bamboo shoots and mushrooms, plus the diced meat of the *sazae*.

Past another point, and we had come to Arari, buried deep in the land. Gradually the outer approach narrowed, finally squeezing us between a tiny island to port and a stone break-water to starboard. The island was no bigger than *Andrea Gail.* It looked as though it should have been enclosed in a glass case. At the water's edge was a scarlet *torii,* the sacred arch of the Shinto shrine. A miniature bridge arched across a step-deep chasm. Above, a single pine tree topped a wall of ancient asymmetric stonework. The effect was like a flower arrangement.

As in Mediterranean ports, the system of mooring in Japan is to drop a bow anchor and maneuver the stern to the quay. But there the resemblance ceases, for while French and Italian Riviera ports are so crowded with yachts that late arrivals can find no place, Japanese ports like Arari are empty except for fishing vessels. A cruising yacht is a rarity and therefore a curiosity. As we approached, men sauntered over from nearby trawlers, women—many carrying babies in sashes slung over the hips—abandoned their shopping to have a look, while button-eyed moppets seriously watched every move. As always; everyone on the dock wanted to be helpful, scurrying to make lines fast, and anticipating any assistance that could be rendered.

Gradually the welcoming committee drifted away, and *Andrea Gail'*s cockpit became a front-row seat on the life of a remote Oriental fishing village. We were moored opposite the most imposing house along the quay, which John Laffin thought was probably the residence of the mayor or head of the fishing union. Almost under our counter was a cement trough with brass water faucets, gleaming from use. Householders arrived with covered buckets to fill and carry away. A few did minor bits of laundry. Through open *shoji* screens we could see into nearby rooms, where three or four generations sprawled on the *tatami* mats, sipping tea, smoking, but principally—I must report—watching television. For

TV is the national passion, the greatest apparent influence in contemporary life; American westerns with dubbed dialogue are favorites, and no one has experienced the height of drama without hearing the sheriff call to the posse in Japanese: "We'll cut 'em off at the pass, boys!"

Couples strolled by in the gathering dusk. Crewmen from trawlers tossed a baseball as long as there was light to see, then began fishing just for fun. Mama-*san* and papa-*san* and a stairstep of children came out of the facing house with short bamboo poles to try their luck along the quay, too. No one paid any attention to us in the cockpit. We had dinner and walked to the inn for an *o-furo*, groping through unlighted alleys and streets past houses unaltered in form or style for hundreds of years, except for the TV antennas recently sprouted from every roof.

With dawn the situation of the evening was reversed. Now the quay was the first-row orchestra and *Andrea Gail* the stage. Jim Hoffman, sleeping wrapped in a blanket on deck, opened his eyes with the first light and stared into thirty pairs of eyes opposite. Gradually, our audience increased, until it seemed that the entire village had assembled. Respectfully they watched us breakfast in the cockpit and helpfully they handed our lines on departure, all in an aura of friendly curiosity.

Outside, the southerly swells had increased—rather inexplicably, as typhoon Bess was well past. Slugging our way southward to again round Irō Saki, I was reminded of conditions off the British Isles or coast of France: strong currents, gales originating in polar regions, a leeward position in relation to prevailing winds, a steeply rising ocean floor. Except that Japan also receives the full force of circular storms sweeping up from the tropics. Offshore sailing can be rugged, even lethal. Eleven lives were lost when two small yachts foundered during a single race across Sagami Bay.

Spring and fall are the best seasons for boating in Japan. The typhoon season parallels that of the Caribbean—July through September. In October the days are clear and crisp. The foliage takes on its autumnal tints, so it is known as "the time of maples in flame." Winds are reliable. Good sailing conditions extend through November, although the nights are likely to be chill. Most boats are laid up from December through March, appearing with the spring buds of April. Then cruising conditions are delightful until the rainy season commences in mid-June, running for about a month. Mid-July through August is not ideal, being on the warm and humid side, but perfectly agreeable, always with the proviso a daily typhoon check is maintained. In September the prudent skipper stays close to dependable home moorings.

As *Andrea Gail* again rounded the Horn of Irō Saki, we seemed to encounter the weather of all seasons. The sea rose to smite us, from all sides. But again the breeze faired as we turned the corner. We were enjoying a spirited sail between the rocks of Yoko Ne when without warning the wind shifted 180 degrees, from south to north. The crests of what had been following seas blew into our faces. Just as quickly, landmarks were swallowed in fog as the temperature dropped 20 degrees.

But the lighthouse perched above the entrance to Shimoda was already over the bow, and soon we picked up the island marking the turn into the river anchorage. Entering, Mike and Jim were amazed by new construction along the harbor's rim. Japan, along with the rest of the world, has learned to make the most of leisure. Hotels are mushrooming in places considered remote only yesterday. We found a berth wedged among sampans and settled snugly below, while overhead the rigging whined the universal song of the nor'easter.

Shimoda was the site of the first American consulate. In the afternoon we made a shore expedition to the temple of Gyokusen, where Townsend Harris set up residence after Commodore Perry signed an agreement with the Tokugawa Shogunate under the guns of the Black Ships, the Japanese name for the steam frigates of Perry's fleet. Prophetically,

Harris noted in his diary on 4 September 1856: "This day I hoist the first Consular flag ever seen in this Empire. Grim reflections—ominous of change—undoubted beginning of the end. Query—if for real good of Japan." Strangely, Gyokusen-Ji has become a shrine for Japanese sightseers, too, perhaps because of the legend of Tojin Okiti, Harris's housekeeper, a romantic attachment not only forming the theme of a favorite *kabuki* drama, but setting an agreeable precedent followed by successive waves of visitors. Tojin Okiti has her own shrine on the other side of town.

It continued to blow hard the following day, so I was happy to confine my research to Japanese food. Among the plaques at Gyokusen-Ji honoring Townsend Harris, one especially caught my eye. It was lettered in English and Japanese calligraphy: "This monument, erected in 1931 by the butchers of Tokyo, marks the spot on which the first cow in Japan was slaughtered for human consumption." As an afterthought, the inscription adds parenthetically, "eaten by Harris and Heusken," the consular secretary. Then, Japanese did not eat beef. They have come a long way since the original sirloin was consumed with diplomatic immunity. There are almost as many steak houses in Tokyo as New York. A special breed of cattle has been developed to please Nipponese connoiseurs. Kobe steers should be foremost among the world's contented cows. They receive beer with their meals, and are massaged twice daily.

But away from tourist trails fish reigns supreme. On a street behind the waterfront Jim and I found a tiny *sushi* bar called the Irifune, "the boat came in." Outside it was plain enough, merely a calligraphic sign above the door. Inside it was simple, too, but charming: a pine counter scrubbed white, wicker stools in front, a low glass case above. Under the case as part of the counter was a trough filled with black pebbles, over which water jetted from a hidden pipe—a running water finger-bowl, so to speak, useful as well as ornamental. *Sushi* is eaten with the fingers.

In the refrigerated case in front of us were things to be combined with rice in the nearest approach to a sandwich in the Japanese diet: slices of octopus, shrimp, squid, tuna, sea-bream, abalone and eel, fresh roe and edible portions of sea-urchins. Jim and I had entered with the intention of having *sushi* as hors d'oeuvre before continuing on to a hotel on the bayfront for lunch, but we got no farther than the Irifune, sampling almost everything. Among others, there was a wonderful tid-bit called *une*, a patty of rice wrapped in paper-thin seaweed topped with sea-urchin, and another with the French sounding name of *avec*: seaweed and raw tuna and hot sauce and cucumber slices and rice arranged in layers on a tiny bamboo mat which was then rolled and pressed, and afterwards sliced in the form of a miniature jellyroll.

The Irifune typifies the Japanese custom of specialization by small restaurants, or "bars." Each serves one dish. There are *tempura* bars, where fish and vegetables are deep but lightly fried; *sukiyaki* bars—pronounced *skee-yaki*, beef and vegetables sizzled in a broth in front of the diner, probably the most familiar Japanese dish to foreigners; *soba* bars, whose specialty is noodles, hot or cold, and on through establishments serving only roast chicken or eel. In each little bar, a snack may be eaten, leaving room for another course down the street, or a whole meal may be made.

The next morning it was a bit harder to hoist sails than usual. Above, the sky was clear except for scattered cirrus, although in the distance the shore was touched by a frosty haze. Course now east, breeze now east, reminding me of Sherman Hoyt's old dictum that the trouble with sailing is that the wind is either dead ahead or dead astern, and there is always too little or too much. Setting main, forestaysail and big jibtopsail, we began a slow beat towards the volcanic island of Oshima, hidden by haze.

For the first time the ocean was reasonably calm, the nor'easter having managed to level the chronic southerly swell. As I sat on the deckhouse, the volcanic cones of Nii Shima and

Kōzu Shima became visible as the port tack carried us southward, part of a chain of seven islands extending some 150 miles to sea—and all part of metropolitan Tokyo. Soon afterwards, Oshima appeared, to rapidly rise as the breeze freshened.

When we neared a plume of smoke lifted from Oshima's central mountain core to join the cloud cover. The upper slopes were barren lava, but there was a verdant green belt girdling the shore. We swung into Habu, the only protected port on the island. Here, by agreement, I jumped ship to taxi to Okada for an early morning assault on Mt. Mihara. "The present crater is reached by passing through a lava bed of two miles on the summit," states *Japan, The Official Guide*, published by the Japan Travel Bureau. "A fine view of Mt. Fuji and other islands can be obtained. . . ." It should have been information enough, but I had to see for myself.

Although the guidebook does not say so, before the big eruption in 1957, when the crater was deeper and steeper, dispairing lovers bought one-way steamer tickets to Oshima to jump into the volcano. These romantically frustrated pairs usually were practical enough to spend a few nights at one of the inns before taking the plunge, leaving behind an unpaid bill. The suicide rate was drastically reduced when the steamship company refused to sell young couples anything but unrefundable round-trip tickets, while room clerks developed the habit of demanding cash in advance.

Morning found this dauntless mountineer, nourished by seaweed and rice, toiling upwards through a landscape by Dante out of Hollywood. High above in the mists tiny figures plodded even higher. The Japanese curiosity surmounts all. Each time I was tempted to stop, a family group ambled by. Toddlers, clutching their mother's skirts, stared enigmatically as they passed, spurring me on. Finally I achieved the lip of the crater crab-wise to peer down into a pit of boiling rock and steam. Desperately I looked around for something to grab. The suicide guard on patrol with binoculars and a power megaphone to discourage those wanting to jump was unnecessary in my case. Just when I was wondering why I had deserted a cushioned cockpit to climb a pile of hot rock, there was a rift in the clouds and it was all worthwhile. With a dramatic vividness impossible to describe, I could see back along our wake to the whole jutting Izu Peninsula, a rich green against the blue of sea and sky, while the majestic cone of Fuji dominated the coastal plains to the north.

By the time I had descended, *Andrea Gail* waited at the quay of Okada. With little delay we cast off as we had in prospect light winds for the 30 mile passage to Eno Shima, site of Olympic Yachting in the '64 Games. It was another lazy day, and I was content to compare the relative merits of sailing and mountain climbing from a supine position on the deckhouse. Fish came flapping in over the stern as Mike tended the line, while the wind gradually hauled into the south and put little cresting wavelets on the backs of the swells.

Eno Shima means "Picture Island," and in many ways lives up to its name, typical of those wooded rocky cones that delight the passing cruiser's eye. Shrines are tucked among trees magnificant even for Japan. There is a cave where once a dragon lived, according to legend, which now is occupied by an image of Benton, one of the Seven Deities of Good Luck. Unfortunately, Eno Shima, like Capri, is an island whose beauty has become its undoing: Coney Island crossed with a bit of Waikiki Beach; three levels of escalators finally debauching into an amusement park complete with botanical gardens and a zoo. There is even a miniature Eiffel Tower on the summit.

After a look at the splendid basin and facilities constructed for the Olympics, we continued a few miles across the head of Sagami Bay to Hayama. The protected area behind a stone breakwater was packed by small racing classes. Dropping anchor off to one side, we lunched in the cockpit while Japanese boys and girls practiced starts in a flurry of broken battens and dunkings, as the afternoon breeze had reached the force of a Buzzards Bay sou'wester. Outside, later, *Andrea Gail* had all the sail she wanted with working lowers and a small jibtopsail, driving rail down into the path of the sun, our bow wave glittering diamonds against the majesty of Mount Fuji.

One long leg carried us well down the coast of Tsurugu Peninsula, where *Andrea Gail*'s home port opened over the bows—Aburatsubo, cradled by surrounding hills, one of those rare sanctuaries truly safe in any wind. Even a typhoon. At Aburatsubo are maintenance facilities, as well as a clubhouse on a bluff, its front porch jutting over the moored fleet. It is a harbor exuding tranquility.

By way of contrast, a short sail down the coast lies the fishing port of Misaki. Here converges much of the fleet supplying the huge Tokyo metropolitan area, more than ten million fish-hungry humans. Vessels of every type shuttle to the docks, where a shed the size of a football field cannot begin to accommodate the daily catch: swordfish with the bills hacked off for more compact storage, tuna, shark—monsters of the deep from every ocean of the world side by side with small mackeral, baskets of shrimp and tubs of squid, caught within sight of the nearby island of Joga Shima.

The quays of Misaki have something of the air which must have pervaded New Bedford and Nantucket during the voyages of the whalers. Crews work over gear, open-air shops make repairs, stores are taken aboard. Vendors of *sushi* and sheath knives and ice cream push little carts from gangplank to gangplank. Children are led aboard for a look. Wives and sweethearts in kimonos stand under paper umbrellas, waiting. For the high-bowed white ships of Misaki make voyages lasting two years or more, and each departure and return is a local event. We watched *Bōchō Maru No. 3* cast off. Loudspeakers played the atonal music of the Orient for a crowd of several hundred on the quay. Code flags and pennants snapped from masts while colored paper streamers were thrown across the opening gap to the crew waving good-bye from the stern.

South of Misaki, as we reached across the steamer channel leading to Yokohama and Tokyo, freighters and tankers passed bow to stern, like circus elephants on parade. Gradually the wind increased until the liferail stanchions disappeared; eased by striking the jibtop, *Gail* swooped over the crests almost as fast and certainly more comfortably. It doesn't pay to bury a boat by overdriving to windward, racing or cruising on either side of the world. Rapidly we crossed Uraga Channel to enter the flat, dusty port of Tateyama. After walking a gray beach rimmed by drab bathhouses, I was on the point of returning aboard when I happened to glance through a gate, and was reminded of a Japanese truism: beauty is never openly displayed, for behind a high wall was hidden a final priceless vignette of old Japan: a serene and lovely garden, its grass velvet smooth, pine trees artfully spaced and pruned, a perfect composition in the texture of granite, raked pebbles, and weathered wood. Over all lifted the sweeping curves of the tile roof, the most unforgettable detail of Japanese architecture, summed up by the name of a pagoda at Nara, which translates as "Frozen Music."

That night we lay snug in harbor while wind whistled through the rigging, but next morning the breeze was light as we sailed northwards into Tokyo Bay. Around noon it dropped out completely, and we unfurled the cockpit awning against waves of heat reaching out from the city pavements ahead. Sampans drooped against the shore of Chiba, while the wakes of passing steamers curled as lazy undulations. We passed the tumbled ruins of island fortifications shown on the chart simply as Forts 1, 2, and 3, navigational hazards that were not victims of war but of the great earthquake of 1923, when most of Tokyo was leveled.

Then the afternoon southerly suddenly struck in, and we scrambled to set the genoa for a final sail. Out of a complex of factories and chimneys and miles of ship loading facilities appeared a small building on a point, flags flying from a tall staff in front. At a puff of smoke the fleet of Yokohama Yacht Club converged on a mark, just as in a race at home. But not quite like home, I thought, looking backward across the bay at the bat-wing sampans plying among the shipping. Definitely not, I decided at last, reflecting upon a cruise whose sights and mood had been like nothing in the world but the woodblock prints of Hiroshige come to life.

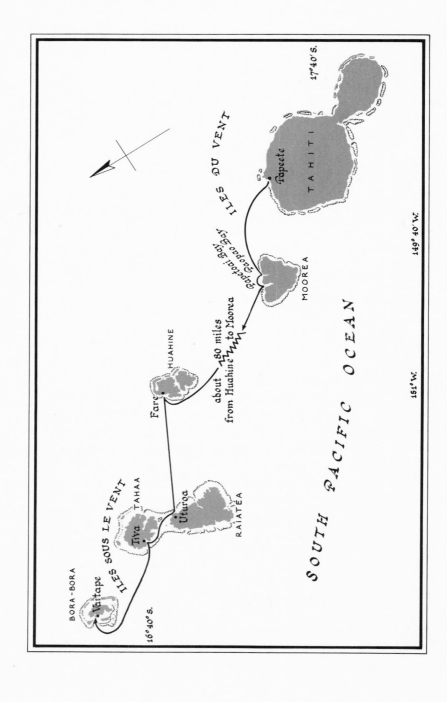

14

The Enchanted Suburbs of Tahiti

THE SOUTH PACIFIC

When *Staghound* neared the opening in the barrier reef off Paopao Bay, we were a silver ship on a silver sea. The last of the rose and gold had faded from the clouds over Tahiti, ten miles astern, although the silhouette of the island was still plain, a jagged black cut-out hung against the sky.

Over the bowsprit, Moorea seemed to float just beyond the smooth lagoon, palm trees spilling down the mountainsides to fringe gleaming beaches, valleys receding mysteriously into shadow. It was the full moon of August. Lazily the swell lifted to break on the coral reef to port, white water marking the area of danger, a clear line guiding us on our way. We navigated as sailors had for generations, before buoys, before lights, when the look of the sea was its own chart. Above the masthead hung the Southern Cross, and strong in the warm air was the scene of flowers piled on deck from our Papeete farewell, *heis* of tiare

Tahiti and frangipani and hibiscus mixed carelessly with coils of line and fenders and the rest of the assorted gear of a small ship off on an ocean voyage.

We did not mean to be so late in making port. But any departure from Tahiti is an event, and this was a special one. For two years *Staghound* had swung around an anchor in the multihued waters off the valley of Taapuna, one of those wandering yachts which make Tahiti a port of missing ships, for no one ever wants to leave and sailors drown in a lagoon of pure content. "You find you were never truly happy any place before," I was told on arrival by Paul Hurst, owner of *Staghound*, "and then you begin to question whether you can be happy anywhere else after you go."

Paul spoke from experience. Originally from Santa Barbara, he first saw *Les Iles sous le Vent*— "The Islands below the Wind," The Leeward Islands, their official title in French— on the Honolulu-to-Tahiti race of 1956. He promptly returned to California and bought *Staghound*, to come back on what was ostensibly the lead-off leg of a voyage round the world. Now, when he announced the previous week to his island cronies that the sailing date to continue his voyage would be Tuesday, scoffers laughed: "Which Tuesday?"

But more than a hundred friends had gathered on the quay during the afternoon. Hands were clasped and cheeks kissed as the floral *heis* of farewell were placed over the heads of the departing. *Staghound*'s crew on the continued voyage toward the setting sun consisted of Paul, Plazi Miller, an American who had sailed out from California with Paul and likewise succumbed to the lotus of the islands, and two native Tahitians, Terii and Sam. While the langurous music of Polynesia drifted faintly from nearby Restaurant Vaiharia, the *au revoirs* spun on and on, as flower laden late arrivals came aboard. The sun was low when lines were cast off. As we powered away, Terii slowly lifted the flowered circlets from her shoulders one by one and dropped them in our wake, already wet with her tears. Like perfumed stepping stones they lay on the water, symbolically linking us with the shore of Tahiti forever, for Polynesians believe that if you cast your *heis* astern as you leave, you must return.

After setting sails to a faint breeze, as long as there was light we stared nostalgically at the receding panorama of vessels moored stern-to along the Papeete waterfront, and the red-roofed buildings peeping through the trees, and the mountains lifting to the cloud cover, their colors changing as the sun set. For me, there was an aura of unreality about the whole thing. Always I had thought of Tahiti and the islands of *Polynésie Française* as a someday cruise, but the dream had come true with staggering swiftness. Months before I had received a letter from an unknown yachtsman in the Pacific asking for information on *Finisterre*'s mechanical refrigeration system, which I had mentioned in an article; correspondence had developed, ending on a note of invitation to cruise should I ever come to his side of the world. Then suddenly I found myself in Honolulu after crewing the Transpac Race aboard *Nam Sang*. Why I thought to take advantage of Paul Hurst's casual suggestion I am not sure, except that I had fallen in love with the Pacific and wanted to see more of it, but a cablegram brought a prompt reply: "SAILING FOR SUVA FIJU MID-AUGUST. COME ABOARD STAGHOUND TO BORA BORA." It was '59, when airplane travel to Tahiti was circuitous and infrequent, but I was aboard the next weekly flight.

Long ago a kindly power fashioned islands in anticipation of the day when the continents would become suburbs and the cities unbearable cauldrons of noise and hurry. Islands mean escape, and part of their fascination lies in the fact that no two—much less any two archipelagos—are ever really alike. But even the connoisseur will concede a very special position in the hierarchy to those reef-girt jewels in the Pacific, whose crowning orb is Tahiti. And so, somewhat unbelievably, I found myself outward bound aboard a staunch little ship, in the company of people who knew and loved the islands as no outsider could.

The parting mood aboard *Staghound* was sadness, which I shared even as a newcomer. But when the moon lifted above the horizon the spell was magically broken. Terii dried her tears with the hem of her *pareu* and went forward to sit on the bowsprit pulpit, obeying the advice of Paul: "Don't look back." Soon, in the lighthearted manner of *vahines* she was laughing with Sam.

We crept along the reef until a gap appeared in the breakers, a dark lane where swells undulated smoothly toward a darker cleft beyond. Turning, we followed the channel, awed to silence by the beauty of the night and the majesty of the land. Mountains towered on both sides and ahead, so steep and so high as to eclipse the moon. Under us the lagoon water lay luminascent and mercurial, reflecting the silver sky except where canoes fishing by torchlight cast long golden spears. Thus I imagined it must have been in 1769 when Captain Cook conned *Endeavour* into Paopao Bay, thenceforth to add his own name to the charts.

Quietly we furled the sails and dropped anchor. After dinner Sam perched in the port upper berth and began to play his guitar, softly singing ancient songs in the ancient tongue. Rolling and repeated vowels give the Polynesian language a liquid flow, yet when put to music it turns into a pulsing beat impossible to resist. The wicker covered "dam John" of Algerian red wine was brought from the cockpit, and the table moved into the forepeak. We clapped hands in time to the music, until suddenly Terii was in the center of the cabin, dancing the strongly emphasized hula of Tahiti, eyes flashing, dark unbound hair flowing, the traditional frangipani blossom behind one ear.

It was not until next morning I fully realized the drama of our anchorage. By moonlight it had been ethereal. Flooded with sunshine, it was overwhelming. On three sides the mountains seemed to touch the sky, verdant to the summit. Smoke lifted lazily from thatch roofed huts almost hidden by flowers. In every vista swirled the colors captured on canvas by the inspired genius of Gauguin: the hot reds, the brilliant greens, the vivid yellows, even the startling purples and oranges and shades of pink.

Paul came up the companionway. He sensed what I was feeling, and grinned. "It's beautiful," he said, "but wait. After breakfast we'll go round to the next bay, and you'll really flip. I'll put *Staghound* alongside a beach where you can pick coconuts from the rigging."

Still I was not prepared for the spectacular loveliness of Papetoai Bay. Many times in my travels local guides have proudly pointed out "the most beautiful place in the world." Perhaps this is really it. There was a feeling of majesty in the towering mountains at the end of a narrow lane of water akin to that of a Norwegian fjord, but here even the upper slopes had been touched by the magic wand of the tropics. Everything I looked upon was rich, warm and alive, rather than cold and austere: small clouds reflected in the blue water, palms waved in the soft breeze, a floral canopy extended from sand beach to summit. Only Capri, in the distant Mediterranean, could compare, and then only because its natural beauty is enhanced by some of the nobler works of man: castles, religious edifices, and lovely villas.

Slowly *Staghound* bore us farther into the bay, dwarfed by the culminating pinnacle of Tohivea at the head. True to his promise, Paul came to rest in a cove where the bow touched white sand, while a coconut palm hung over the main rigging. Like Tahiti, Moorea is not a place left astern lightly. For days we shuttled between the neighboring bays. It did not seem necessary to go fast or far, for nothing distant seemed important. The only factor finally sending us forth upon the broad Pacific was the sailor's age-old restlessness, the indefinable need to see what else lies beyond the horizon. Thus finally we slipped through the opening in the reef at sunset, bound for the harbor of Fare on the island of Huahine, 82 miles to the west.

Clear of the land, a long sea was running. While we lay snug a *maraamu* had begun to blow, the fresh southerly accompanied by overcast skies and misting rain which occasionally displaces the normal trade wind during the southern hemisphere winter. It was still a fair slant for the islands to the west, so the breaking crests which burst under the counter shouldered *Staghound* on her way. Happily she rolled along, and I felt happy and at home. In the fading light I looked around the deck. Bunches of bananas swung in the main rigging, coconuts were heaped on deck forward of the skylight, a basket of mangoes and *pamplemousse* rode aft of the cockpit, and red wine sloshed in the "dam John" lashed at my side. Not yachty, but right, as a small ship should cruise, and I felt even more the kinship between *Staghound* and my own *Finisterre*, both sturdy live-aboard go-anywhere vessels of 38-feet overall, both with a turn of speed. *Staghound* had twice won the Transpacific Race before coming to Paul Hurst.

Under short canvas we clipped off the miles. Moorea was in sight astern at dark, but when the moon arose at the end of my wheel trick, the sea was empty. At 4:00, when I came back on deck Huahine was plain on the starboard bow. Yet in the moonlight it was unreal. As each passing sea raised above the horizon, the jagged outline of the mountains merged into the tumbling crests, to disappear until the next trough, when the peaks lifted again to look like a wave suddenly turned to stone. Watching, I was hardly aware of a change in the quality of the light. At dawn, the first moments of sun were not brighter than the moonlight, only different in texture. But suddenly the clouds over Huahine glowed, and it was day, brilliant day, with the glorious soft warmth of the tropics.

The barrier reef of Huahine stretched far beyond the shore,

with a dogleg turn to enter. At 6:45 we jibed and stood in close to the breakers, then had to jibe again. Rounding the corner into the lee, the water smoothed, and we saw clearly defined the opening of the pass leading to Fare Bay.

I wish I could say something pleasant about the village of Fare, beyond the giant mangoes purchased at the open marketplace, but it is indeed a fatuous lover who can find no fault. Seeking escape from staring children on the dock, I retreated to a room in the Hawaii Hotel, upstairs over the Restaurant-Café-Bar and General Store of Ah-Kim. The walls were of pale blue fibreboard, and the single light bulb overhead formed one corner of a suspension system for the mosquito net. From hooks by the door depended bent and rusted hangers. A single yellowing sheet covered the mattress of the bed, which took up most of the floor, leaving space only for a single chair and low round table. Through the uncurtained window came sounds of hammering; of voices speaking Chinese, Tahitian, and French; of babies crying, flies buzzing, and roosters crowing without cease.

Seeking escape again, I hired an ancient Ford with Plazi and Sam for the trip to Maeva, a fishing village on a tidal lake, where houses are built on stilts over the water. Outside of Fare, Polynesia was again Polynesia. At Maeva we found not only a labyrinth of stone fish weirs dating from ancient times, but the ruins of a *marae*, a pagan shrine. In the afternoon we explored the other end of the island by outboard, and found it lovely. Wide, white beaches sheltered by towering palms opened into deep bays, especially at Porte du Bourayne, which connected by a shallow passage with the Bay de Maroe on the other side. Huahine is shown as two islands on the chart, Huahine-Nui and Ito, Huahine Great and Small, although they look like one from the deck of a passing vessel.

Not so our next pair of islands, Raiatea and Tahaa. As we left Fare Bay, they stood bold and separate on the horizon ahead, although they were embraced by a single giant barrier reef in the shape of an hourglass. Small, creaming wavelets raced us to the pass. The *maraamu* still blew. *Staghound* was ready for rough going, South Sea fashion, the bananas in her rigging securely lashed to the ratlines, the drinking coconuts at the foot of the mainmast well chocked down, a carved Tiki in the cabin to bring her luck.

There was less wind and sea outside than we expected. The blasts funneling through the valleys had been stronger than the true offshore breeze. *Staghound* rolled along with flying fish skittering under the bow as the white crests of long Pacific rollers lifted the stern. Seabirds circled and dived over schools of bonito. Lazily we watched, bestirring ourselves only enough to put out a fishline, while the purple haze of distance melted from the volcanic cones of Raiatea, and transmuted the emerald-green slopes of Huahine astern.

When we neared Raiatea the symmetrical cone of a long dead volcano lined up with a pair of palm crowned islets as a range guiding us into the pass. Entering, *Staghound* was immediately in smooth water. Everywhere the Polynesian barrier reef, invisible above the surface, was a curiously effective buffer against the seas outside. It took time to adjust to lying at anchor seemingly exposed to the open ocean. Yet the encircling reefs magically tamed long swells into ripples. And the sound of surf became an ineffable memory of the South Seas, never absent, even ashore.

Raiatea was not only the second largest island in the group after Tahiti, but the town of Uturoa the second largest metropolis. Although it is no Papeete, I found it had unexpected amenities, including a room with private bath at the Hotel Hinano. Again I moved ashore. "Hinano" is a useful word. It is the name of the national brew, a strong beer made in Papeete, which uses a native girl in *pareu* as a trade-mark, and also is the name of many *vahines* who might have posed for the ad. Loudly calling "Hinano" in any bar is certain to produce results one way or another, possibly both.

It was Saturday, and Saturday night is Saturday night the world over. After dinner in the hotel restaurant the crew of *Staghound* joined the crew of a New Zealand yacht at the Vairahi Bar. To phrase it delicately, the joint was jumping. And no joint anywhere can outjump a Tahitian nightspot when the drums get rolling. In Tahiti, people have fun. As sailors have found through the years, there are few taboos and no inhibitions. This expresses itself in a unique form of dancing. In Hawaii, visitors are told to watch the hands. Here there was no such nonsense. Hinano flowed. The drums increased tempo. The joint got jumpier. And when it finally closed, we jumped our way back to *Staghound*, to move the cabin table and go on dancing to Sam's guitar.

By way of contrast, a few miles from Uturoa is the famous *marae* of Taputapuatea, once the center of learning and worship for all Polynesia, the vast triangle extending from Hawaii to Samoa to Easter Island. More than 600 years ago the Aotea canoe set off from Raiatea for New Zealand, and the Maori people still consider it an ancient seat of knowledge. Archeologists have discovered sacred stones from Taputapuatea in lesser *maraes* thousands of miles away, additional proof that during the centuries before the coming of Europeans, the Polynesians were skilled in construction, navigation, and seamanship.

In the morning we visited Taputapuatea by outboard. Landing in a nearby village we walked past groves of coconuts and copra drying sheds to a point of land extending into the lagoon. A soft wind blew through the trees, and the roar of surf was loud. Carried away by visiting whalers was the decoration of human skulls described by the Reverend William Ellis, the great Polynesian scholar who visited it in 1819, but still in existence were the ruins of extensive coral and stone platforms. Also remaining was the tall pillar on which the ancient kings were presented to their subjects. Local legend has it the same stone was used to measure the height of warriors; any man who could not top it was likely to become a victim of the nearby ceremonial oven. If true, former inhabitants of Raiatea must have been supermen, as the stone was nearly nine feet high.

On our return to Uturoa for lunch, *Staghound* acquired a passenger, Repeta, who was proving an embarrassment of riches to one of the crew of the New Zealand yacht which had helped us observe Saturday night. His Papeete girl had arrived by mail boat. So Paul agreed to take Repeta home to Tiva, on Tahaa, which we had already planned as the next stop.

Repeta was sixteen, a typical *vahine.* Her skin was soft brown, perhaps a shade darker than a brunette American girl might achieve from a summer on the beach, and her dark hair hung in a thick braid to her waist. Her eyes were large and expressive, and her smile as innocent and shy as a child's. She loved flowers. She was completely unaffected in manner and dress, and without visible complications. Immorality, as such, for her simply did not exist.

It was a glorious sail to Tiva. Leaving Uturoa, Plazi Miller went aloft to con *Staghound* through scattered coral clumps, but in the open lagoon between the islands the water was deep and free from danger, at once sheltered from ocean seas by the barrier reef, yet open to the full sweep of breeze. As on the Bahama Banks, the color of the water was governed by the depth, so *Staghound* reached across a quilt of blue and green, with purple patches of deep coral to either side.

Terii and Repeta chattered in the shade of the mainsail while Tahaa lifted higher. Although there is a basic similarity to the islands of the Society group, each is individual. Tahaa was scalloped by deep bays, a cruising man's dream of snug harbors, all with romantic names: Tapuamu, Apu, Teoneroa-Haaoa, Hamene. Coconut trees grew not only along the shore, but to the tops of the lower hills. And coming around the southern point there was a vision of distant loveliness, the towering twin peaks of Bora Bora, rising above the shimmering horizon.

Tahaa was an island rarely visited by yachts. A crowd gathered as *Staghound* made fast to the small quay. The people seemed curious but quiet, and soon drifted away. "They'll be back," predicted Paul. We swam and drank sundown rum punches in the cockpit as Terii cooked dinner. The village appeared deserted. But as we sat around the table in the cabin after the dishes had been stowed the tentative chords of a ukulele began to sound from the shore. Sam took his guitar and went on deck.

Gathered on the quay was a solid mass of people, "like a dark wall," as Paul commented. Sam perched on top of the trunk cabin amidships and began to play. Soon the man with the ukulele sat alongside. Another man ventured aboard, and began to sing. He left to return with a guitar, and a wonderful night began. Tahitian music is less plaintive than Hawaiian; there are few sad songs, laments for lost loves and the sorrows of parting. It is gay, and always there is the beat, the vibrant pulse of life. Almost everyone could sing. From the shore voices joined, or began a new song when the musicians paused.

The crowd on the quay moved in time, an unconscious mass response to music. Ashore couples began to dance. Slowly big-eyed children stole into the cockpit, peering below but vanishing like moths if invited farther. *Vahines* giggled from the shadows, and gradually came aboard. Men followed, until our decks were crowded and *Staghound* took a heavy list. A waning moon peeped over the horizon. Cigarettes glowed. All was laughter and good humor: how long would we stay, where were we going, whose girl was Repeta? The three musicians played steadily, voices soft and caressing. Below, the pat of bare feet on deck in time was like the sound of muffled drums.

It was a moment of glory for Repeta. As we docked in her

home village she had displayed a fine proprietary air. Now she sat next to Sam. When he rested she took over the guitar, and played it well. She sang every song. For hours the music continued, while the moon lifted above the spreaders and began to drop on the other side of the sky. The music began to soften as the crowd drifted away, until finally there was only the sound of surf on the reef, and the village slept under the palms.

Next morning, I was awakened at sunrise by the tentative plunking of a ukulele from the dock. But this time no one stirred in welcome, and the player went away. Later, I lighted the stove to make early tea, had a swim while the water was heating, and went ashore. People smiled as I passed and called *"Ia ora na,"* the Tahitian greeting which means "May you live," and is used in the sense of both hello and welcome. Under the palms, the village was awakening, and the simple chores of a simple life were underway.

When time came to sail after breakfast we still had a passenger. Repeta was ready to continue the voyage—have *pareu,* will travel. It took some time for Paul to explain in French that from Bora Bora *Staghound* was making a long trip, and there wasn't space for a *vahine,* however charming. Reluctantly she went ashore, possessions in a small basket. She stayed on the quay to cast off our lines, gave us a final quiet, shy smile, and disappeared as a kitten might wander away.

All along Bora Bora had had a special allure. From the first I had heard of the drums of Bora Bora, the girls of Bora Bora, the beauty of the twin peaks and the islands of the lagoon. It being my birthday, the weather gods decided to give me a perfect final sail. The *maraamu* had lost most of its punch and the sky had cleared except for a few puffy cumulus clouds to lend emphasis to the blue. The seas were lazy instead of cresting, yet overhead the sails filled snug and taut without slatting.

The closer we sailed to Bora Bora, the more perfect it

looked, a Bali H'ai come true. Fisherman walked the reef as
we entered the pass, darting long spears into tidal pools. Others dragged nets. Outrigger canoes drifted across the lagoon.
And to starboard lay Motu Tapu, The Forbidden Isle, where,
according to legend, young girls were sent to stay out of the
sun, and thereby became paler and more alluring. Crowned
by palms, ringing by white sand and water of many colors,
Motu Tapu epitomizes the South Seas. Years ago it formed
the locale of the famous motion picture *Tabu*.

Inside the lagoon, Paul swung *Staghound* to starboard and
followed a line of deep blue water. Skirting a sunken coral
ledge, we came to anchor in eight fathoms. I had asked for
poisson cru, and it was up to us to get the *poisson*. Nor was it
difficult, thanks to Sam. With his home-made wooden spear-
gun, he was uncanny at stalking and long-range shooting.
Contrary to expectation, reef fish in Tahiti run scarce, small
and wary. Sam's technique was to dive well away from prey
he had spotted, then move flat along the bottom, seeking coral
clumps for cover. At times he would hide behind a branching
coral tree until a fish swam within range; watching him from
the surface, my lungs began to ache in sympathy. Rarely did
he release the spear without making a hit.

Leaving the affairs of the pot in the hands of a master, I
swam further along the reef, occasionally diving down for a
better look. There were tiny fish by thousands, flecks of blue,
of purple, of yellow, of red, of green, of stripes and spots and
iridescence, for nothing in nature rivals the pigmentation of
the smaller denizens of a tropic reef. Some hung together in
dense clouds and others peered in lonely suspicion from minute caverns, while my favorites—inch-long, pale-blue characters—appeared and disappeared from a thicket of coral like a
covey of quail in pine woods.

Swimming back to *Staghound*, I was reminded that less innocent creatures share the same waters. Far below, shadowy
in the depths, a huge horned ray flapped along the bottom.

The tempo of my strokes unconsciously quickened. Yet a half-hour later Sam and Plazi were completely unconcerned when from the deck Paul spotted the tall sickle fin of a cruising shark. At our shouted warning, they turned for a look, then resumed swimming at the same leisurely pace. "He smelled our fish," commented Sam contemptuously on coming to the boarding ladder.

Poisson cru—called *e i'a ota* in Tahitian, plain "raw fish" in English—had become my favorite Polynesian dish. Nothing is more delicious. Nor is it raw, except in the sense it is not cooked by heat. Now at last I was to see it made, as Terii took over the string Sam lifted aboard.

Almost any sort of fish may be used, although bonito is considered best by Tahitians. After cleaning, scaling and dicing into small cubes, it was put in a bowl, and the juice of perhaps a dozen limes squeezed over—enough to thoroughly dampen the flesh. Terii anointed a layer, salted it generously, and turned it with a fork, making sure none was missed. Onions were sliced in, and given a thorough tossing to mix. The bowl was covered to marinate. Thirty minutes is sufficient to cook to the taste of a true convert; after an hour the meat is done enough for almost anyone. It has the taste and texture of cooked fish, and the flavor is not strong. Excess juice is drained off, and salad ingredients added—sliced tomatoes, more chopped onions, diced carrot, halved hard boiled eggs, lettuce—none or all, as fancy dictates. Ideally, milk from pressed coconut meat should be poured over just before serving, but this is not essential.

Paul had arranged for an evening birthday party at the Hotel Tiare Tahiti, on the waterfront of the village of Vaitope. Candles had been added to the oil lamps, and our table was strewn with flowers. As usual in Polynesia, the dining room was a palm thatch-roof supported by palm trunks, open on all sides. A warm perfumed breeze blew through, and we could see the lights of fishing canoes across the lagoon.

Soon the drums warmed up. Every night is dance night on Bora Bora. As we dined—on more *poisson cru*—I was aware of movement in the outside darkness. There was no moon, but I thought I saw people crossing stray shafts of lantern light. Still, I wondered if there would be enough for a dance. Indeed! At the first sound of music couples flowed to the floor, until even the orchestra was innundated.

Bora Bora belles practice a no-wall-flowers system. They cluster in deep shadows beyond the ring of light from the room. They will dance when asked, but selection of a partner becomes a chancy affair. The crew of one yacht was reported to have solved the problem by the use of a Polaroid camera and flash gun: on development, the print was inspected, and each man made his choice: "I'll take the second from the left . . . I'll take the one by the tree . . ." The system worked fine until the *vahines*, with a fine Polynesian sense of humor, shifted positions in the darkness as soon as a picture was made.

Viatape, seen by daylight the next morning, turned out to be a village a single street wide. The beach was its front yard and the lagoon its swimming pool. Behind the last row of huts steeply soared the twin volcanic peaks which make the island's silhouette unforgettable. They are not cast in the familiar shape of cones, but are free-form, mammoth monoliths chiseled by a laughing god. There could be no finer monument for a sailor, and in the coral-girt depths below rests one of the great ocean wanderers. Alain Gerbault was a Frenchman who achieved fame on tennis courts; seeking escape and solitude, he widened his boundaries. His first exploit, a one-hundred day crossing of the Atlantic aboard an ancient and unsuitable cutter called *Firecrest*, was awarded the Blue Water Medal of the Cruising Club of America. Later he circumnavigated the globe, looking for the ideal final home port. It was Bora Bora.

There was some discussion as to how we should spend our

last day together. Paul planned a dawn departure for Raro-
tonga, 600 miles to the west, while I returned to Papeete. Sam
and Plazi solved the problem by finding an outrigger canoe
of a type unchanged since the great era of Polynesian seafaring, when early European explorers watched in awe as their
swift vessels sped past.

After tucking a few cans of bully beef and a jar of water in
a sack, we took off across the lagoon, seven people aboard a
craft only 18 feet overall, and no more than 18 inches wide.
Even overloaded there was an astonishing sensation of speed.
As each williwaw rifled down the slopes, the slim hull jetted
ahead, Sam scrambling outboard to add stability. A small
streamlined log extended on wooden poles acted as a second
hull, or outrigger, to port; but to starboard there was only a
stubby extension to take the stays of an unusual doublemasted
rig—which consisted of a short, thick spar stepped through
a thwart, and a second, longer and lighter mast acting like a
tall gaff. The result was a sail of high aspect ratio and drive.

It was swift and exciting sailing, over water clear as glass.
Heads of coral reached for the keel, sea fans seemed to brush
the steering paddle, patches of grass and schools of small fish
zipped by with kaleidoscopic forms and colors. When we
lifted our heads from the underwater garden, there was sunlight dancing on the fronds of palms rimming the sand
beaches, and splintering on the crests of tiny wavelets. Looking astern, Raiatea and Tahaa were indistinct through the
spume of breakers crashing on the barrier reef.

Soon we came to Point Matria, a finger of dazzling white
sand which disappeared under the surface without seeming to
get wet, as it hardly changed color. When we felt the canoe
touch, we stepped out to haul it ahead, then went back in the
water to swim. As we did, the Polynesian owner of the canoe
went a few yards inland, to where laden palms stood in a row.
Without ado he walked up a sloping trunk, as easily as a
bygone Jack Tar might go aloft by the ratlines.

By the time Paul and I arrived in the shade of a sea grape tree, green coconuts were waiting, tops neatly lopped off. Terii spread a straw mat on the sand, and began opening the cans of bully beef. I turned to see Paul grinning at me, again reading my thoughts. Raising his coconut, he said: "Here's to Tahiti. And Paradise."

For me, at the moment, they were one and the same.

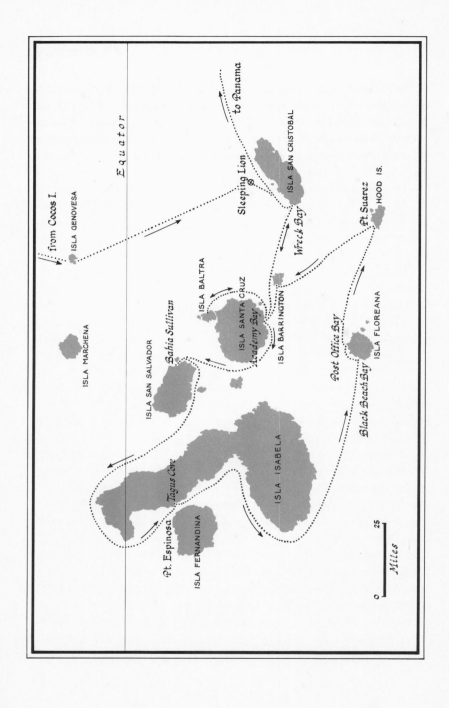

15

A Strange Cyclopean Scene

THE GALAPAGOS

The first European to set eyes on the Galapagos wrote home, "It looks as though God had caused it to rain stones."

Ever since Fray Tomás de Berlanga, Bishop of Panama, put that down in a letter to the King of Spain in 1535, travelers have been struggling to say it better. No one has. I am not going to try. For my cruise to the archipelago was a subjective experience, a phenomenon which took place out of the ordinary context of place and time, and I am still groping to sort out what I saw and felt. If in the process I can pass along some of either or both, I will be satisfied, for descriptive words alone cannot do justice to the Galapagos.

It was the birds which got to me first. They came out to meet us, even before dawn, as *Sans Terre* plowed rhythmically through Pacific swells. Astern our wake faded quickly, swallowed by the vastness, as invisible as vacuum closing behind a space ship. Already there seemed nothing remaining to form a point of reference. So I looked up at the stars for familiar faces. There were none. The Great Bear and Polaris had dropped below the horizon, and the rising Southern Cross brought along unknown galaxies. But as I looked, I was conscious of shapes moving amongst them, sensed rather than seen, while occasionally came the sibilant whisper of swift wings. Land could not be far.

Yet it was impossible to be sure. *Las Islas Encantadas,* The Enchanted Islands, early Spanish navigators had called the Galapagos, implying that along with other strange characteristics they had the power of changing position. Certainly many an ancient mariner had suffered thirst and hunger scanning an empty ocean after arriving where he believed them to be. Currents were to blame, decla ed later sailing directions: the Humboldt, the South Equatorial, the Equatorial Countercurrent, and even the destructive *El Niño*, named after the Holy Child, which some years around Christmas brings warm currents from the Gulf of Panama, upsetting nature's bizarre experiment of polar chill in the heart of the tropics. All these mighty swirls of ocean flow in different directions at different times and are subject to no known laws.

Again I scanned the chart. Genovesa should be there, I assured myself, staring over the bow, and Marchena somewhere in the blackness off to starboard. How to explain that less than a degree from the equator the name Marchena brought a shiver, or that it symbolized what I was expecting to find in the yet unseen archipelago? For many years before I had looked at macabre photographs of two thirst-parched sun-shriveled bodies lying on a beach, the last act of a celebrated mystery which had begun on another island of the Galapagos. Through a chain of circumstances still unexplained, the men had gone ashore at Marchena. It was less the fact of their death which lingered in my mind than the impression I had formed of the setting; barren, arid, tortured; neither sand desert nor stark unrelieved rock, but alien—a strange glimpse of another world, not really part of planet

Earth. What affected me most was the feeling that somehow it was a landscape in which the corpses of men seemed to belong.

In my reverie, I was almost unaware the night weld of sea and sky had dissolved into a horizon. Alvie Daniels had to remind me it was time for morning sights. Taking the sextant from its case, I looked aloft. What drew my attention were not the remote lifeless points of brilliance, light years away, but a profusion of life just overhead. Frigate birds beyond count soared in layers, the lowest seemingly attracted by the button on the tip of our radio antenna, the highest minute swept-wing silhouettes against the fast paling clouds. Across this serene warp scurried a busy woof of booby birds, beguiling clowns I had grown fond of as they escorted *Sans Terre* along the Mexican coast. Between the two darted gulls and cormorants, while tiny Galapagos storm petrels sipped at plankton in the swells, as delicate and precise as hummingbirds poised over a blossom.

Following the flight of a snow white booby, I had my Galapagos landfall, Genovesa, low on the horizon to port. Outlined against the dawn sky, it was not what I expected. No clusters of volcanic cones as serrated as the dorsal spines of some antediluvian monster, not even a single symmetric peak, a chalice inverted after the fires of Hell had poured forth. Instead, Genovesa looked as innocent as an oversize birthday cake with pale chocolate frosting.

It had its crater, all right, but it went down, not up. *Sans Terre* entered Darwin Bay over a lip rising almost to the surface; after we passed over the shallow doorstep without tripping the keel, the depth recorder showed the bottom plunging beyond its maximum range. All the line aboard would not have held us to an anchor in the center, but the *Sailing Directions* noted a ledge in the northeastern corner of the bay for "small craft with local knowledge."

For long minutes after coming to rest my shipmates and I

leaned on the rail and stared. Veteran wanderers of the Pacific wastes, Alvin Daniels and his wife Eula had previously visited the Galapagos, but still they shared my awe at our surroundings. An aura of unreality always sets in at the finish of a long ocean passage in a small boat, a feeling of strangeness at the cessation of an accustomed routine, a sensation of not belonging—of wanting yet not wanting the voyage to end. Suddenly the sea was almost wholly shut out. Darwin Bay formed a nearly perfect circle. Its walls were gray-black rock, not tall, but steep. The only thing which showed man had ever intruded were the painted names of passing yachts, saved from being offending graffiti by being reassuring links with the familiar world.

Lowering the dinghy, we began rowing toward a small wedge of sand, the only break in the encircling walls. As we neared, the way was blocked by an amorphous dark cloud roiling in the shallows. Alvie lay-to on the oars, trying to make out what it was. As we drifted closer, dorsal fins cut through the froth of churning tails. At that moment, it did not seem out of character to have the way blocked by a convocation of sharks, but later it appeared as a prank of the odd gods watching over this odd corner of the world. In five weeks, we did not see another shark. Now we had to wait until the pack moved away before we could get to shore and drag the dinghy above the tide line. For awhile we stood beside it, as though loath to abandon our symbol of escape.

Yet for us, quite literally, there was no escape. The Galapagos lie beyond the range of most small engine driven craft, and even we had passed the point of no return. *Sans Terre* could not make the return passage to Panama without taking on fuel. Our voyage to the Galapagos had depended in part on the fragile thread of a ham radio contact. While still in Costa Rica, uncertain of the course to pursue, chance put me on the frequency of station HC8FN. The operator identified himself as Forest Nelson, and reminded me that 20 years before we had spent part of the winter anchored near each other in the Bahamas. Afterwards, he had made three extended cruises to the Galapagos; finally he had sold his boat and was now settled ashore on Isla Santa Cruz: could he be of help?

I explained we lacked papers to enter, and were reluctant to detour to Panama for them, as it would mean bypassing Cocos Island, and also that we would need fuel after making the run direct. "No problem," Forest came back across the intervening miles, whittled to nothing by the miracle of single-sideband transmission. Forest would arrange to have drums of diesel aboard the rusted World War II tank landing craft which waddled out from Guayaquil each month, and would ask the *comandante* of the Ecuadoran navy stationed in Wreck Bay, who had local jurisdiction, to allow us to enter without visas from Panama. We arranged a schedule for the following day.

Next morning, HC8FN again came in loud and clear. All was arranged, reported Forest jubilantly. The *Cristobal Carrier* would bring out fuel on her next trip; and the commanding officer of the naval station had messaged his superior in Guayaquil, who had granted permission to waive the usual requirements for visiting yachts. We signed off on a joyous note, promising to keep in touch on the way out. I never heard Forest again. His transmitter packed up the same afternoon. Thus we did not know that the Chief of Naval Operations had countermanded the orders of his junior officers when they arrived on his desk in the capital city of Quito; so we did not have permission to enter; nor that the skipper of the *Cristobal Carrier* had refused to take aboard the drums of diesel oil consigned to us, as he already had too much cargo, so we could not leave.

Sans Terre, swinging at anchor in Darwin Bay, had cruised from Los Angeles southward along the west coast of Mexico and the Central American republics to Golfito, Costa Rica, before taking off for Cocos Island, and thence to the Galapagos. With occasional fueling stops our shakedown voyage had already covered 4000 miles, enough to cross the Atlantic Ocean with plenty to spare. The coastwise part of the cruise had been made more pleasurable due to Alvin Daniels' familiarity with the coast, the result of serving as mate on a small cargo vessel which wartime demand for bananas had sent into every bight where donkeys could bring down stems from the hills.

Thus the theories which had gone into a thick envelope marked Project Home Afloat—signalizing my transition from sail to power—were now successful realities. In comfort—nay, luxury—*Sans Terre* had carried us past the semi-desert lands of Baja California, and into lush tropic bays indenting the Isthmus of Panama, living up to the meaning of her name: "Free from the Land." A Grand Banks 42, extra fuel tanks for extra range had been added when she was built in Hong Kong, but even a camel—or a Galapagos tortoise—must drink sometime.

It was probably just as well we did not know the complications awaiting us in Wreck Bay as we stood on the beach of Isla Genovesa, called *Quito Sueño*, Nightmare Island, on some early Spanish charts. To be confronted by nature Galapagos-style was enough as a starter. But again the birds came out to meet us, to guide us, to make clear that the island was not a desolate waste, but a veritable Garden of Eden for those who belonged. And we were welcome. The first greeters were a pair of swallow-tail gulls, noisy little fellows with big bright eyes rimmed with orange. They are night feeders, and might have considered our pre-dawn meeting offshore sufficient introduction. They advanced to our feet and retreated, leading us up the beach, to proudly present a ball of fluff in a nest under a thorn bush where the beach ended. While we admired, they stood on tiptoes and bragged loudly.

Next came the mockers, which we were soon to think of as

dead end kids, precocious but naughty urchins, at once amusing and infuriating. The advance guard deployed in the dinghy as we alighted, peeking into camera cases and trying to sip from the water bottle; others scurried away from under each footfall, darting back to investigate a shoelace or discarded matchstick. Meanwhile the main body marched along as a flanking escort, chattering among themselves, obviously discussing what the strange bipeds who walked instead of flew away from the sea would do next. Obviously they did not recognize us as Man, the Destroyer.

Swiftly I realized the stories I had read about the lack of fear shown by Galapagos life were true. It had been a source of wonder to the earliest explorers even as they slaughtered for food, and Charles Darwin, whose observations in 1835 led to the theory of evolution, felt it necessary to conclude his "description of the natural history of these islands by giving an account of the extreme tameness of the birds." Although the archipelago is among the few places on earth where aboriginal man never existed, it has served as a larder for over four centuries of buccaneers, whalers, sealers, turtlers, tuna fishermen, and assorted outcasts from civilization. Since World War II, the Galapagos can no longer be considered uninhabited. Yet we could walk among the birds like a latter-day St. Francis of Assisi.

On either hand birds by the hundreds went on with the ritual of display courtship, the brooding of eggs, the feeding of young, as we passed within touching distance. We paused to see the outcome of raucous arguments over choice building sites, and laughed at titanic struggles over shards of nesting materials. So far as the local residents of Genovesa were concerned, we were only birds of passage in strange plumage, not worthy of rank in the pecking order which regulates avian society.

Even frigates guarding chicks paid no attention, imposing characters with wingspans wider than our outstretched arms, staring over blood-red air bladders, basketball size, inflated under long hooked beaks. One slash would have cut like a razor, but they watched us approach within striking distance without moving. It was the same with boobies—red-footed, blue-footed, and white—and gannets and gulls and other varieties I did not recognize. Naturalist William Beebe recorded 24 species on Genovesa during a short visit, but what impressed him more than the profusion was the unreality of being able to study specimens which did not flee on approach.

The rookery noises arose in a cacaphony nowise related to familiar bird sounds. I could detect peanut stand peeps, castanet clicks, rusty door hinge squeaks, baby rattles, wolf whistles, the mewing of kittens, sheep bleats, hog-wallow grunts, and rasping blasts like old-fashion hand-operated automobile horns.

Sea lions watching from the perimeter added to the bedlam. In the Galapagos, they are almost as curious as the birds, but more circumspect, as befits a species which survives solely because it is neither good to eat nor looks pretty around a woman's neck, while their cousins, the fur-bearing seals, are almost extinct. Females and their pups tagged along behind like dogs, whiskered faces peering up from the waters just offshore. Only bulls guarding harems were touchy, but we knew from the islands of Mexico that their bark was worse than their bite.

At the far boundary of the rookery the lava was pierced by a series of tidal pools. All were occupied. Yet we desperately wanted a swim, and despite the bellowing as we shed our clothes, felt the climate more friendly than at the beach, where fins still protruded. When I eased into an oversize bathtub, an entire family of sea lions scrambled up the far side. They stopped before going far, with an air of waiting for me to finish, and hurry up about it.

I was slow, because the other end of the pool was draped with marine iguanas, basking on the rocks. Looking at them,

I was for the first time fully aware of the landscape. Earlier I had been too fascinated by the birds to get the full impact. But the hideous reptiles, lying in the sun to warm blood corpsecold, were reminders of the photographs from Marchena. They, too, seemed to fit the setting. For I floated in my pool looking out at unimaginable desolation. Perhaps in retrospect less spectacular than other islands pocked with towering volcanic cauldrons, Genovesa's origin was nevertheless unmistakable: molten rock flowing like pitch, cooling layer on layer into forms tortured and fantastic beyond description. An astronaut saw the moon's surface as "pale gray cement chopped at with a pick-ax." Had he glimpsed this equally alien world, he would have been harder put for a comparison. Everywhere spills of lava are spiked, crenellated, twisted, bubbled, shattered, tumbled, into a million-million bizarre forms, a nowhere-flat surface where in places walking a hundred yards could take a day and cost a man his life, because he could not carry enough drinking water to get back.

In terms of the earth's timetable, the Galapagos are newly minted. Studies put the age of most of the islands at less than a million years, and none much more than two. They surged from ocean depths in a mighty display of primordial fireworks—2,000 volcanos, estimated Darwin, and the figure has never been challenged. When the eruptions ended, there were 13 major islands, plus innumerable islets and rocks, totaling some 3,000 square miles. Another freak of nature placed them in an atmospheric vacuum. Gales are unknown, and even normal winds are fickle and for long periods can disappear entirely. Rain is a rarity. Thus neither erosion from the sea or sky has taken place, nor has the accumulation of humas and detritus through the decomposition of organic matter. Except for a very few areas, the Galapagos remain creation in the raw, not yet ready for man. Perhaps it is this which makes them frightening.

When we went back to *Sans Terre*, we found the birds had

taken over. Pelicans roosted on awning supports over the after deck, and the bow pulpit was festooned with boobies. Those who had first achieved a foothold on the slippery stainless steel tubing had developed a fine proprietary air. Interlopers were warned off with shrill squawks and rapier beaks. The same group seemed there next morning when we got under way to circumnavigate the island. Neither the clanking anchor chain nor swells outside dislodged some hard-core survivors, who had to flap their wings without cease to maintain balance. Still, they refused space to potential hitch-hikers from our swarming escort, which was constantly augmented. As we followed each squiggle of coastline, barely clear of backwash from surf dashing against sheer walls, clouds rose from other rookeries to join the parade. Genovesa will always remain in my memory as the island of birds.

By slipping away at midnight, finding our way out of the crater-harbor by radar and fathometer, we avoided prolonged farewells. Only the stars were with us when *Sans Terre* crossed the equator. It was too early for Father Neptune to come aboard, but we were in time to see the Sleeping Lion awaken with the dawn. In soft morning light we crept between two rock pinnacles, unknown and unheralded, which dwarfed the Faraglioni of Capri, a tourist wonder of the Mediterranean world. It was not until we launched the dinghy, and I took photographs from a quarter-mile away, that my eye succeeded in grasping the true scale. When Alvie steered *Sans Terre* through the cleft, our sturdy ocean-going vessel was reduced to a barely visible speck.

Leon Dormiente lay not far off the coast of Isla San Cristobal, where man has establihed himself, both on the shore and in the highlands. The anchor had no sooner plummeted into Wreck Bay than a launch approached from the naval administration building. In the stern was a lieutenant, very courteous and efficient, who took our unstamped passports and said in excellent English that everything would probably be all right.

I missed the stress toward the end of the sentence, and forthwith entered in the log a note of thanksgiving. Soon afterward the launch came out again, bearing a young lieutenant commander, who introduced himself as the *commandante*. We soon learned everything was far from all right. He began by apologizing, then told us what had happened along the chain of command. Now that we had actually arrived, he would send a dispatch to the Chief of Naval Operations, asking reconsideration. Meanwhile, we could come ashore—but not leave port.

After a look at the drab settlement, I prodded to find how soon a reply might be expected. The *comandante* shrugged. It was sometimes hard to get through to Quito by radio, and anyway there would be no way of telling when the admiral might make up his mind. But meanwhile, we had the freedom of Wreck Bay. He started to leave, but paused at the rail to add it was most unusual for small vessels requiring substantial amounts of fuel to come to the Galapagos—in fact, *Sans Terre* was the first of her kind to arrive on a pleasure cruise. Thus there might be a little difficulty in getting the required quantity. Then he let us have the second bit of news: the *Cristobal Carrier* would not be bringing the drums Forest Nelson had ordered. Further, there was such a shortage of diesel oil in the islands that the Wreck Bay municipal electric generating plant had curtailed its schedule, so there was none to buy ashore, and he had none to spare from the navy's operating allowance. But a supply ship might be coming out soon —by the end of the month—and he would try to arrange enough for us.

We went ashore rather chastened to find Wreck Bay a frontier settlement of frame houses and rusting corrugated iron roofs, token of increasing population pressures driving men further afield. Approximately 3,500 *Galapageños*—mostly Ecuadoran, but embracing 14 nationalities—now eke out an existence in the archipelago. They are concentrated almost entirely on San Cristobal and Santa Cruz islands, where cloud covered uplands provide some soil and moisture. As we walked the street rimming the beach, we found shops selling onions and potatoes, dried fish and beans, canned beef and flour. One time through and we had done the town. Thus on the fourth day our gratitude was boundless when the *comandante* took the responsibility of granting "provisional" clearance for Academy Bay. Quito had still not responded.

Liberation added spice to the January day, mid-summer on our side of the equator. A mild breeze kicked up little wavelets, which *Sans Terre* drove through without wetting the deck, despite a flurry of white water under the bluff bow. Almost on course lay Isla Santa Fe, more commonly called Barrington. A confusing detail is that all the islands have both Spanish and English names, the latter carrying the ring of nobility although mostly bestowed by buccaneers. Thinking we could have a look without violating our parole, we nosed in close, to find a paradise for sea lions. Large colonies snoozed in rock girt coves, or body-surfed in the creaming breakers, while bulls maintained a ceaseless offshore patrol, bellowing lustily at the intruding bulk of *Sans Terre*. It was a place to return to.

Forest Nelson was waiting to indicate the best anchorage when we entered Academy Bay. After three protracted cruises to the Galapagos, he had sold his boat to become a pioneer in tourism. Ashore he showed us cottages he was constructing around a central dining room-lounge, at the tip of a lava rock flow into the sea. Forest envisioned small groups flying from Quito to Isla Baltra, where the Ecuadoran government had enlarged an airstrip built by the United States to patrol the approaches to the Panama Canal during World War II; thence they would be brought by boat to Academy Bay. Later would come an overnight expedition on horseback to the highlands of Santa Cruz, and finally a visit to Floreana.

Academy Bay we found to have charm, despite having

mushroomed even more swiftly than Wreck Bay. Our near neighbors ashore were the Angermeyer brothers, Carl, Gus, and Fritz, who had arrived from Germany in 1938. We were anchored so close to their houses that Carl's pet marine iguanas swam under *Sans Terre* whenever they foraged for algae on the harbor bottom. Carl painted, struggling to capture on canvas the special quality of the local landscapes, while Gus collected Galapagos curiosa—shells, weird formations of lava, driftwood. Together they know the islands as no others.

Despite a hospitable welcome, our glimpses of the uninhabited islands made the haunts of man pall. Salvation came sooner than hoped. The lieutenant who had first boarded in Wreck Bay arrived in an ancient river patrol boat to assume command of the naval station. He invited us alongside to take on a bit of fuel for a cruise, and afterwards his first official act was to extend our clearance to visit any islands we wished. While our permit remained "provisional," we were free. The sole stipulation was that before leaving for Panama we report again to the navy. It was an unnecessary proviso, as we both knew.

The same afternoon we watched the pigmy traces of civilization drop astern. As soon as *Sans Terre* turned the corner of the bay, we looked upon terrain unchanged since the first awed intruder had sailed past. To starboard, Isla Santa Cruz towered as an almost perfect cone, except for being divided into twin craters at the very summit. Today it was clear of cloud, and we could see green. Yet I was not fooled by the aspect of vegetation on the lower slopes. Up close, only spike-leaved opuntia cactus could find a foothold in the lava, alternating with thorny shrubs, which never develop into trees. They are covered with bark as tough as armor plate, and put forth a few green shoots only at the tips of their branches. Their ability to survive depends on their capacity to absorb and retain the scant moisture falling during the season of the *garua* drizzles, May to November. There would be no shade and no water under them for a castaway. Let disaster strike *Sans Terre*—a fire in the engine compartment, for example, knocking out our ability to communicate while putting us at the mercy of the currents—and we would be no better off than earlier victims of these inhospitable shores.

Yet there is a magnifiance about the Galapagos—a starkness, an austerity, a purity of line—which fascinates more than it repels, unique among the cruising areas of the world. Charles Darwin, in *The Voyage of the Beagle*, called it "a strange Cyclopean scene," but perhaps its peculiar appeal is hinted in another observation of the great naturalist: "Here . . . both in space and time, we seem to be brought somewhat near to that great fact—that mystery of mysteries—the first appearance of new beings on this earth."

Islands literally lay at every point of the compass, although many were out of sight over the horizon. The larger of those we could see from the flying bridge conformed to the description in the U.S. Navy *Sailing Directions:* "roughly circular in shape . . . (having) one or more principal craters towards their centers with several smaller ones on their flanks." The exception to the rule is Isabela, lifting to port, which consists of five major craters and lesser beyond count. Some geologists believe the flow of lava was so great five separate islands were joined together at their bases, forming a contiguous land mass 80 miles in length, by far the largest of the Galapagos islands. As the highest cone towers to 5,540 feet, and depths of nearly 2,000 fathoms are found close offshore, it means that the eruptions lifted some three miles above the ocean floor.

Before sunset we anchored under a dramatic symbol of fiery creation. At one corner of Bahia Sullivan rose a monolith of black rock, not much bigger at the base in proportion to its height than the Empire State building, and seemingly nearly as tall. Looking up as we sipped an evening cocktail, Alvie and I decided even a wee tremor could put the whole mass across our deck. But it was mosquitoes coming off Isla

Bartholomé which caused us to shift our anchorage farther offshore, we told ourselves.

On leaving Academy Bay a rendezvous had been arranged with Carl and Gus Angermeyer. They were undertaking a round trip voyage of some 300 miles in their little ketch *Simba* in the hope of selling paintings and artifacts to tourists aboard a cruise ship scheduled to make a three-hour stop in Tagus Cove, on Isla Isabela. Getting there, *Sans Terre* crossed the equator twice, as the magic dividing line cuts across the northern tip of Isabela. When we entered Tagus Cove from one side, the huge cruise liner was steaming out the other, looking like a child's wind-up toy in comparison to the towering walls.

The Angermeyers had been disappointed. Due to a change in the ships' announced departure time, they had hardly gotten aboard when it was time to leave. They were somewhat cheered by our arrival, and happy to accompany us to Point Espinosa, on Isla Fernandina: our good fortune, as they showed us details we might otherwise have overlooked. For as Genovesa in my mind symbolizes birds, Punta Espinosa is fixed as the extraordinary showcase of bizarre Galapagos life. Several species do not even exist elsewhere in the archipelago. Crossing Canal Bolivar, the volcanic slopes of Fernandina loomed ever more barren. But on coming to anchor near *Simba,* we found ourselves off a rare oasis of greenery, a mangrove swamp lying between the lava wastes and the sea. The point itself was an outstretched arm of black sand and ground-up seashells, making it a mottled gray; the outer extremity was like a hand spread open, with surf creaming into coves formed by the fingers.

My introduction to local phenomenon came even before going ashore. In the lee of the point, the sun was scorching. A swim to cool off had afforded more than the anticipated effect. Diving from the stern platform, I came up gasping. In comparison to the air, the water was icy. Then I remembered the Humboldt current, the great surge from the Antarctic which flows northward along the coast of South America without losing its polar chill. Drying hastily, I found among the navigational gadgets the same sensitive thermometer which had located the Gulf Stream for *Finisterre* on three races to Bermuda. Lowered over the side, the mercury barely topped 60 degrees—exactly 16 miles from the equator.

Long ago penguins had been swept away from their ice fields at the bottom of the world by the same current, and ashore we were greeted by the most northerly colony in existence, winsome little fellows whose ancestors had adapted to a strange new home. They regarded us with the gravity of judges as we approached small islets fringing the mangrove swamp. Sharing their ledges were birds hardly deserving to retain the title. Elsewhere, cormorants are aerial acrobats, swooping to snatch fish from cresting seas. On Point Espinosa a species has evolved which uses the remaining stumps of wings only for balance when hopping toward the water. Once submerged, webbed feet which grew larger as the wings became vestigial, take over. So profuse was the food supply due to the feeding chain based on plankton borne by the Humboldt Current, their ancestors had simply given up flying, doubtless on the theory there is no use going to the grocery when the icebox is full at home.

Totally different forms of life awaited us on the barren peninsula forming Point Espinosa. Marine iguanas were massed on the rim of the cove we chose for landing. When we pulled the dinghy clear of the water, they retreated, then formed a circle. Most individuals were approximately three feet in length, but many were larger. Like miniature dragons, ugly and black and scaly, they stared at us through slitted reptilian eyes. A ridge of horny dorsal spines bristled along their backs from neck to tail as they raised the fore-part of their bodies on taloned feet. I had hardly thought that all necessary to complete the medieval notion of a dragon would be the ability to breathe steam, when several did—if disturbed, the marine iguana ejects a vapor-fine spray of salt water from its nostrils.

Trudging through the coarse volcanic sand of Punta Espinosa with the Angermeyers, I felt as close to being in a Lost World as could exist on planet Earth. Flightless cormorants and marine iguanas are indigenous to the Galapagos, yet show their resemblance to similar species elsewhere. In fact, naturalists agree that the forebearers of all living things in the archipelago except a few long-range flying and swimming creatures arrived as flotsam borne by currents, castaways who survived by being able to adapt to the conditions they found. Little wonder Charles Darwin was startled into questioning the tenant of faith which maintained that the world and its denizens had been created complete in 4004 B.C. Darwin believed the Bible, but after he cataloged thirteen species of finches obviously descended from a common ancestor, each of which had developed beaks of different shape and size to survive by different means, he had noted in his diary: "One might really fancy that from an original paucity of birds, one species had been taken and modified for different ends." A quarter-century later his observation in the Galapagos formed the basis for *The Origin of Species*. The revolution of thought it engendered had such a profound effect on the future of mankind that some historians rate the humble *Beagle*'s cruise among the islands as second in importance only to the voyages of Columbus.

Of the exotic creatures described by Darwin, the most difficult to find today are the giant land tortoises. I was content to settle for the examples roaming enclosures at the Charles Darwin Research Station in Academy Bay. Others survive on Santa Cruz and Isla Isabela, but in such inaccessible upland fastnesses only dedicated naturalists are likely to seek them out. Unfortunately, the *galápagos*, once so numerous as to give the archipelago its name, possessed characteristics guaranteeing virtual extinction—they were not only good to eat, but could be kept for long periods, before the days of refrigeration. Commander David Porter, U.S.N., captain of the frigate *Essex,* wrote in 1815: "Vessels on whaling voyages among these islands generally take on board from two to three hundred . . . and stow them in the hold, where, strange as it may appear, they have been known to live for a year, without food or water."

Behind us as we explored Punta Espinosa reared a volcano which had last erupted six months earlier. Carl Angermeyer had seen a mushroom cloud and heard an explosion on 11 June 1968; he had sailed over from Academy Bay a few days later to find that although there was no fresh lava flow, the bottom of the crater had lowered nearly 1,000 feet. And across Canal Bolivar, we looked upon a part of Isla Isabela which had been sea-floor not many years before. A subterranean convulsion had caused a section of coast to rise so swiftly that fish were left stranded, and langouste died in their caverns. Nature is not yet finished with the Galapagos.

Perhaps a tree standing almost at the tip of Punta Espinosa came closest to symbolizing for me the wonder and mystery of the archipelago. Equatorial sun burned my bare shoulders as I looked upon swimming penguins. Sea lions by the hundreds ranged between the fingers of the outermost ledges, the bulls roaring ceaselessly at invaders real or imaginary, while mothers nursed pups in the coves. Scarlet crabs, bright as painted tin, darted in and out of surf creaming onto coal-black lava. Frigate birds wheeled and bobbies plummeted from a blue sky into green shallows. And there before me were the stark skeleton branches of a tree which somehow had managed to achieve maturity in sand laved by salt water. As I came closer, sea lions sleeping at the base lifted their heads, and marine iguanas, which had climbed into the branches to come closer to the warming sun, spat at me through their nostrils. The tree and its denizens vividly recalled that I was an intruder.

Man's existence in such surroundings is tenuous. The past history of the Galapagos is one of strife, suffering, and bloodshed. Humans arrived in small waves through the centuries, briefly clinging to the inhospitable shores before being flung back into the sea. Ability to survive came from discovery of an oasis providing drinking water, which still limits settlement to a few parts of very few islands. One of them is Isla Santa Maria, or Floreana, whither *Sans Terre* bore us after Punta Espinosa. It is the island of the Galapagos which summarizes for me the complex creature cataloged by zoologists as Homo sapiens.

The first mention of an inhabitant on Floreana was contained in the log of Captain Porter of the *Essex*, who put in at Post Office Bay to find a marooned Irishman named Patrick Watkins, clad in "ragged clothes, scarce sufficient to cover his nakedness, and covered with vermin; his red hair and beard matted, his skin much burnt, from constant exposure to the sun, and so wild and savage . . . that he struck everyone with horror." Watkins grew vegetables which he traded passing whalers for rum; his garden, hidden in the inaccessible uplands, was tended by unfortunate sailors who had been stretching their legs on shore after weeks at sea, when Watkins captured them at gunpoint. His tenure ended in 1809 when he sailed for Guayaquil with five of his impressed workers. They were either eaten or forced overboard when water ran short, as Watkins arrived alone.

Next came one General José Villamil in 1832, who had arranged with the Ecuadoran government to provide political prisoners to establish a plantation. On Darwin's visit three years later, 300 men were grubbing in the sparse soil, no better off than the slaves of Watkins. On Villamil's death, a successor made life even more miserable for the enforced colonists. They were mercilessly flogged, and on attempting escape were hunted with dogs. A revolt caused the project and the island to be abandoned, but in 1870 another attempt was made at colonization with convicted labor. This time the overseer was murdered by his charges, and again the island lay empty.

So it was in September 1929 when a German dentist, Karl Friedrich Ritter, came ashore with a former patient, Dora Koerwin. In bleak post-World War I Berlin, Dr. Ritter had evolved a philosophy of return to nature which involved eating only vegetables and fruit produced by his own toil, discarding unnecessary clothing, and shunning contact with other humans. Why he had chosen Floreana for his experiment is unclear, but he had chosen well: when he arrived it was wholly his, an incipient Paradise or an intractable Purgatory, depending upon the point of view. Part of the doctor's meticulous preparation for passing the remainder of his life away from civilization was to have all his teeth extracted, and replaced by plates of stainless steel.

In the summer of 1932 he was astounded and upset by the arrival of another German couple, Heinz and Margret Wittmer. By this time, Dr. Ritter was well established in a cottage in the semi-fertile uplands near a trickle of potable water. His industry had been rewarded by a thriving garden. Far from welcoming company, when the Wittmers called, he made it clear that he and Dora wished to remain alone. Frau Wittmer was pregnant. When she asked if he would help when the time came, Dr. Ritter replied brusquely he had not come to the Galapagos to practice medicine.

The Wittmers departed, and before long, with matching Teutonic zeal, had established themselves on the shore of Blackbeach Bay. Water had to be transported, but they managed to start a garden and begin construction of a house. Floreana at that juncture might have become the Paradise each couple sought in its own fashion, but Satan arrived that same October—a veritable devil incarnate in the guise of an unbeautiful woman calling herself Baroness Eloise Bosquet de Wagner Wehrborn. She had three companions, Robert Phillipson, Alfred Lorenz, and an Ecuadoran who had joined the entourage in Paris. In both dress and actions the group was apparently the forerunner of the hippy "family."

Before leaving Guayaquil for Floreana—and no one knows why she picked that particular island, either—the Baroness had announced grandiose plans for building a resort hotel which would make Floreana the Mecca of the Pacific. She and her helpers were to make preliminary plans. From the first, she regarded the island as her exclusive property, with the prior settlers allowed to remain on sufferance. Her usual costume was a brassiere and shorts, but, as beads had not yet come into vogue, she packed a pistol. She brandished it frequently, and used it on occasion, usually on animals, which she then attempted to nurse back to health. But a peon working for the Baroness apparently fell victim to the small automatic, and the Ecuadoran in her family was shipped out with a bullet in his stomach. Lorenz was beaten and frequently threatened with worse after he had been displaced as favorite by the huskier Phillipson.

The Baroness promoted herself in dispatches to Empress of the Galapagos, and even before the denouement, the world press blossomed with plans for Hotel Paradiso and details of the idyllic life on Floreana, usually subtitled Eden Isle, Utopia, or the Island of Love. Despite the nearest thing to a mail service being a barrel set on a platform in Post Office Bay —holdover from whaling days, when outbound vessels left letters for homeward-bound ships to pick up—the Baroness managed to file hot copy with the skill of a Madison Avenue publicist.

Then in March 1934 the Baroness and Phillipson suddenly vanished, a drama still ranking among the outstanding causes célèbres of the twentieth century. The world press never gave more space to a mystery. The Ecuadoran government appointed a commission to investigate. Its reports were seized upon by journalists liberated from the shackles of verifiable facts by distance and the difficulties of communications.

263

Speculation filled endless columns, making the Galapagos more famous than the discoveries by Darwin. Back on Floreana, Lorenz was distraught; Dr. Ritter wrote a letter implicating Heinz Wittmer, then died, ostensibly from eating tainted chicken—odd diet for an avowed vegetarian; and a mysterious American yacht was reported to have taken off the missing pair, impossible to verify.

Even across the years the details came back vividly as *Sans Terre* closed Blackbeach Bay. A boat put off as we dropped anchor, and Rolf Wittmer introduced himself as he climbed aboard. He was the baby Margret had been carrying when she visited Dr. Ritter, and met the curt refusal to help. At the last moment, when Frau Wittmer was in great pain, during labor, and normal delivery seemed hopeless, Heinz Wittmer left her to plead with Dr. Ritter. The physician had responded without delay, and descended from his aerie to save the lives of mother and child.

Rolf rowed us ashore. Margret Wittmer welcomed us, a sweetfaced *hausfrau* grandmother who had survived pioneer hardships perhaps unequaled among her generation of women. Sipping homemade wine in a curtained dining room, surrounded by nostalgic reminders of a homeland far away, it was hard to remember the hostile environment beyond the tiny clearing, or conceive what carving it from the wilderness had cost in human terms. Outside, chickens cackled, a cow grazed, children played, and Rolf had gone back to hammering on a boat he was building in the side yard.

Thus the following morning, going ashore at Post Office Bay, I had a feeling of closer association with the mystery of Floreana than when face to face with the surviving protagonists. For Lorenz had crossed the same sliver of beach to go aboard *Dinamita*, which was to carry him to Marchena, and in the scrub and cactus thickets nearby the Baroness had lived and planned Hotel Paradiso—and undoubtedly is still there,

close, a bundle of bones stuffed into a lava cave alongside what
is left of her last lover, Phillipson.

Although elsewhere Lorenz probably would have been
jailed on circumstantial evidence, he remained free for a fate
more in keeping with the setting of the drama. In July a
Norwegian named Nuggerud, member of a colony which had
established itself in Academy Bay, happened to stop in
Dinamita, a small boat he used for fishing. Lorenz begged to
be taken to Wreck Bay, where he could find means to leave
the Galapagos. They paused briefly at Santa Cruz, and continued on what should have been an overnight passage. The
next morning they were sighted from Wreck Bay, becalmed.
No further thought was given *Dinamita*, which might have
been fishing, but an old tragedy of the islands was repeating
itself: no wind, no motor, no means to make headway, the keel
gripped by currents; sooner or later, no food and no water.
On 17 November 1934 an American tuna clipper sighted a rag
on a pole at Marchena, some hundred miles to the northwest.
Going ashore, the captain found the bodies. Later, photographs were made, the visual images I carried approaching
Genovesa.

At Post Office Bay we went through the ritual of leaving
a packet of letters in the barrel, and taking out some to mail
that had been left by a Tahitibound yacht several weeks
before, but I could not shake a sense of malevolence. If it is
possible for an island to be accursed, Floreana qualifies—and
its dire history goes on. Not long before our arrival a woman
visitor walking with a group at Post Office Bay failed to
return with the others when the boat was ready to leave, and
was never seen again—"captured by the Baroness, who is not
dead, but lurks in a cave," explained Carl Angermeyer with
mock seriousness on our return to Academy Bay—and before
Sans Terre had even arrived at the Panama Canal there was
another mysterious disappearance. An Ecuadoran vanished
while hunting in the uplands. No one knows more than that

his donkey came down to the shore with waterbottles still tied to the saddle, the sure kiss of death in the Galapagos.

On our departure, Floreana—the Island of Love, Eden Isle, Utopia—was shrouded by unseasonal *garua* clouds as it lowered into the sea, apt symbolism. We were happy to drop anchor behind Point Suaréz, on Hood Island, fifty miles to the eastward, back among the sea lions and the birds. Hood is the sole nesting site of the majestic waved albatross, which roams the vast and lonely southern oceans on wings spanning eight feet, but always finds its way back to the same infinitesimal dot on the chart. White bobbies—to me the most beautiful and graceful of all the sea birds—watched curiously as we picked up barnacles torn loose by surf and tossed to the elevated nesting plateau. As I held giant shells in cupped hands I was able to understand for the first time accounts in old log books of ancient wooden ships remaining trapped in areas of light winds until they sank under their crews; barnacles larger than demi-tasse cups, growing in clusters on a hull, would reduce the smartest sailer to a sluggish hulk, while the teredos—voracious shipworms—bored through the planking from below.

About when it looked like *Sans Terre* might be trapped, too, the Ecuadoran navy came to the rescue. After pausing at Barrington to get acquainted with the acquatic artists we had seen outward bound, we arrived in Academy Bay to find the supply ship on schedule, with fuel aboard for us, as the *comandante* had promised. Nuzzling against her iron flank, *Sans Terre* was efficiently given a transfusion of 500 gallons. We had covered 661 miles cruising between islands. It is a sizable archipelago. Astern lay 17 anchorages on 12 islands, yet we had encountered humans ashore in only three places.

After we had returned to Wreck Bay to thank our Navy benefactors and depart with our papers in proper order, we made a detour to pass once more through the mighty cleft of the Sleeping Lion. As well as any other single phenomenon, it symbolized the natural forces which had created the Galapagos. And while Marchena lay far to the west of our course for Panama, I had not forgotten its spell or symbolism, either. The Galapagos are a memory which will never fade. And the birds followed us a long way, as reminders.

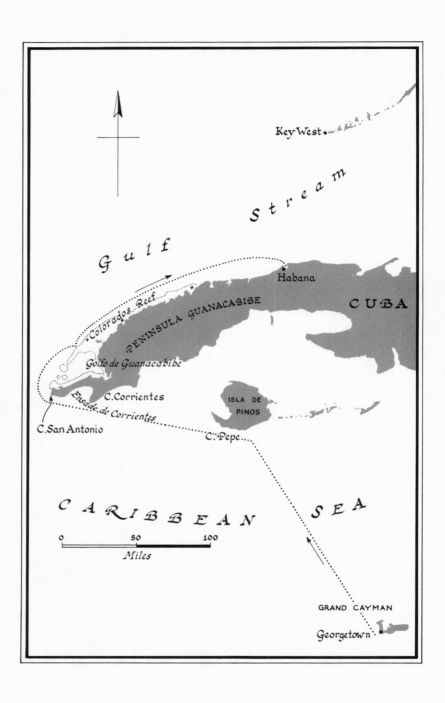

16
Twenty-four Hours
THE YUCATAN CHANNEL

This is the story of a day. Not a special day, just a day at sea. The story could be about the day before, or the day after, and it would be nearly the same. Days at sea can be pretty much alike, so long as the weather is good. But not exactly alike. No two are ever exactly alike.

This story is about Wednesday, 27 March 1946.

At noon Hod Fuller noted in the log: "Flying fish weather." Years later on browsing through the salt-stained book—a wonderful winter evening pastime, for so much of sailing is remembering—the phrase caught my attention. "Flying fish weather," and all it implies to a sailor: the blue of the sea, flecked by white, the pause and thrust of a boat off before a steady warm breeze, the fall of water under the bow, the iridescent darts of flying fish skittering from crest to crest. I read the rest of the entries, and located in an attic locker the chart cross-hatched and circled by our navigator on that particular day, and it came back to me, clear and perfect. It was like living it again.

Usually, at the end of a passage you remember only the passage. The individual days go along, good or bad. Watch follows watch. There are the jobs of ship keeping and checking, the routine chores of maintaining a crew. Time telescopes. At the moment each day has a sense of novelty, but later you think of the whole while the parts are forgotten. The longer the voyage, the more this is true, until a nomad of the ocean wastes like Conor O'Brien writes: "The homeward passage was entirely orthodox . . . I put in, most properly, to the Falkland Islands, being again short of potatoes."

So I am reversing the process and making this the story of a day rather than of a passage.

We had left Georgetown, Grand Cayman, shortly before sunset on Monday, after a winter of cruising the waters of Haiti and Jamaica. On the advice of the captain of a Cayman Island turtling schooner we had laid a course for Cape Pepe, Isle of Pines. By so doing we lengthened our passage to Cape San Antonio, the western tip of Cuba, but gained a lee and possible shelter if the weather gods should decide to package and deliver a late season norther.

Our indefatigable navigator, John Cowperthwaite, plotted a series of sun lines on Tuesday, and at twilight added a batch of stars. During his Navy years aboard a weather ship stationed in the Aleutians John had ample time to perfect his use of a sextant. I trusted his sights, and all of them put us off to the eastward of the rhumb line. The current *Sailing Directions* said that "the current on the southern side of Cuba is variable and generally very strong. Its usual course is to the westward. . . ." But the 1827 edition of Blunt's *Coast Pilot* quoted "the great Captain Livingston" as observing an "easterly current, which often runs very strong," causing shipmasters to make the Isle of Pines when expecting Cape San Antonio, with fatal results, as was "the case of a very fine ship a few years since."

So during the afternoon we had altered course slightly, and at 9:30 that night, after running out our distance, we swung sharply to parallel the unseen coast. At 11:00 Cape Pepe came abeam, a weak flicker instead of the 16 mile light promised by the chart. An easterly current had been setting us outside the circle of visibility, a potentially dangerous place to be.

After midnight the breeze had dropped but the sea had not. To stop slatting we lowered the main and ran the engine slowly. At dawn on Wednesday the wind came back to gradually freshen; at 10:00 we set a cruising spinnaker. At noon Hod made his entry, "Flying fish weather." And that is where this particular day begins:

Carib's position was logged as 21 degrees 37 minutes north latitude, 84 degrees 04 minutes west latitude. Some 17 miles to starboard lay the Guanacabibe Peninsula, a narrow finger of land terminating in Cape San Antonio, the western extremity of Cuba. The wind was east-southeast Force 3–4, the barometer stood at 30:02, the sky was clear, the course west by north. We were carrying the small spinnaker. On the basis of the previous two hours, we were making slightly better than 7 knots.

By a similar process of assumption based on past performance the usual noon ship routine was under way. The six of us aboard had covered quite a few miles together during the winter. We were fairly well shaken down into a system. Although the log does not record all the details, I took over the wheel from Hod while John readied for his sight. Charlie, the professional, checked leads and chafing gear, while from the galley issued various clanks and clinks as Zib and Vicki readied lunch. Also on the basis of usual fair weather routine, it was more than possible that frosted glasses made an appearance. Ice had been taken aboard at Grand Cayman. When that manna of the tropics is available it is sheer ingratitude to let it go to waste.

We slid along before a moderate easterly, a true spring

trade wind. It is during the winter months of December and January that the "Christmas winds," the strong trades, harass the small boat sailor. By the end of February reasonable breezes are likely to be in order. During a good spell there is a fairly regular pattern to the daily weather cycle, especially close to the shores of the larger islands: the wind drops off before midnight, comes up again with the sun, freshens during the day to its maximum velocity about four, and gradually eases down again with sunset. That is what you can expect. It is not necessarily what you get. Some have the idea that progress in a trade wind area is a matter of trimming the sheets once and then a few days later making certain there is no chafe. Near the islands, where the warming and cooling of the land mass affect conditions, nothing is farther from reality.

On this particular day, just to prove its independence and disregard of convention, the breeze began to lighten after lunch. Not only did the wind refuse to abide by the book, but a gray haze appeared to obscure the sun. It gradually spread across the sky, thickening and deepening. Our morale dropped with the temperature. There are few places in the Western Hemisphere—with part of the Eastern thrown in for good measure—that could be nastier in a blow than that particular patch of water. Off Guanacabibe the currents are indeed "strong and irregular." Seas can roll down from the Gulf of Mexico, or the Straits of Florida, or across the whole sweep of Caribbean. The Gulf Stream, which has its birth hereabouts, is hardly to be counted upon as a soothing influence.

Once the Isle of Pines is astern, there are no true harbors along the southern coast of Cuba. There is an indentation shown on the chart as Corrientes Bay between the cape of that name and Cape San Antonio, dignified by the title of an anchorage in the *Sailing Directions*. However, it is nothing but a narrow ledge of sand on the east side of a wide bay which shoals rapidly from depths of several hundred fathoms. I knew from experience that the comment of the *Sailing Directions*, "winds from the south and southwest cause heavy swells," would be an understatement. More than once during the winter I had crouched over a bar-taut chain with my heart in my throat, and I had no desire to enter another such trap.

So it was with apprehension that we watched the clouds gather, the breeze drop, and the barometer take a deeper-than-diurnal dip. Towards four o'clock the wind left us entirely. There began a period of rolling *Carib* rarely equaled in an honorable career. The 1600 log entry commented: "Wallowing in backwash of large and confused sea which can be seen breaking heavily along rocky coast. Cape Corrientes light bears approximately west-by-north." The sea *was* breaking heavily, and it *was* a rocky coast. Rocky and inhospitable. We didn't even like to look at it. Hod started the engine. My personal log calls it "a low moment."

At 1800 a hopeful note appeared in the ship's log: "Sea somewhat less confused. On Mainsail." and lo! at 2000: "Under working lowers. Engine off. Beam wind and sea." Five minutes later another entry: "Sighted Cape San Antonio Light. Good sailing."

That's the way it goes: the bitter with the sweet, the darkest before dawn sort of thing. At noon we had been sliding along basking in the sun, pitying poor landsmen; at four we would have given our all for a chicken farm; at eight we were happy again.

During the afternoon we had been steering due west. That end of Cuba is shaped like a wedge of pie. Cape San Antonio lighthouse stands out at the apex. To get around, coming up from Jamaica or the Caymans, the course is some slight variation on a theme of west; beyond, the coast between Cape San Antonio and Bahia Honda trends back to the northeast. So far, easy enough, but there is one complication: north of San Antonio extends the Colorado Reef, a thoroughly dangerous line of coral thrusting steeply up from great depths, and so far offshore that land cannot be seen beyond. The trick is to stay in as close as possible, as every foot means easting, yet not to get too close. Because of the vagaries of the currents the proper balance is not always easy.

By ten the brilliant light of Cape San Antonio was around on the starboard quarter. It was blowing fresh from the southeast. Our course of west brought the wind broad on the port quarter. On her best point of sailing, *Carib* roared through the night, a wide band of phosphorescence streaking the black water astern. There was a fair amount of sea. We were rolling and going. No thoughts of a chicken farm now!

I came on deck at ten to relieve Charlie. At that moment it seemed to be blowing too hard to risk a jibe without calling others, so at 10:15, when the light bore northeast, the two of us tacked ship and set a course of north. This put the wind in exactly the same position on the starboard quarter. Nothing was changed except the tack.

At 11:35 I entered: "Wind southeast force 4. Log 328.6. Completed doubling angle on bow—light now abeam, distance off 6.9 miles. Safe enough. Wonderful sailing. Wind fresh yet sea smooth."

As we had come under the land the sea had dropped, a welcome change from usual Caribbean conditions. It was glorious. The breeze was warm, a few stars glittered through the parting overcast, and we tore off the miles towards Havana.

Hod Fuller came on deck at midnight to take over. It was still blowing a good force 4, still from the southeast. The midnight log entry caroled: "Under lee of reef—sea calm. Wind perfect reaching breeze. Boiling along. We're being lucky." Lucky was almost an understatement. *Carib* did not relish going to windward. Neither did we. Previously during the winter we had rounded the western tip of Haiti and Jamaica in pursuit of a port to the east; each time the whole

Caribbean had reared up and flung itself on our necks. Ever since leaving Montego Bay we had been thinking apprehensively of this moment. And now we reached along, decks dry, practically burning out the bearings on the taffrail log.

John relieved Hod at two. Through their watches conditions stayed the same. The log notes: "Strong reaching breeze with almost no sea." Charlie relieved John at four, and course was altered to northeast by north.

When I came on at six I found that the breeze had died with the first glow of light. We had bare steerageway. I sat at the wheel enjoying the morning. People can talk about dawn in the mountains, or on the desert, but I'll take mine at the wheel of a boat somewhere on the equator side of latitude 23 degrees 27 minutes. There is a feel to an early tropic morning that nothing else has: a wonderful promise, a peaceful content, a satisfaction. Especially when the wind is light and the sea is smooth, and it is possible to leave the helm and putter around the deck, and perhaps sneak down into the galley to swipe an orange and start a pot of coffee.

But after the morning was well established I happened to notice that we weren't getting anywhere. The breeze had completely vanished. I pressed the button that called our faithful gasoline slave into action. The log line began to angle out astern. We moved again.

Soon I got to thinking that we had perhaps been overcautious during the night, and had stayed on the course of north too long. We wanted easting—all we could get. At any moment the wind might strike in from dead ahead. So, although at 0600 the course had been changed to northeast at the navigator's order, I began to bend over more to starboard on my own. After all, I reasoned, there couldn't be any danger. There were places where a boat of *Carib*'s draft could get in trouble, but tropic reefs always give plenty of warning if visibility is good. If there is a sea there will be breakers; if it is calm, the color of the water is a sure guide. The Colorado

Reef would show plainly against the deep blue of the outer water. I came around to east-northeast.

Towards the end of my trick the breeze began to come in again from the southeast. At first it was very faint, but it gradually hardened. As soon as it had enough weight to give us full steerageway I cut off the engine. Within a few minutes Hod came up to take over.

Breakfast was nearly ready. Hod, John and I sat in the cockpit, considering whether the big jibtopsail should be set at the moment or after breakfast. The former motion carried. Languidly Hod and John put it on the stay. John happened to glance under the bowsprit. "Hey! You're on soundings!" he yelled aft. "There's bottom!"

And so it was. I could see it by leaning outboard from the wheel. Nice unyielding clumps of coral, and waving sea fans, and patches of grass, all rather hazy and misty because of the depth, but real enough. We did not tarry. I spun the wheel to a reverse course. Within minutes the last trace of land vanished below. But looking astern we could not make out the reef line by color. The morning sun was still too low on the horizon for safe pilotage to the eastward. Another lesson.

John was forgiving, although he did look at me with the reproachful expression the scientific navigator reserves for the rule-of-thumber. The log recorded a mere: "Altered course. Too close to reef." But through the years I remembered why.

The wind stayed in the southeast during the early morning. The big jib swelled against a bright cloudless sky. Flying fish skittered from crest to crest. Sights showed that the Gulf Stream was helping us on our way, a power below as silent and effortless as the breeze above. The log spun merrily. It was hot in the sun, cool in the shade.

Watch followed watch. The little ship jobs got themselves done: chafing gear renewed, a drop of oil on a snapshackle, a new whipping on a rope end, dinghy lashings tightened, jib leads changed. A sailing vessel is still a bundle of sticks held together by strings, and the strings need minding. And down below the girls did their share: sweeping, cleaning, washing and readying for the next onslaught of seagoing appetites.

In the late morning the breeze began to haul. The regular track of the barograph was interrupted. A wind south of southeast could mean that it was going all the way around; that we might get a norther cycle of south, southwest, west, northwest and north. All would be fair winds for Havana. Or the breeze might go into the south and die to come blasting back from the east like the furies of hell. Only the future held the answer.

Meantime we reached across the sea, across the morning. Never was sailing more perfect. At noon John entered the log: "Sea smooth. Beautiful going." And so it was. Ahead lay another day, another twenty-four hours, bringing along different circumstances, different problems and different pleasures. Another day, and perhaps another hundred or so miles of passage. Or perhaps no miles at all.

But this was to be the story of just one day. The day ended at noon.

Afterword

As I reread these accounts of cruises, a fact occurs to me: many of the far places are less distant than when I visited them. The combination of ocean spanning jets and the growing availability of yachts for charter opens new parts of the world to casual exploration each year.

After returning from a cruise of the Windward and Leeward Islands at the end of World War II, I received a letter from the Collector of Customs in Grenada saying that *Carib* had been the sole yacht to put into St. George's during the winter, but he "hoped others would follow in the future." Only one other pleasure craft was encountered between Trinidad and St. Thomas, and there was not a single vessel for charter in all the West Indies. Today, while it would be an exaggeration to say that the Caribbean is full of yachts, it is dotted with them like raisins in a windjammer's Christmas pudding, and a large percentage of them can be chartered. Anyone with a week to spare can fly to almost any major island and commence yachting, in a wide range of vessels, depending on personal preference, knowledge, and pocketbook. Most come complete with crew, but increasingly there are "bareboats," the nautical equivalent of the drive-yourself automobile, ready stocked: hoist the sails and off you go.

The Mediterranean, the Aegean, and the Baltic all have yacht chartering agencies, so arrangements can be made to begin or end a cruise in almost any port of Europe or the British Isles. Bareboats are available along the Riviera. And while it might take a bit of digging by correspondence, boats often can be found in Panama for a passage to the Galapagos, or in Tahiti for a cruise through *Les Iles sous le Vent*—frequently a bogged-down circumnavigator needs funds to continue the voyage. Many such wanderers are crackpots with unsuitable vessels, but others would be ideal companions. Japan is becoming possible as yachting flourishes as a sport.

Many owners have cruised distant waters in their own boats by shipping them as deck cargo on freighters, and going along on the same ship, or flying over to save time. Another possibility beginning to become a reality is airlifting. Giant cargo planes have been developed, partially as an adjunct to the space and missile programs, and already yachts have crossed oceans above the clouds. Those with the leisure can choose the best method of getting from one area of gunk-holes to another yet devised: in your own portable castle. But however, the title of the Cruising Club of America's official history should serve as the inspiration: "Nowhere is too far."